THE WRITINGS OF ELIZABETH WEBB

The Writings of Elizabeth Webb

A Quaker Missionary in America, 1697–1726

EDITED BY RACHEL COPE
AND ZACHARY MCLEOD HUTCHINS

THE PENNSYLVANIA STATE UNIVERSITY PRESS
UNIVERSITY PARK, PENNSYLVANIA

Library of Congress Cataloging-in-Publication Data

Names: Webb, Elizabeth, active 1712, author. | Cope, Rachel, editor. | Hutchins, Zachary McLeod, editor.
Title: The writings of Elizabeth Webb : a Quaker missionary in America, 1697–1726 / edited by Rachel Cope and Zachary McLeod Hutchins.
Description: University Park, Pennsylvania : The Pennsylvania State University Press, [2019] | Includes bibliographical references and index.
Summary: "A comprehensive collection of the writings of Elizabeth Webb, a Quaker missionary who traveled and taught in England and America during the seventeenth and eighteenth centuries"—Provided by publisher.
Identifiers: LCCN 2018035755 | ISBN 9780271082226 (cloth : alk. paper) | ISBN 9780271082233 (pbk. : alk. paper)
Subjects: LCSH: Webb, Elizabeth, active 1712. | Society of Friends. | Spiritual life—Society of Friends.
Classification: LCC BX7617.W43 W67 2018 | DDC 289.6092—dc23
LC record available at https://lccn.loc.gov/2018035755

Printed in the United States of America
Published by
The Pennsylvania State University Press,
University Park, PA 16802–1003

The Pennsylvania State University Press is a member of the Association of University Presses.

It is the policy of The Pennsylvania State University Press to use acid-free paper. Publications on uncoated stock satisfy the minimum requirements of American National Standard for Information Sciences—Permanence of Paper for Printed Library Material, ANSI Z39.48–1992.

CONTENTS

ACKNOWLEDGMENTS

We—Rachel and Zachary—are tremendously grateful to have had the opportunity to work together on this project, a natural extension of our friendship and shared interests in early American religion. We would also like to acknowledge the assistance of those who have helped us in various ways as we have engaged with Elizabeth Webb's writings. Specifically, we would like to express appreciation for the direction we have received from archivists at the West Chester County Historical Society, Haverford College, and Swarthmore College. We are also grateful for the meticulous efforts of our research assistants, Elizabeth Cope and Ian McLaughlin, and for the Religious Studies Center at Brigham Young University for providing funding for this project. A broad network of colleagues and friends too numerous to name have offered each of us support throughout this process, and we express thanks for their aid.

We both owe a debt of gratitude to those who fostered our interest in Quaker history. Zachary's interest in the topic has early roots. As a child, his mother told him that he was a descendant of Katherine and Patience Scott and regaled him with stories from early Quaker history. Later, Laurie Maffly-Kipp read a draft of his first book and asked him what the Quakers thought about Puritan ideas of Eden and the end times. At the time, he could not answer her with any sophistication, but he never forgot her question and hopes that she might regard this edition of Elizabeth Webb's writings as a belated response to the inquiry. Rachel's interest in Quakerism originated with her research on women's religious experiences in upstate New York—Quakers quickly figured into the story. Carol Faulkner, a generous mentor, encouraged Rachel to apply for a Gest Fellowship at Haverford College. The wonderful archivists and librarians at Haverford introduced her to a wealth of manuscript sources that further sparked her interest in the Quaker experience.

Finally, we would like to thank our reviewers—Reiner Smolinski and Thomas Hamm—and the staff at Penn State University Press. Our editor, Kathryn Yahner, deserves particular thanks for her dedication, encouragement, support, and assistance. It has been a pleasure to work with her.

NOTE ON THE TEXT

The Writings of Elizabeth Webb is a comprehensive collection, bringing together every extant text known to have been penned by Elizabeth Webb. The collection begins with Webb's public works—texts that were prepared for publication and that circulated widely. The first of these two texts is a letter written by Webb to Anthony Boehm in 1712, a confessional account of her struggle for faith that introduced her to a broader reading public. This letter inspired thousands of readers and was often reprinted in the eighteenth and nineteenth centuries; it is the only one of Webb's works previously available to readers in a modern, print edition. The second, *Some Meditations with Some Observations upon the Revelations of Jesus Christ*, is a commentary on the biblical book of Revelation—Webb's *magnum opus.* Although Webb prepared her commentary for the press during the early eighteenth century, it was never published.

Following these works, the collection proceeds to a chronological presentation of three manuscripts intended for smaller audiences. The first, a travel diary, recounts Webb's travels throughout North America as a missionary between 1697 and 1699. The second, "Short Memorial," is a narrative account of Webb's life that she prepared for her children, recounting her conversion, her marriage to Richard Webb, and her life on both sides of the Atlantic. The third, a brief letter written to her children in 1724, was eventually published in a nineteenth-century Quaker periodical.

Two of these texts—*Some Meditations* and her travel diary—have been abridged. In the case of Webb's travel diary, this abridgment is a matter of necessity; two pages of the manuscript are missing, and several pages are damaged. We include the entirety of her extant narrative account but omit material at the end of the manuscript, including a series of log-based entries documenting her return voyage to England in 1699, both because it is fragmentary and because the log largely records distances traveled rather than her deeds, thoughts, and experiences. In the case of Webb's commentary on Revelation, we present her reflections on scripture in their entirety but have chosen to omit her transcriptions of the Revelation itself, confident that readers will have ready access to a copy of the King James Version, which she seems to have relied on and from whose language she deviates only rarely in presenting the text of that book.

For the ease of our readers, spelling has been modernized, including U.K. spellings, and we have inserted end-stop punctuation in order to make sentences more comprehensible. Ambiguous nouns that Webb had capitalized have been changed to lowercase, unless they are proper nouns or nouns that are always capitalized in religious usage, such as New Jerusalem, or mentions of God's name and its variants. Ellipses indicate brief missing passages where damage has made the manuscript illegible; brackets indicate that our insertion or reconstruction of a word or phrase is conjectural. Throughout, we avoid the insertion of quotation marks because Webb often thought of herself as quoting when she wasn't using the exact language of an extant biblical translation, and more importantly, she very rarely used quotation marks in her writing. Perhaps she thought of her own quotations or paraphrases as newly inspired scripture, the words of God being spoken as if for the first time, through her own mouth, and therefore not in need of attribution to some prior speaker. We have moved almost all scriptural citations—including the vast majority of those Webb cites in the main text of her various writings—to the footnotes, except when doing so would impair the sense of Webb's words.

WEBB AND HER WORLD

An Introduction

As a young woman in Gloucestershire, England, Elizabeth [Hoopes?] Webb (1663–1726) joined the Society of Friends, convinced that it contained the religious truth for which she had been searching. Her conversion took place over the course of months; the Society of Friends or Quaker message, which she likened to "bread cast upon the waters, for it was found after many days," resonated with her only after a period of deep introspection (33). In addition to being drawn to Quaker doctrine, Webb found deep meaning in the religious life that her newfound faith offered, particularly its emphasis on inward experience and spiritual equality. She recalled feeling the divine presence as she attended Quaker meetings, experienced symbolically powerful dreams and visions that shaped her own spiritual journey, and committed herself to the work of fostering religious community. As her faith developed, Quakerism became more than a message she had embraced; Webb came to believe that God had called her to share this message with others, through the spoken and written word, on both sides of the Atlantic.

George Fox founded the Society of Friends in the seventeenth century within the volatile political and social climate created by the English Civil War. The Civil War period gave momentum to radical discussions about religion—discussions that, for many groups, offered a new sense of possibility. The Society of Friends, along with several other radical sects, including Levellers, Diggers, Ranters, Shakers, and Fifth Monarchists, emerged at a time when many Christians were seeking new understandings of liturgical form and ecclesiastical governance.[1] As a result, several groups, including the

1. Christopher Hill, *The World Turned Upside Down: Radical Ideas During the English Revolution* (1972; repr., New York: Penguin, 1991), 87–258.

Quakers, claimed the role of the "new true church, the model of the fully reformed Church" in a context of religious dissent and change.[2]

The first Quakers believed they were preparing the way for the imminent, physical return of Jesus Christ—an event Christians had anticipated since his resurrection and ascension into heaven during New Testament times. But starting in the 1660s, Friends turned traditional interpretations about Christ's return on their head; drawing on biblical texts such as Jeremiah, Isaiah, and especially Revelation, they concluded that the Second Coming was an inward experience available to all. In essence, they proposed that God could communicate directly with humanity, that everyone could experience the Light of Christ, or God's presence, and be spiritually transformed in the process. Formal priests, sermons, and outward sacraments, Quakers proposed, were not needed. As England wrestled with the social and ecclesiastical unrest caused by civil war, Fox and the Society of Friends taught that Christ would come to all.

Because the early Society of Friends empowered all Quakers to participate in its liturgical life and proselytizing work, women like Elizabeth Webb enjoyed the opportunity to assume roles from which they had been precluded in other Christian traditions prior to the social breakdown of the English Civil War. In 1697, for example, Webb had a vision persuading her that she needed to travel in the American wilderness so she could share her faith—a vision whose fulfillment was possible because of Fox's emphasis on evangelical outreach. From early on, Quakers traveled to America, where they preached the gospel and looked for locations where they could settle. Since the ministry was open to all, women as well as men made such journeys. Although Webb's husband, Richard, initially opposed her desire to preach the gospel in America, she convinced him that God had called her to make this significant journey. Webb, along with her traveling companion and fellow evangelist, Mary Rogers, arrived in America in December of 1697. For eighteen months, Webb (accompanied by Rogers until Rogers left to minister in the West Indies) traveled by boat and horseback, preaching at Quaker meetings along the way, with stops in North Carolina, Virginia, Maryland, Pennsylvania, New Jersey, New York, Rhode Island, Massachusetts, and New Hampshire. Throughout this period of time, Webb kept a journal recounting

2. Pink Dandelion, *The Quakers: A Very Short Introduction* (Oxford: Oxford University Press, 2008), 8.

her ministry, personal religious experiences, and the divine inspiration that guided her work while preaching in the American colonies.

Webb crossed the Atlantic a second time and returned to England in 1699. Shortly thereafter, in 1700, she emigrated from England to Pennsylvania with her husband and children, ultimately settling in Chester County. Over the course of the next decade, Webb continued to travel and preach throughout the colonies until the Holy Spirit called her to return to England in 1710. Upon receiving this call, she once again crossed the Atlantic so she could proselytize among those she considered to be in need of the gospel message. This time, she spent eighteen months preaching in England before returning home to Pennsylvania.

While sharing the gospel in London, Webb met the German pietist Anthony Boehm, who served as chaplain to Prince George of Denmark, the consort of Queen Anne of England.[3] Their friendship was memorialized in an autobiographical narrative Webb wrote for Boehm in a letter, following her return to Pennsylvania. This important account was printed after Webb's death and familiarized Quakers on both sides of the Atlantic with her life story. The letter she wrote to Boehm was read as a spiritual guide to social upheaval in the age of revolution. During the American War of Independence, Friends also read, in manuscript, another treatise written by Webb. In the years prior to her passing, she wrote a commentary on Revelation, titled *Some Meditations with Some Observations upon the Revelations of Jesus Christ*, and prepared it for publication. The Pennsylvania Yearly Meeting gave Webb permission to bring the commentary to press but refused to fund its publication, so it remained unpublished when she died in 1726. Like *Some Meditations*, Webb's other autobiographical writings, now collected in this volume, circulated in manuscript during her lifetime, and during the nineteenth century, excerpts appeared in *The Friend*, a popular Quaker periodical. Although Webb's work circulated widely for more than a century after her death, only her letter to Boehm has been republished in the twentieth and twenty-first centuries.

Well known in her lifetime, Webb is now familiar only to a handful of specialists.[4] But her writings, collected here, deserve a broader audience. Her

3. Pietism was a movement that originated in the Lutheran Church in Germany in the seventeenth century. It stressed personal piety over religious formality and orthodoxy.

4. For scholarly treatments of Webb, see Rebecca Larson, *Daughters of Light: Quaker Women Preaching and Prophesying in the Colonies and Abroad, 1700–1775* (New York:

work sheds significant light on both Quaker theology and the lived experience of colonial American women and will be a significant addition to our understanding of women's religious thought during the period. Texts like those written by Webb are rare for a number of reasons. The scant number of records by (and even about) colonial Quaker women is due in part to the unique nature of Quaker meetings—during which participants awaited the inspiration of the Holy Spirit and then spoke extemporaneously. The words they spoke, their theological positions, and the ways in which they experienced their faith are too often unrecoverable. In his comprehensive index of Quaker sermons recorded between 1671 and 1700, for example, Michael Graves identifies just seventy-nine surviving texts, all authored by men and only one, by Thomas Chalkley, preached in colonial America. (By comparison, many hundreds of sermons preached by male Puritan ministers in New England survive from this period.)[5] In making available the breadth of Webb's work, *The Writings of Elizabeth Webb* highlights the theological and ecclesiastical contributions of women in colonial America. The collection includes every extant text known to have been penned by Webb, including the journal of her mission to the colonies with Mary Rogers, her letter to Boehm, her commentary on Revelation, and several works addressed to her children and close friends. Three of those texts—her commentary, travel journal, and an autobiographical account penned for her family—have been transcribed from manuscript and are now published for the first time.

Webb's commentary on Revelation will be of significant interest to scholars and students in the fields of Quaker studies and millennialism—often regarded as the most important strand of thought in early American religious history because of the ways in which the American Revolution was framed by some as a precursor to the Millennium. Her travel journal, letters, and other autobiographical narratives will, on the other hand, resonate with those studying early American literature. They illustrate the role that women played in developing transatlantic religious and social networks as well as the importance of ecstatic or visionary experiences in the construction of Quaker identity. The afterword of her commentary on Revelation includes a particu-

---

Alfred A. Knopf, 1999); Phyllis Mack, *Visionary Women: Ecstastic Prophecy in Seventeenth-Century England* (Berkeley: University of California Press, 1992); and Carla Gerona, *Night Journeys: The Power of Dreams in Transatlantic Quaker Culture* (Charlottesville: University of Virginia Press, 2004).

5. Michael P. Graves, *Preaching the Inward Light: Early Quaker Rhetoric* (Waco: Baylor University Press, 2009).

larly beautiful passage in which Webb experiences the transcendent pleasures of nature through an "inward eye," an episode that will recall, for students and scholars of American literature, both the ecstatic wanderings of Sarah Pierrepont and the transparent eyeball of Ralph Waldo Emerson (174).

Together, this collection of texts introduces Webb as a major contributor to the literary and religious history of colonial North America; her life and words should stand beside those of women such as Anne Hutchinson, Anne Bradstreet, Mary Rowlandson, Sarah Kemble Knight, and Abigaill Levy Franks. Webb's life story and her views on slavery in Virginia, religious persecution in Massachusetts, and the apocalyptic significance of American history are now accessible to readers for the first time. *The Writings of Elizabeth Webb* is the earliest extant collection of colonial Quaker writings and an important window onto the lived experience of women in the eighteenth-century Atlantic world. It is a volume that promises to revolutionize our understanding of Quaker eschatology and to reintroduce, for modern audiences, a woman who was well known to religious communities on both sides of the ocean during her life and for decades afterward.

WOMEN AND THE SOCIETY OF FRIENDS

When George Fox began to preach publicly, toward the end of the English Civil War, he soon developed a significant following. Many of those who identified themselves as "Friends of the Truth" were women. Their tendency to quake and swoon under the influence of religious conviction led Fox's critics to coin a new epithet, describing his disciples as *Quakers*. These women were drawn to his budding movement, at least in part, because Fox taught that God called women, as well as men, as preachers and evangelists. From the beginning of his ministry, Fox encouraged women moved by the spirit or Light of Christ to testify publicly of their experiences. By the time of Elizabeth Webb's convincement, the Quaker term for conversion, their involvement in the Society of Friends's liturgy and governance had been codified.[6]

6. As Kate Peters notes, Fox's support for the participation of women in the ministry was hardly universal, and their public activities were circumscribed into carefully defined roles after the 1650s. See Kate Peters, *Print Culture and the Early Quakers* (New York: Cambridge University Press, 2005), 124–50.

Early female Friends pressured the Protectorate of Oliver Cromwell and the restored monarchy of Charles II on questions of public policy and religious freedom, presenting themselves as mouthpieces for a movement. In 1659, Mary Westwood and others published a petition protesting tithes levied in support of the Church of England above the signatures of more than seven thousand Quaker women. Although these "Hand-Maids and Daughters of the Lord" acknowledged that "it may seem strange to some that women should appear in so publick a manner," they insisted on their collective authority as "the Seed of the Woman, which bruiseth the Serpents head, to which the Promise is, Christ Jesus in the Male and in the Female."[7] This assertion of spiritual power, which is typical of early Quaker writings, challenged conventional readings of the creation narrative in Genesis. Most Christian sects regarded women as frail and fallible because of Eve's example, but Quaker leaders taught that convincement purified women of any inherent weaknesses. This theology emboldened female converts to participate actively in public life.[8]

Margaret Fell, who was one of Fox's early supporters and eventually became his wife, offered the most substantive defense of preaching by Quaker women. Her 1666 tract, *Women's Speaking Justified*, builds on the language of Westwood's 1659 proclamation and other early pamphlets, declaring that "those who speak against the Woman and her Seeds Speaking, speak out of the enmity of the old Serpents Seed." Fell and other early Quaker writers turned to Genesis so frequently because they saw its narrative, which recounted Eve's struggle with the serpent, as a preface to the account in Revelation 12 and "the enmity God put between the woman and the Dragon."[9] Genesis and Revelation thus became biblical bookends for the spiritual identities of early modern Quaker women, who understood their participation in liturgical and evangelical activities as an extension of the cosmic drama begun in Eden and concluded, anticipatorily, in the record of John's vision on Patmos. Webb's lifelong interest in the book of Revelation, as demonstrated by her commentary and frequent references to it in autobiographical accounts,

7. *7000 Handmaids of the Lord*, in *Hidden in Plain Sight: Quaker Women's Writings, 1650–1700*, ed. Mary Garman et al. (Wallingford, Pa.: Pendle Hill, 1996), 58–59, 64.

8. On contemporary readings of Genesis, see Philip C. Almond, *Adam and Eve in Seventeenth-Century Thought* (Cambridge: Cambridge University Press, 1999), and Zachary McLeod Hutchins, *Inventing Eden: Primitivism, Millennialism, and the Making of New England* (New York: Oxford University Press, 2014).

9. Margaret Fell, *Women's Speaking Justified* (London, 1666), 4.

reflects this belief, suggesting that her convincement and evangelical outreach are part of a larger biblical narrative in which women play a central role. In a letter to her children, Webb speaks of God acting "as a tender Father" and then immediately transitions into a discussion of her own role "as a tender mother," establishing a rough equivalency between these gendered identities (217–18). She taught both publicly and privately, acting as an agent of deity and on an equal spiritual footing with male Friends.

In her writing, Webb readily acknowledges biblically based arguments for the spiritual debility of women, but she also insists that any weakness she might suffer is a function of mortality and the flesh, not her sex. In her commentary on Revelation 2:22–25, writing of Peter's characterization of woman as "the weaker part of mankind," Webb argues that "men are concerned in false doctrine as well as women—all make up the false church which the spirit foresaw" (64–65).[10] Although she accepts the title of "weaker vessel" in her autobiographical letter to Boehm, Webb likely thought of her weakness in social or bodily terms, rather than as a spiritual handicap (28). During her missionary service with Mary Rogers, for example, Webb complained that she found herself "both sick and lame, for I had traveled hard, beyond the ability of my body" (188). When she "traveled alone," without the protection of men, and arrived at her destination in good health, she "set it down as a memorial of the goodness of God to a poor young creature of the weaker sex" (202). On another occasion, after preaching successfully before an angry minister in Puritan Boston, Webb wanted to travel throughout the region but felt acutely the limitations imposed on her by her sex. Many colonists in rural Massachusetts "were got into garrisons for fear of the Indians," and Webb apparently felt unable to preach as widely as she would have liked because she was a woman and might have been unable to defend herself if attacked. Wishing that she could wander freely through the countryside, Webb declared in her journal that "had I been a man I thought I could have went into all corners of the land to declare of it, for indeed it is the great day of New England's visitation to them that will receive the truth in the love of it" (138–84). She defended the spiritual capacity of women, fighting against common allegations of spiritual inferiority, but she also acknowledged that her sex imposed physical or social limitations no eloquence could remove.

Webb's ministry in New England was made possible by the evangelical efforts—and sufferings—of prior Quaker women. In 1656, Mary Fisher and

10. See 1 Peter 3:7.

Anne Austin became the first Friends to set foot in Puritan Massachusetts; they were immediately imprisoned. Other fearless women followed, crying repentance. When, for example, Katherine Scott learned that Puritan magistrates had sentenced three male Friends to have their ears cropped, she walked from Providence to Boston to demand their release and was herself imprisoned; her eleven-year-old daughter, Patience, promptly followed in Scott's footsteps and was likewise incarcerated. On other occasions, Quaker women created a public spectacle to protest Puritan rule. Imitating the example of the prophet Isaiah, who remained naked for three years as a sign from God, Deborah Wilson and Lydia Wardell walked naked through the streets of Massachusetts. For their actions, Wilson, Wardell, Elizabeth Hooton, and other female Friends who testified of the sins of Puritan magistrates were forcibly stripped and whipped through the town. For her repeated, outspoken criticisms of the Massachusetts Bay Colony, Mary Dyer was executed. These pioneering women established Quaker congregations in Salem and other cities, paving the way for Webb's later ministry. With the Toleration Act of 1689, Parliament granted nonconformists such as the Quakers the right to worship as they saw fit, and by the time Webb arrived in Massachusetts ten years later, religious persecution was largely a thing of the past. As she wrote in her journal, "It is the day of Boston's visitation, after her great cruelty to the servants of the Lord" (186). Webb's journey was difficult but, because of the women who went before her, not particularly dangerous.

During her travels through the colonies, Webb gathered in a wide variety of meetings with local groups of Quakers and "with the world's people"—a mixture of religious seekers and hecklers (192). In addition to her regular weekly worship meetings on land and on sea ("twice in the week all the voyage on board"), Webb attended youth meetings, monthly women's meetings, and larger quarterly or yearly meetings, to which each Quaker congregation in the county or colony sent male and female delegates (180). The development of women's meetings allowed Webb and other women to participate in the business of the Society of Friends, as well as its worship services. Women's meetings, which were established by Fox and Fell, disciplined erring Friends, investigated the lives of individuals wishing to marry, collected money for a separate women's treasury, and distributed goods to the poor. These meetings provided Webb opportunities to connect with a local network of women and to participate in ecclesiastical governance.

Because common law held that a woman's legal and fiscal identity was subsumed into that of her husband at marriage, participation in the Society's financial and disciplinary matters provided women an opportunity to exercise authority beyond that allowed them in civic life. When Webb and Rogers arrived in Maryland, for example, they "met with a greater body of Friends, and . . . there were some disorderly spirits amongst them which had cast stumbling blocks in the way of the weak, and they were not taken away, which the Lord gave us a sense of. And so we made inquiry into those matters and were made instrumental in helping to remove these causes, and to lay judgment where it was due, that so the true innocent seed might be set at liberty" (181). Although Webb could not serve on a jury because of her sex, the establishment of women's meetings provided her with an opportunity to sit in judgment on both men and women if they violated Society expectations. As a Quaker, she achieved a measure of social prominence and authority that might otherwise have eluded her.

Webb's influence expanded with the circulation of her writings in manuscript, a form of publication that prevailed, David Hall explains, when "the economics of the book trade stood in the way of some manuscripts passing into print."[11] Her letter to Boehm, commentary on Revelation, and other writings circulated in manuscript for decades before "some devout persons, who have been edified by the spiritual experiences" they contain, sought to publish her work and correct the mistakes or "inconveniencies to which manuscripts are liable, through the negligence and inattention of transcribers" (27). This form of circulation was typical for all colonial writers in the early eighteenth century, when there was a shortage of printing presses and disposable income to spend on local works, but women struggled even more than men to usher their words into print. William Frost notes that of the twenty-eight tracts, journals, or broadsides published by New Jersey or Pennsylvania Quakers between 1683 and 1776, only three were associated with women, and in two of those three cases, men published their work posthumously.[12]

Before they could proceed with publication, Quaker authors required the approval of a body charged with reviewing the content of manuscripts.

11. David D. Hall, *Ways of Writing: The Practice and Politics of Text-Making in Seventeenth-Century New England* (Philadelphia: University of Pennsylvania Press, 2008), 16. This form of publication was particularly common for women writers; see Caroline Wigginton, *In the Neighborhood: Women's Publication in Early America* (Amherst: University of Massachusetts Press, 2016).

12. See J. William Frost, "Quaker Books in Colonial Pennsylvania," *Quaker History* 80, no. 1 (1991): 4.

In England, the Second Day Morning Meeting determined whether manuscripts reflected the Society's values, while a committee of Philadelphia overseers regulated Quaker publishing in colonial North America—processes instituted after a slew of inflammatory publications stirred up considerable controversy in the seventeenth century.[13] Although Webb received approval from the Philadelphia Overseers of the Press for the publication of her commentary, her work was one of many cases in which Quaker overseers "approved a manuscript for publication but did not recommend that the Society should bear the cost."[14] Without Society funding, colonial authors rarely found a printer willing to invest in Quaker writing, and a number of scholars have suggested that women like Webb were disproportionately marginalized by Society censorship.[15] Webb's words would continue to be read in manuscript, but they would not achieve the broader circulation of print until after her death.

Nevertheless, Webb and other female Friends persisted. Although her commentary was never published, she continued to write for family and Friends on both sides of the Atlantic until her death, trusting that manuscript accounts of her life and witness would find their way to interested parties.

13. In 1672, under the direction of the Yearly Meeting, the Second Day Morning Meeting was given the task of censoring all manuscripts published with the Society's name. As Luella M. Wright explains, they "checked fanatical tendencies, held the diction up to higher standards, and helped authors to clarify the points at issue" but by so doing "stressed only the interests of the group" which "hasten[ed] the day of eighteenth century exclusiveness and of barrenness in literary productivity." In particular, the Second Day Morning Meeting became cautious about circulating records they considered to be too enthusiastic, ecstatic, or extreme in nature: records of "visions, prophecies, lamentations, healings and fasts" were deemed too radical for publication. Such an approach both wittingly and unwittingly discriminated against women's writing—their voices and their messages were often considered too extreme to be in print. See Luella M. Wright, *The Literary Life of the Early Friends, 1650–1725* (New York: AMS Press, 1966), 97–109.

14. David J. Hall, "'The fiery Tryal of their Infallible Examination': Self-Control in the Regulation of Quaker Publishing in England from the 1670s to the mid 19th Century," in *Censorship and the Control of Print in England and France, 1600–1910*, ed. Robin Myers and Michael Harris (Winchester, U.K.: St. Paul's Bibliographies, 1992), 66.

15. See Betty Hagglund, "Quakers and Print Culture," in *The Oxford Handbook of Quaker Studies*, ed. Stephen W. Angell and Pink Dandelion (New York: Oxford University Press, 2013), 485–86.

As a traveling minister who was often away from her family for extended periods of time, Webb was well aware of the limitations that distance posed on all kinds of relationships, including those forged in religious contexts. When she preached, she knew that she might never see her audience again. She was aware of the loneliness many converts felt—particularly those who lacked ready access to a supportive spiritual community. And she knew that her fellow Quakers needed to experience spiritual kinship because such relationships were a key part of fostering faith. Unable to be everywhere she wanted to be, and with everyone she wanted to be with, Webb found creative ways to offer fellowship and encourage the formation of community with her pen. The pages she wrote throughout the course of her life thus offer more than travel logs and autobiographical details; these accounts capture how Webb's sense of community was cultivated through her personal reception of the Light of Christ, while also demonstrating how writing about and sharing such religious experiences with others enabled her to stretch the boundaries of Quaker community into a transatlantic context.

While sharing the Quaker message in the American colonies, for example, Webb decided to keep a record of her experiences. The writing of journals, diaries, letters, memoirs, and autobiographies was an important practice among educated early modern women—a means for them to highlight the challenges of exercising agency in their daily lives, to engage with a modern transoceanic world, and to situate their identities as relational or communal constructs rather than the product of a singular genius or solitary individual.[16] Religious women, in particular, did not see the words they penned as depictions of cloistered experiences and used personal writing to portray the unification of lives that resulted from a mutual commitment to the same beliefs and ideals. As various examples of life writing demonstrate, many of the stories women told were contingent upon and thus inextricably linked to other stories—indeed, personal accounts were often filled with details that

16. D. Bruce Hindmarsh, *The Evangelical Conversion Narrative: Spiritual Autobiography in Early Modern England* (Oxford: Oxford University Press, 2005); Catherine Brekus, *Sarah Osborn's World: The Rise of Evangelical Christianity in Early America* (New Haven: Yale University Press, 2013); Candy Gunther, "The Spiritual Pilgrimage of Rachel Stearns, 1834–1837: Reinterpreting Women's Religious and Social Experiences in the Methodist Revivals of Nineteenth-Century America," *Church History* (December 1996): 577–95.

made it clear that women thought about their lives in the context of a shared identity. These kinds of relational details are evident in the writings of early Quaker women, especially those who crossed back and forth between England and America as they sought to share their beliefs with friends and family members an ocean away.[17] In her journals and letters, Webb wrote not just about her own experiences but about the spiritual community of which she was a part. As a female preacher, she found ways to write lives together, both at home and abroad.

Webb's partnership with fellow preacher Mary Rogers is one of the first relationships discussed in the 1697 travel journal—her earliest surviving text. Throughout the course of this journal, she consistently uses the first-person plural, identifying as part of the larger whole that was her relationship with Rogers. Webb writes not just about what they did together; she also attaches "we" or "us" to their subjective experiences and feelings. For example, in a moment of distress Webb noted that she and Rogers "trusted in him, and [he] gave us a strong evidence of his preserving hand and arm of power which was about us" (180). On another occasion, when Rogers announced her intention to depart for Barbados, Webb received a confirming revelation that Rogers should leave, and together "we were sensible that it was of the Lord" (188). This corporate sense of self is consistent with the life writings of her contemporaries—she and other female Friends "created a transatlantic network of women who shared a similar 'calling.'" Webb and Rogers, like other Quaker preachers treated by Rebecca Larson, had traveled extensively, "unifying Friends in faith and practice" on both sides of the Atlantic.[18] By writing in the first-person plural, then, Webb not only highlighted the unity she felt with Rogers but also spoke on behalf of a transatlantic Quaker community of which she was a part. Webb's travel journal and her other writings make it clear that she was involved in an active, rather than a passive, faith. By responding to the Light of Christ, she had an opportunity to preach, travel, and write—to share her faith with others in a variety of contexts. Webb asked, "For why should I be as one that turns aside from the flocks of the companions? Oh! The drawing cords of divine love! How did it draw my soul

17. Larson, *Daughters of Light*; Mack, *Visionary Women*; Catherine Brekus, *Strangers and Pilgrims: Female Preaching in America, 1740–1845* (Chapel Hill: University of North Carolina Press, 1998).

18. Larson, *Daughters of Light*, 11, 9.

with longings" (197). In the accounts that she penned, therefore, it is clear that Webb saw herself as a full participant in her faith—a spiritual companion to her fellow believers, women and men who felt called to do the same things she felt called to do. "We," and not "I," described Webb's experience as a Quaker evangelist.

Indeed, much of Webb's writing makes it clear, both implicitly and explicitly, that she wanted those to whom she ministered to understand the importance of religious community. While detailing her experiences as a traveling preacher, for example, Webb takes note of the time she spent exhorting groups of Friends to "sit down together" (184). In other words, she wrote to encourage believers to nurture and support one another—a principle that is woven throughout many accounts she penned. Webb also recalled writing "many letters to Friends and kin," an act that both encouraged and exemplified the forging of spiritual community (192).[19] On one occasion, the first line she wrote in a letter to recent converts stated: "I have traveled in the path that you are now entering into" (184). By foregrounding their shared experience of convincement, Webb became one with new members of her faith, suggesting that they were now a part of her extended kin. This powerful relational sensibility continues throughout the remainder of the letter as Webb relates to her new friends while also encouraging them to align with other members of their religious community so they can establish a network of spiritual relationships with those who live within closer geographic proximity. Although distance limited her long-term physical interaction with those she ministered to throughout the course of her travels, correspondence allowed Webb to foster and maintain relationships across time and space, and it became a means through which she could continue to teach others about the importance of fellowship.[20]

19. Although we have yet to locate Webb's letters in manuscript form, it is clear that she kept an extensive correspondence. Webb, like other Quakers (particularly women), created Quaker networks through letter writing. See, for example, Marjon Ames, *Margaret Fell, Letters, and the Making of Quakerism* (New York: Routledge, 2017).

20. On the importance of letter writing in establishing eighteenth-century networks, see William Merrill Decker, *Epistolary Practices: Letter Writing in America Before Telecommunications* (Chapel Hill: University of North Carolina Press, 1998); Dena Goodman, *Becoming a Woman in the Age of Letters* (Ithaca: Cornell University Press, 2009); and Sarah M. Pearsall, *Atlantic Families: Lives and Letters in the Later Eighteenth Century* (Oxford: Oxford University Press, 2008).

Webb's focus on community began well before her journey to America; the importance of relationships is manifest throughout the story of her convincement in England and is woven into her call to preach. Specifically, her autobiographical narratives foreground the ways in which her sense of community is forged by a personal reception of the Light of Christ. In her letter to Anthony Boehm, for example, Webb's account of her convincement seems typical in that she writes of spiritual indifference, religious awakening, and eventual acceptance of God's grace and mercy. She is, like many other religious converts of the time, telling her own story and, thus, focusing on personal development. However, the very framework of the story she tells hints at her budding devotion to community. As Webb contemplated her own spiritual state, she received impressions from the divine that encouraged her to think beyond herself. Even while in the process of discovering her own spiritual journey, she felt called to comfort the children of God. It would not be long after she developed a deep commitment to Quakerism that she was "drawn by the spirit of love, to travel into the north of England," where she would begin preaching (43). While responding to the influence of the Light of Christ in her own life, Webb later recognized, she was also being prepared to invite others to do likewise. The journey she was making and the inspiration she was receiving extended well beyond her personal sphere—she believed she had been called to foster feelings of "universal love" so she could could nurture a vast network of committed believers (29).

The call to preach and establish community, Webb's writings make clear, often came in the form of a dream or vision—mediums through which, according to Quaker belief, God communicated with mortals. Indeed, Webb recorded multiple dreams and visionary or ecstatic experiences, noting, "in those days I had certain manifestations of many things in dreams" (44). Through her dreams she further cultivated feelings of that universal love, grounding her within a larger spiritual community.[21] The act of recording dream narratives was common in the seventeenth and eighteenth centuries; many autobiographical accounts written during Webb's lifetime contained detailed reports and interpretations of dreams and visions. Quakers, in particular, valued dreams, viewing them as powerful spiritual experiences

21. Mechal Sobel, *Teach Me Dreams: The Search for Self in the Revolutionary Era* (Princeton: Princeton University Press, 2000); Gerona, *Night Journeys*.

through which they received divine inspiration. Because these dreams often involved travel of some kind, they were frequently referred to as "night journeys," and these imaginative trips provided guidance on major decisions: as Carla Gerona attests, "dream interpretations plotted courses for people to take in their everyday lives on earth." Ultimately, the dreams of Friends "enabled them to better identify with and construct the identity of their group in a collective fashion." Quakers transformed "their dreams into creative stories that allowed Friends to define and redefine themselves, as well as their relationship to each other, to their nation, and to non-Quaker others."[22] Night journeys, then, encouraged Quakers to establish networks of relationships.

Like other itinerant preachers, Webb had dreams that guided her travels. While journeying in Northern England, for example, Webb had dreams that forewarned her of pending danger and seemed to offer protection. "I had many visions of spiritual things when the outward man was asleep," she explains, "and sometimes it seemed as though I was in great combats with evil spirits, and the good spirit used to give my soul the victory many times when the body was asleep, which used to be comfortable to me when I did awake" (202). She described the spirit that led her as being akin to a compass, pointing her in the direction that she should go. In 1697, she had dreams and visions through which she was called to share the gospel in America. Despite her husband's initial misgivings, and her own bout of illness before departure, Webb was determined to heed the call she had received. She thus crossed the Atlantic, and began preaching in the colonial context—a space that slowly expanded her sense of community to encompass another land and other racial groups.

While preaching in the American colonies, Webb felt the guidance of the Light of Christ woven throughout several significant dreams she had, many of which further expanded her understanding of Quaker community. Upon arriving in Virginia, for example, Webb was surprised by the number of slaves she encountered and wondered if "the visitation of the grace of God were afforded to them or not" (203). Virginia legislators, who had passed a law in 1667 stipulating that conversion to Christianity would not alter a slave's legal status, seemed to say no. Webb, however, wanted to know whether Christianity was indeed universal—could anything limit the boundaries of the

22. Gerona, *Night Journeys*, 2, 9, 3.

community of which she had become a part? Personal encounters with slaves did not answer Webb's question, but an eventual dream did. She recalled:

> I fell into a slumber, and dreamed I was a servant in a great man's house, and that I was drawing water at a well to wash the uppermost rooms of the house, and when I was at the well, a voice came to me, which bid me go and call other servants to help me and I went presently; but as I was going along in a very pleasant green meadow, a great light shined about me, which exceeded the light of the sun, and I walked in the midst, and as I went on in the way, I saw a chariot drawn with horses coming to meet me, and I was in care lest the light that shone about me, should frighten the horses, and cause them to throw down the people which I saw in the chariot; when I came to them, I looked on them, and I knew they were the servants, I was sent to call, and I saw they were both white and black people, and I said unto them, why have you stayed so long? And they said the buckets were frozen, we could come no sooner, so I was satisfied the call of the Lord was unto the black people as well as the white. (45)

In the context of her fascinating dream, Webb's questions about God's universal love had been answered. Her vision hinted at spiritual equality, which assured Webb that the message she had been called to share was indeed meant to be extended to all. Her dream also spoke to the expansive possibilities of a Quaker community unbounded by limits of race or gender and assured her that her efforts as a preacher would prove unifying. It confirmed to her that she had the responsibility to foster faith and forge relational ties.

Ultimately, Webb's dream indeed proved to be more than an answer to a question. She acted on the message she had received in this dream by embracing a more expansive meaning of universal love and weaving it into the context of her daily life. She did not passively accept that "the call of God was to the black people as well as to the white"; she actively extended the call, participating in the creation of that unlimited community she believed God had revealed to her. In a memoir written for her children, Webb explained,

> I saw the fulfilling of the vision in part before I returned to Old England, for we had an evening meeting at a Friend's house in New England and the Negros came in, and I felt a stream of divine love run to them. And one young man, a black, was so reached to by the love of God through

> Jesus Christ that his heart was so broken that the tears did run down like rain. And he was convinced of the truth and lived honestly in it and walked among Friends to his dying day and left a good savor behind him, and his wife and children kept to meetings when he was gone. These things have lived on my mind, to set them down as a memorial of the great and universal love of God, who would not that any should perish, but that all should come to the knowledge of the truth and be saved. (204–5)

As a result of her visionary dream, Webb incorporated African Americans into her own personal circles. By doing so, she remembered the overlooked and helped create a more inclusive Quakerism—a community that became willing to welcome all into gospel fellowship.

As a Quaker, as a preacher, as a writer, and as a visionary, Webb responded to the call of the Light of Christ, which encouraged her to build a powerful spiritual community. The stories she shared and the dreams she recounted were read by contemporary Friends and helped them establish a sense of purpose, identity, and community. Through her personal writings Webb offered members of her faith community a better sense of what it meant to be a Quaker. Many accepted her implicit invitation to become a part of her spiritual kin. Her words, and her dreams, helped connect Quakers on both sides of the Atlantic.

FROM REVELATION TO REVOLUTION

Included among Webb's various dreams is a visionary episode in which she imagines herself as the protagonist of Revelation 12, where a "woman fled into the wilderness" to escape the persecutions of Antichrist and raise a child variously identified as Christ or his church (101–2).[23] In her letter to Boehm, Webb recounts that during a period of intense spiritual struggle, "my soul was led into a wilderness" until a personal judgment day couched in the language of scripture. She recalls that "the day of the Lord came upon me, which burnt as an oven in my bosom, till all pride and vanity were burnt up, my former delights were gone, my old heavens were passed away within me, as with fire" (35). At the end of this personal apocalypse, Webb

23. Revelation 12:6.

experienced a rebirth and found "entrance into the heavenly kingdom or New Jerusalem" (43). For Webb, as for so many early Quakers, Revelation was the blueprint for her individual experience of the Light of Christ as well as a guide to the eschatological destiny of all earth.

This sense of Revelation's dual significance is evident both in her personal writings and in her verse-by-verse commentary on Revelation. For example, in her autobiographical "Short Memorial," Webb discusses John's account of being carried "away in the spirit into the wilderness," where a woman Webb identifies as "Mystery Babylon was seen . . . upon a scarlet colored beast, and now judgment is gone forth. . . . These things are and will be without, in the great world, but let me come nearer and desire to know the judgments of God to dwell in my heart, that hath been as a wilderness" (206).[24] Even more than she wanted to understand the geopolitical implications of John's prophecy in the "great world," Webb wanted to recognize its patterns "nearer," in her own life. Revelation provided Webb with an interpretive key to both history and current affairs, but it also facilitated introspection because "as it is in the great world, so it is in every obedient child of God and follower of the Lamb" (76). Each of the texts included in this compilation of Webb's work references the imagery or language of Revelation; it was a touchstone of Webb's theology and a baseline against which she evaluated her experience of the world.

Although she frequently describes her struggle with sin in metaphorical terms, identifying with the woman of Revelation 12 for spiritual reasons, Webb also experienced wilderness in a visceral, bodily sense. In the journal recounting her travels through colonial America with Rogers, Webb records experiences that she might have regarded as a literal fulfillment of scripture. Having left papacy and national churches—visible manifestations of Antichrist—an ocean away, Webb walked across the pathless landscape of North America to nurture "the children of [light]" as though she were the very woman John dreamed of on Patmos (186). En route to a monthly meeting in Maryland, she writes, "we traveled about fifty miles through the wilderness; about ten miles of the way there was no path" (189). This parallel between Revelation and reality begat other, metaphorical parallels; after her various journeys, when Webb worshipped with these children of light, she observed that many were "much tendered by the sweet streams of life that ran through the meeting," characterizing their experience of the Light of Christ as an encounter with

24. Revelation 17:3.

John's "pure river of water of life" (186).[25] Entries surrounding these excerpts from her journal make no mention of eschatology, but given Webb's decades-long fascination with the book of Revelation and the way in which her experience parallels a key scriptural narrative, her record seems evidence of a self-conscious identification with the woman in Revelation 12. Britain's American colonies became, for Webb, the wilderness envisioned by John.

Webb's effort to locate North America in sacred time and space reflects a common desire, among colonists, for an understanding of how the landscape and its Native inhabitants fit into the biblical narrative of creation, fall, and redemption. For some, who regarded these lands as the future home of the New Jerusalem, designating the Americas a *New World* was more than just an acknowledgment of their unfamiliarity; it was an expression of hope in the "new heaven and a new earth" promised by John.[26] However, Joseph Mede and others regarded the Americas as a bastion of satanic power that would need to be checked or overcome completely before the end times arrived. Determining how best to incorporate American lands and peoples into the eschatological tradition was a popular pursuit among Webb's contemporaries and, after her death, throughout the tumultuous eighteenth century.[27]

Some Meditations with Some Observations Upon the Revelations of Jesus Christ identifies the sufferings of early Friends preaching to the Massachusetts Bay Colony as events foreseen in John's dream. The angel that John saw, who flew "in the midst of heaven, having the everlasting gospel to preach unto them that dwell on the earth," was for Webb a representation of Quaker missionaries called to preach in Britain and the colonies.[28] God, she writes, "raised up able ministers of the gospel in the morning of this dispensation and sent them forth as sheep among wolves, in and amongst the natives of Old England; and sent them also to New England, and to other lands. Now here is the foundation of the everlasting gospel which the angel proclaimed" (115). Webb reads Revelation with an eye for specific historical parallels and an interest in her own role as a missionary to the North American colonies.

25. Revelation 22:1.

26. Revelation 21:1.

27. For a primer on the competing viewpoints of Protestant and especially Puritan exegetes, who regarded the Americas, alternately, as a promised land or hellscape, see Reiner Smolinski, "Israel Redivivus: The Eschatological Limits of Puritan Typology in New England," *New England Quarterly* 63, no. 3 (1990): 357–95.

28. Revelation 14:6.

In her commentary on chapters sixteen and seventeen of Revelation, Webb expands on this initial link to the New World with idiosyncratic commentary deviating from the views presented in popular Protestant commentaries on John's vision. In Revelation 17, after seeing a beast with seven heads and ten horns, John hears an angel explain, "the ten horns which thou sawest are ten kings. . . . These shall make war with the Lamb."[29] In his widely read exegesis on the passage, Matthew Henry speculates that the kings may be those that rise up after "the *Roman* empire be broken in pieces" or who will yet rise up "near the End of Antichrist's Reign"; he can offer no specifics, no certainty.[30] Similarly the collaborative *Annotations upon the Holy Bible* begun by Matthew Poole confesses that "who these Ten Monarchs be, or what these Ten Governments are, I must confess my self at a loss to determine."[31] However, Webb identifies these rulers with some specificity as "the kings of the national churches that are separated from the mother church and yet are her daughters." Like other radical Protestants, Quakers treated the Church of England with suspicion, regarding it as an outgrowth of the Roman Catholic church. And because the English monarch is the titular head of the Church of England, Webb identified "these kings, who seem to me to be in our day the persecuting power . . . both in Old England, and in New England, which will stand on record in ages to come together with the faithfulness of the sufferers" (140). Persecutions directed by Oliver Cromwell, King Charles II, Queen Anne, and Governor John Endecott of the Massachusetts Bay Colony were, for Webb, clearly prefigured in the Bible.

Believing that Revelation spoke of both Christ's physical arrival in a world devastated by conflict and the arrival of his spirit in the hearts of believers, Webb straddled a theological divide. Her desire to particularize and identify political actors is consonant with early Quaker eschatology, but scholars allege that the Quaker obsession with end times waned in the late seventeenth and early eighteenth century, a period when Friends increasingly focused on their experience of a personal Second Coming and not Christ's millennial reign over all the earth. Douglas Gwyn argues that

29. Revelation 17:12, 14.

30. Matthew Henry, *Exposition of the Old and New Testaments*, vol. 6, *An Exposition of the Several Epistles Contained in the New Testament* (London, 1721), 713.

31. Matthew Poole et al., *Annotations upon the Holy Bible*, vol. 2 (Edinburgh, 1701), n.p.

second-generation Friends such as Webb were quietists promoting "a static spatial teleology (a sanctified communal space in which God's will is realized) more than a temporal eschatology (a sense of God's will revealed in historical events)."[32] Webb clearly believed that the cosmic drama narrated in Revelation was playing out in her own life and heart, but she also sought to ground her reading of Revelation in both history and current events.

Tracing signs of "the Roman heathenish emperors" (80) and the rise of "the holy Catholic Church" (82) in John's dream, Webb places the sounding of the sixth trumpet, in Revelation 9, during "the time of the first Reformers"—locating England's embrace of Protestantism as a key point in sacred time (85). The rise of reformed national churches, and the persecution of Quaker preachers during Webb's lifetime constituted additional signs of the end times. So, too, the cessation of persecution; Webb believed that the Toleration Act of 1689 fulfilled John's promise that "the civil power will yet remain, only deprived of the dragon's power or persecuting spirit. So it may be said (and yet is), for though the persecuting power is not, yet the kingly power is yet remaining, for that is ordained of God" (138–39). Although Webb frequently condemns national churches, she celebrated the British nation as a divinely ordained state because it provided a measure of religious freedom to noncomformists. A careful reading of Revelation became the basis for her political views, as Webb waited for the "winnowing and trying day [to] come; and many in such a day will turn to the national churches," and "the cities of the national churches will fall" (141). Although she believed Britain to be a nation divinely ordained, she apparently expected London and other national centers of religious worship to be destroyed at the Judgment Day.

Webb's writing on Revelation and the future of nations like Britain found renewed interest among American Friends during the social upheaval of the American Revolution, when Quakers turned to her commentary as a guide to current events. In addition to the manuscript prepared by Webb for the press during her lifetime, a second known copy of *Some Meditations* was made during the course of the war by Joseph Buffington (1737–1785), a

32. Douglas Gwyn, "Quakers, Eschatology, and Time," in Angel and Dandelion, *Oxford Handbook of Quaker Studies*, 208.

Pennsylvania Friend who kept a store in East Bradford.[33] Buffington's annotation indicates that he copied the first part of Webb's account, through her comments on Revelation 11:11, "in the Spring of the year 1775." In other words, Buffington likely turned to Webb for guidance after the battle of Lexington and Concord, regarding the onset of war as a sign of the end times. He returned to Webb six years later and finished copying *Some Meditations* on "the 17th Day of February Anno Dom. 1781," just weeks before his nephew Richard, also of East Bradford, would be publicly accused of treason, having "willingly aided and assisted the enemies of this state."[34] Another nephew, named Joseph, fought with a South Carolina regiment in the Continental Army, and Buffington likely regarded this division in his family as a fulfillment of Webb's declaration that "when the seventh vial of God's wrath shall be poured out . . . there will be great searchings of heart, and divisions . . . among men" (141). Copying Webb's commentary allowed Buffington to make eschatological sense of the personal and public turmoil surrounding him.

In turning to *Some Meditations* and the book of Revelation for guidance during the war, Buffington participated in a religious movement that has long fascinated historians. Indeed, Gordon Wood suggests that the "historical literature on Revolutionary millennialism is approaching in complexity and sophistication the finespun discussions eighteenth-century clergymen themselves had on the subject."[35] These discussions regularly marginalize

33. In a nineteenth-century genealogical account, Lewis Palmer describes Buffington as "being of a benevolent nature, and often concerned to administer to the wants of the needy in the surrounding neighborhood. He remained a bachelor during life." Buffington also was a horse enthusiast who wrote *The Citizen and Countryman's Experienced Farrier* in 1784. See Lewis Palmer, *A Genealogical Record of the Descendants of John and Mary Palmer* (Philadelphia, 1875), 38.

34. Elizabeth Webb, *Some Meditations with Some Observations upon the Revelations of Jesus Christ*, manuscript, Chester County Historical Society, ms. 77111, pp. 69, 141; *Pennsylvania Packet*, 24 March 1781.

35. Gordon S. Wood, "Religion and the American Revolution," in *New Directions in American Religious History*, ed. Harry S. Stout and D. G. Hart (New York: Oxford University Press, 1997), 197. For the most significant overviews of millennial thought in North America during the late eighteenth century, see Alan Heimert, *Religion and the American Mind: From the Great Awakening to the Revolution* (Cambridge: Harvard University Press, 1966), 59–94, 413–509; Nathan O. Hatch, *The Sacred Cause of Liberty: Republican Thought and the Millennium in Revolutionary New England* (New Haven: Yale University Press, 1977); Ruth H. Bloch, *Visionary Republic: Millennial Themes in American Thought, 1756–1800* (Cambridge: Harvard University Press, 1985);

Quaker views on the subject, but Buffington's keen interest in Webb's commentary suggests that colonial Friends, like their Protestant counterparts, sought a divine perspective on the war and its eschatological significance.

In all of her writings, Webb consistently expressed a hope that her readers, correspondents, friends, and family members would keep the message of Revelation foremost in their minds, as she had throughout her life. In a letter to Jacob Morel and his wife, whom she helped to convert in New England, Webb teaches that they "will see that all these things that have been set up in the night of apostasy must be done away, both the old heavens and the old earth wherein unrighteousness dwelleth, and new heavens and a new earth will be created, wherein dwelleth righteousness" (184). Webb also held out John's promise of a new heaven and new earth to her children, exhorting them to "often remember your latter end. . . . There the souls of those that have passed through many tribulations, and have known their garments washed and made white in the blood of the Lamb, which taketh away all sins, behold the ineffable glory of God. They sing a new song, even the song of the Lamb, that none can learn, but those who are redeemed from the earth" (219). Her deepest, most frequently expressed desire was that others would reflect on the words of Revelation and come to experience for themselves, through the inner light, the changes that John foretold for the "great world." With the publication of this volume, Webb's eschatological message of admonition and encouragement now reaches a new generation of scholars, students, and Quakers; once again, "she calleth her friends."[36]

Reiner Smolinski, "Apocalypticism in Colonial North America," in *The Encyclopedia of Apocalypticism*, vol. 3, ed. Stephen J. Stein (New York: Continuum, 1998), 36–71; and James P. Byrd, *Sacred Scripture, Sacred War: The Bible and the American Revolution* (New York: Oxford University Press, 2013), 143–63.

36. Luke 15:9.

Works Prepared for Publication

A LETTER FROM ELIZABETH WEBB TO ANTHONY WILLIAM BOEHM, WITH HIS ANSWER

[Copies of this letter, from Webb to Boehm, circulated in manuscript during Webb's life, and in 1781, a Quaker printer and bookseller named Joseph Crookshank made this the first of Webb's works to be published. He sold the letter from his shop in Philadelphia, and it proved popular enough to merit a second edition in 1783; others would reprint it in decades to come. Although capitalization and spelling have been modernized in this text, the preface, punctuation, and paragraphing are those of Crookshank's 1781 edition.—Eds.]

The inducements to the publication of the following letter at this distant period, from the date of it, proceed from a hope entertained by some devout persons, who have been edified by the spiritual experiences it contains, that it may prove instructive and comforting to others alike piously disposed, and to obviate the inconveniences to which manuscripts are liable, through the negligence and inattention of transcribers, incorrect copies having been handed about;—it has therefore been revised, and is now recommended to the serious perusal of those who having entered on a religious life, may find encouragement and instruction to press forward with stability and humble resignation, through the various probations and conflicts attending them in their Christian progress, that they may obtain under their spiritual leader, the grace of God, the end of their faith, the salvation of their souls.

It may also be satisfactory to the readers, to have some account given of the writer, and the person to whom the letter was wrote, they are therefore briefly informed that Elizabeth Webb was an acknowledged minister among the people called Quakers, who from an apprehension of religious duty, and the constraints of gospel love, went from Pennsylvania to Great Britain, to visit her friends there about the year 1712, and in London contracted some acquaintance with Anthony William Boehm, chaplain to prince George of Denmark, the consort of Anne, Queen of England; he was by birth a German, but well acquainted with the English language, and died in the year 1722; the diverse writings on religious subjects he has left, show him to be a man of a truly pious and catholic disposition, which is also confirmed by the testimonials given of him by men of character in that time, who from their personal knowledge, mention him with great respect for his piety to God, and benevolence to mankind.

Philadelphia, eleventh month, 1782.

A LETTER FROM ELIZABETH WEBB TO ANTHONY BOEHM

Worthy Friend,

The kind respect thou showed me, when at London, hath laid me under an obligation wherein I find my mind drawn to communicate to thee in the openings of divine love, on which I must desire thy favorable construction; as I am almost a stranger to thee. What I have to write, hath been on my mind these several weeks, in that pure innocent love, in which is the communion of saints. I have no learned method to deliver my religious experience either by word or writing, but plainly and simply as the spirit of truth directs, and I being the weaker vessel too, have the more need to beg to be excused. I shall not write from notions or speculations; as at a distance, I look on such things as unsafe, and I know they are many times unsound, but I shall write a small part of what I have gone through, and what my soul hath tasted of the good word of life, which is near, that we may have fellowship together in God the Father of our spirits, and in his son Jesus Christ our Lord, whom my soul hath known, both in mercy and in judgment, to the mortifying, in a good degree, the fallen and corrupt nature, and to the purifying of my heart, so far, that I can say to his praise, I do not see HIM through particular forms, sects, party-impressions, or any such thing; no, my dear friend, I never sought after the Lord in these ways, nor for any of these ends, but I sought after him in my young years for salvation, and I still seek to him for the perfect restoration of my soul in him. I have nothing of my own to boast of, unless it be weakness and infirmities; but desire to rejoice in the cross of Christ, by which I am crucified to the world, in a good degree, and the world to me, so that I can say I die daily.

And as touching the fondness for education, religious profession and conversation, these things have cast no mist before my eyes.

I can see, own and love the image of my Lord and Saviour in any sort of profession, if the soul hath been educated in the heavenly university or school of Christ, nevertheless we cannot see God in or have fellowship with all sorts of conversations, that of the wicked is as "if there was no God, God is not in all their thoughts:"[1] and such as despise the image of the meek, humble Jesus, and will follow none of his precepts, nor his self-denying example, whilst they are here; the Lord will hereafter despise their image; for they shall have an image according to the seed or spirit, in which they lay down their body; every seed shall have its own body in the resurrection of the just and the unjust, and every one shall receive his own sentence: Thou well observest that sin, self-love, self-will, etc., contract the soul into a very narrow compress, but the love of God, breaks down all those walls of selfishness by which the soul is hedged in and restrained from universal love and benignity. This is very true, but, there are those who will not receive our love as it is in Jesus, nevertheless some have felt the flowings of the love and compassion of him, "that would not the death of a sinner, but rather that all would return to him, repent and live;" I am a witness for the Lord, that the shedding abroad of his love over the inhabitants of this nation, hath been like showers of rain in the spring time, I well remember that I told a Friend in London, I felt the divine extendings of the love of God, so to flow to the people, as I walked in the streets of the city, that I could have freely published the salvation of God, which is near, and his righteousness which is ready to be revealed, in the public places of concourse; the friend said he hoped it would not be required of me, this I mention to convince thee that universal love prevails in the hearts of some who are unknown to the world, and hardly known to their own brethren, and this is not to be wondered at, Eli did not know the inward exercise of Hannah,[2] and the prophet Elijah thought he had been left alone, until the Lord told him he had seven thousand in Israel who had not bowed to Baal;[3] the prophet Samuel, also when he looked out with an eye of reason

1. See Psalm 10:4.

2. 1 Samuel 1:8.

3. 1 Kings 19:18.

on the goodness of the stature of Eliab said, surely the Lord's anointed is before him;[4] so now unless the Lord be pleased to reveal things to us, we are liable to mistake. But blessed be the name of our most gracious God, who is the same that ever he was, he sees not as man sees, for man looks at the outward appearance, but God looks at the heart.[5]

I received thy second letter just as I was going out of London, of which I have sent thee a copy, with some annotations. My view therein is that if thou thinks it it may be of benefit to any, thou may communicate it; if not let it lie by thee.

I take great notice of thy Christian love and good advice in thy second letter, and do accept of it very heartily, and can assure thee, that my labor is not to gather people into a formality, but I labor according as the Lord enables me to gather souls to Christ, who is able to make the deceitful hearts of the children of men, plain, honest, upright and clean, and "when the inside is clean, the outside will be clean also,"[6] but I freely acknowledge that the glory of the true church or mystical body, or bride of Christ, which is made up of souls, who have entered into covenant with the Lord, to love and serve him forever, is within, her clothing is of wrought gold, and the curious needlework of virgin wisdom is upon her, for she having been stripped of all her old rags or garments of righteousness and unrighteousness, and having been washed in pure water, her bridegroom hath anointed her with holy oil, the holy unction of his spirit, and he is clothing her with the beautiful garment of his salvation, the robe of his righteousness; she is depending on him for her daily bread: So that she is not eating her own bread, nor wearing her own apparel; she cannot be content only with bearing his name, but longs to be made more and more a partaker of his divine nature, and the love of her Lord hath been and still is so largely extended to her, with her love so to him, that she is wholly subject to him, he ruleth in love, and she obeys in love, and this makes all things easy; she hath no will of her own, but the will of her Lord is her will in all things, all his commands are pleasant to her, because she delights to wait on him, and to serve in his presence, and had rather be deprived of all outward enjoyments, than of his presence and the enjoyment of his favor, her conversation is adorned with humility and meekness, her steps are comely in the eyes of her beloved, "all her children are taught of the

4. 1 Samuel 16:6.

5. 1 Samuel 16:7.

6. See Matthew 23:26.

Lord, established in righteousness, and great is their peace."[7] And my soul may say to the praise and glory of God, that no greater comfort can be enjoyed on this side of the grave, than to be a child or member of this church.

And now, my dear friend, I will give thee a short account of the dealings of the Lord with me in my young years, how he brought my soul through fire and water, for what end this hath lived in my mind I know not, except it be for our spiritual communion; but when my soul is lowest and nearest to the Lord in the simplicity of truth, then is my heart opened and my mind filled with divine love respecting this matter. I desire thee to peruse it inwardly, when thou art retired, and not to judge of it before thou hast gone through it, and then judge as freely as thou pleasest: I was baptized and educated in the way of the church of England, I went to school to a minister thereof, and loved and honored him greatly, he showed great kindness and tenderness to me, and in those days I looked on the ministers to be like angels, that brought glad tidings to the children of men;[8] but when I was about fourteen years of age, I went to live at a knight's house who kept a chaplain; I observed his conversation and saw it was vain, and I thought it ought not to be so, and was troubled in my mind, for I then began to think on my latter end, and also on eternity, and I had no assurance of salvation, or a state of happiness, if it should please the Lord to send the messenger of death to call me away. So the fear of the Lord laid hold on my mind, and I began to search the scriptures, and found they testified that the wicked should be turned into hell, and all those that forgot God; and I saw that both priests and people did too generally forget God, as soon as they came off their knees or from their devotion, and I was much afraid of hell, and wanted an assurance of a place in the kingdom of heaven; then I began to think on the great promises that were made for me in my baptism, as they called it, whereby they said I was made a member of Christ, a child of God, etc., and that I should renounce the devil and all his works, the pomps and vanities of this wicked world, and all the sinful lusts of the flesh, and should keep God's holy will and commandments. I thought indeed this was the way to obtain a place in the kingdom of heaven, but I had no power to do what I ought to do, nor to forsake what I ought to forsake, for I was very proud, vain and airy, but as I was thus inwardly exercised, and outwardly searching the scriptures, my understanding was more and more opened. I read and took notice that the ministers of Christ, which

7. See Isaiah 54:13.

8. See Luke 1:19.

he qualified and sent forth to preach were to do it freely, for Christ said, "freely ye have received, freely give,"[9] and that those "who run when the Lord never sent them, should not profit the people at all,"[10] and many such things opened in my mind and I used to ponder them in my heart, and the promises to the flock in Ezekiel 34, where the Lord promised to bind up that which was broken, and to strengthen that which was sick. Those and such like portions of the scriptures, were very comfortable to me, for I was sick of my sins, and my heart was broken many times before the Lord, and I thought, Oh that I had lived in the days of Christ, I would surely have been one of those that followed him, and I grieved because the Jews crucified him, so that I loved Christ in the outward appearance, and could have said (as Peter said) far be it from thee Lord to suffer:[11] Yet I did not know he was so near me by his Holy Spirit; but I was convinced that the hireling shepherds who teach for hire and divine for money[12] were not the ministers of Christ, by the testimony of the prophets and of Christ himself, who said "by their fruits ye shall know them,"[13] so I left going to hear them; and walked alone, for I went so long till a fear followed me into the worship house, and I thought it would be just upon me, if I was made an example for my inattention, to the spirit of truth. And when I was about fifteen years old, it pleased God to send the spirit of grace and supplication, into my heart, by which I prayed fervently unto the Lord; there was a divine breathing in my soul, I had no life in my forms of prayer, except that one which Christ taught his disciples, for which I have always had a reverent esteem, but when I was in a state to pray, I found that the spirit made intercession in me and for me, according to the present want and necessity of my soul, I remember the expressions that used to run through my mind were Oh Lord! preserve me in thy fear and in thy truth. Oh Lord! show me thy way, and make known thy mind and will unto me;—and I thought I was ready to obey it, and much desired to know the people of God, for my soul cried, Oh Lord where dost thou feed thy flock, why should I be as one that is turned aside from the flocks of thy companions. Oh the drawing cords of thy divine love. Oh thou didst draw my soul with long-

9. Matthew 10:8.

10. See Jeremiah 23:21.

11. Matthew 16:22.

12. See Micah 3:11.

13. Matthew 7:20.

ings and breathings after the knowledge of the only true God, and of Jesus Christ. There was then no condemnation for the sins of ignorance which the Lord winked at, but he called me to repent and forsake my pride and vain company, which was a great cross to the will of the flesh, and I took it up for several months, and while I did so, my soul had great peace and divine comfort, so that many times the enjoyment of divine love was more to me than my natural food, or any outward thing. I remember when the family used to ask me why I did not come to meat, I used to think I had meat to eat, they knew nothing of, and in those times of retirement, I had manifestations of sufferings, that I should go through, and a sight of several things which I met with since, and in those times I walked alone; I was convinced that the Quakers held the principles of truth, and that their ministry was the true ministry, but I dwelt then far from any of them, only thus it had happened. When I was about twelve years old, I was at a meeting or two of theirs, and the doctrine of one man that preached there, proved to me (as the wise man terms it) "like bread cast upon the waters, for it was found after many days,"[14] the sound of his voice seemed to be in my mind, when I was alone, and some of his words came fresh into my remembrance, and the voice and the words suited with the exercise of my mind, and at that time I met also with a little book of theirs, which as the doctrine it contained agreed with the doctrine of the apostles, I was confirmed in my judgment, that their profession agreed with the truth, but did not join with them, for by that time flesh and blood began to be very uneasy, under the yoke of retirement, and to groan for liberty. I was about sixteen years old, and the subtle enemy lay near, and did not want instruments; so I was persuaded by reasoning with flesh and blood, that I was young and might take a little more pleasure, and might serve God when I was older; so I let go my exercise of watching and praying, left off retirement, and let my love out to visible objects, pride and vanity grew up again, the divine, sweet, meek, loving spirit withdrew, and I could not find it again when I pleased, although I did seek it sometimes; for I could have been pleased with the sweet comforts of his love, yet I did not like to bear the daily cross, and being convinced that was the Quakers' principles, and believing they did enjoy the sweetness of divine love in their meetings, I went sometimes a great way to a meeting to seek for divine refreshment there, but to no purpose, for I was like some dry stick that had no sap nor virtue, unto which rain or sun shine, summer or winter are all alike; thus it was with me for

14. Ecclesiastes 11:1.

about three years. Oh the remembrance of that misspent time! Oh the tribulation that came on me for my disobedience, is never to be forgotten by me: But when I was about nineteen years of age, it pleased the Almighty to send his quickening spirit again into my heart, and his light shined into my mind, all my transgressions were set in order before me, and I was made deeply sensible of my great loss; and then, Oh! then the vials of the wrath of an angry Father, were poured out on the transgressing nature, Oh! then I cried, woe is me, woe is me, I am undone,[15] I have slain the babe of grace, I have crucified the Lord of life and glory to myself afresh, although I have not put him to open shame,[16] for I had been preserved in moral honesty in all respects, to that degree, that I durst not tell a lie, or speak an evil word, and could be trusted in any place, and in any thing, for this would be in my mind many times, that if I was not faithful in the unrighteous mammon, I should not be trusted with the heavenly treasure, but notwithstanding my righteousness, he whose eye penetrates all hearts found me so guilty, that I thought there was no mercy for me, Oh! that testimony of our blessed Lord Jesus, I found to be true, viz., Except your righteousness exceed the righteousness of the Scribes and Pharisees, there is no admittance into the kingdom of heaven or favor of God.[17] But after many days and nights of sorrow and great anguish, having no soul to speak to, it came into my mind to give myself up into the hands of God, and I said, Oh Lord! if I perish, it shall be at the gate of thy mercy, for if thou cast me into hell, I cannot help myself, therefore I will give up my soul, my life, and all into thy holy hand, do thy pleasure by me, thy judgements are just, for I have slighted thy sweet love, and have slain the babe of grace. And as I sunk down into death, and owned and submitted to the judgments of God, my heart was broken, which before was hard, and it pleased my merciful Father to cause his divine sweet love, to spring again in my hard, dry and barren soul, as a spring of living water, and the fire of the wrath of God was mightily abated, and the compassionate bowels of a tender Savior my soul felt, I had living hope raised in my mind, yet greater afflictions came afterwards, so that I may say by experience, "strait is the gate and narrow is the way indeed, that leads to life;"[18] and I have cause to believe, none but such as are made willing to be stripped of all that belongs to self, or the old man, and do become

15. Isaiah 6:5.

16. See Hebrews 6:6.

17. Matthew 5:20.

18. Matthew 7:14.

as a little child, can rightly or truly enter in at the strait gate. And I do find by experience, that no vulture's eye, no venemous beast, nor lofty lion's whelp, can look into or tread in this holy narrow way, although it is our king's high way:[19] Oh! the longing that there is in my soul, that all might consider it. But to proceed, I thought all was well, the worst is now over, and I am again taken into the favor of God, and so I was led into an elevation of joy, though inwardly in silence; but in a few days my soul was led into a wilderness, where there was no way, no guide, no light, that I could see, but darkness such as might be felt indeed, for the horrors of it were such, that when it was night I wished for morning, and when it was morning I wished for evening, the Lord was near but I knew it not, he had brought my soul into the wilderness, and there he pleaded with me by his fiery law, and righteous judgments; the day of the Lord came upon me, which burnt as an oven in my bosom, till all pride and vanity were burnt up, my former delights were gone, my old heavens were passed away within me, as with fire, and I had as much exercise in my mind of anguish and sorrow as I could bear, day and night, for several months, and not a drop of divine comfort, I could compare my heart to nothing, unless it were a coal of fire, or a hot iron, no brokenness of heart or tenderness of spirit, although I cried to God continually in the deep distress of my soul, yet not one tear could issue from my eyes, Oh! the days of sorrow and nights of anguish, that I went through, no tongue can utter or heart conceive, which hath not gone through the like; I could have wished I had been some other creature, that I might not have known such anguish and sorrow, for I thought all other creatures were in their proper places, but my troubles were aggravated by the strong oppression and temptation of Satan, who was very unwilling to lose his subject, so he raised all his forces, and made use of all his armour, which he had in the house, and I found him to be like a strong man armed indeed, for he would not suffer me to enter into resignation, but would have me look into mysteries that appertain to salvation, with an eye of carnal reason, and because I could not so comprehend, he caused me to question the truth of all things that are left upon record in the holy scriptures, and would have persuaded me into the Jews' opinion concerning Christ, and many other baits and resting places he laid before me, but my soul hungered after the true bread, the bread of life, which came from God out of heaven, which Christ testified of which I had felt near, and my soul had tasted of it.[20] Although the

19. See John 28:7–8.

20. See John 6:27–71.

devil prompted me with his temptations, my soul could not feed on them, but cried continually, thy presence Oh Lord! or else I die. Oh! let me feel thy saving arm or else I perish. Oh Lord! Give me faith. Thus was my soul exercised in earnest supplications unto God night and day, and yet I went about my outward occasions, and made my complaint to none but God only, and I have often since considered that any soul that can be content to feed on any thing below the enjoyment of God, the subtle serpent finds suitable baits for them; so having known the terrors of God and the subtle wiles of satan, I am concerned sometimes to persuade people to repent, and to warn them to flee from the wrath to come. Now all my faith which I had before, whilst in disobedience, proved like building on a sandy foundation, etc.[21] All the comfort I used to have in reading the scriptures, was taken away, and I durst not read for sometime, because it added to my condemnation; so I was left to depend upon God alone, who caused me to feel a little hope at times, like a little glimmering of light underneath my troubles, which was some stay to my mind, and if it had not been so, I had fallen into despair, but I much desired to be brought through my troubles the right way, and not to shake off or get over them in my own time; I had not freedom to make known my condition to any person, for I used to think if the Lord did not help me, in vain was the help of man, and I have since seen it was well I did not upon several accounts, for I might have come to a loss if I had done so; as it was the will of the Lord to humble me, and to turn up and throw down, all that which might be imputed to man or self, that I might know the work or building of the Lord to be raised from the foundation of his own power, where there is none of man's building, that all the glory might be given to him alone, for we are very apt to say in effect, I am of Paul, I am of Apollos, I am of Cephas and I of Christ, as if Christ was divided; but the Lord will not give his glory to another, nor his praise to graven images; for as thou my friend well observest, the chief that we ought to labour for is to make people sensible of their corruption, to direct them to the word nigh, and to be good examples to them; so in the Lord's due and appointed time, when he had seen my suffering of that fiery kind to be sufficient, he was pleased to cause his divine love to flow in my bosom, in an extraordinary manner, and the Holy Spirit of divine light and life, did overcome my soul; then a divine sense and understanding was given me to know the power, and also the love of God in sending his only Son, out of his bosom into the world, to take upon him, a body of flesh, wherein he

21. See Matthew 7:26–27.

did go through the whole progress of suffering, for the salvation of mankind, and so did break through, and break open the gates of death, and repaired the breach that old Adam had made between God and man, and restored the path for souls to come to God.

And the Almighty was pleased at that time to make my simple soul sensible, that he did send the spirit of his Son again into my heart, in order to lead me through the progress of his suffering, that as he died for sin, so I might die to sin, by bearing the daily cross, and living in self denial, humility and obedience to God my Heavenly Father, in all things he should require of me, and then the baptism of the Holy Ghost, compared to water, as well as fire, my soul came to witness, and the ministration of judgment and condemnation, I saw had a glory in it, which made way for the ministration of life, and the ax of God's word was laid to the evil root of the tree, etc.,[22] and the voice of him that preached repentance my soul heard, that called for the mountains to be laid low, and the valleys to be raised,[23] viz., the mountains of my natural temper, that a plain way might be made for the ransomed soul to walk in, and the Lord showed me, how John the Baptist came to be counted the greatest prophet that was born of a woman,[24] viz., because he was the forerunner of Jesus Christ, and is rightly termed the mourner, and how the least in the kingdom of heaven was greater than he that is under his ministration only, which was to decrease, but the ministration of Jesus was to increase,[25] whose baptism is with the Holy Ghost, and with fire, and he will thoroughly purge his floor;[26] then I came to witness that it is indeed the work of God to believe rightly and truly on him whom God hath sent, that this purifying saving faith is the gift of God, and the very spring or vital principle of it (divine love), then I mourned over him whom I had pierced with my unbelief and hardness of heart, and I did eat my bread with weeping and mingled my drink with tears, I was between 19 and 20 years of age, when these great conflicts were on my mind, by which I was brought very humble, and I had entered into solemn covenants with God Almighty, that I would answer his requirings, if it were to the laying down my natural life; but when

22. See Matthew 3:10.

23. See Luke 3:5.

24. See Matthew 11:11.

25. See John 3:30.

26. See Matthew 3:12.

it was showed me that I ought to take up the cross in a little thing, I had like to have hearkened to the reasoner again, and been disobedient in the day of small things;[27] for although I had gone through so much inward exercise, yet I was afraid of displeasing my superiors, being then a servant to great persons. It was showed me, that I should not give flattering titles to man, and I was threatened inwardly that if I would not be obedient to the Lord's requirings, he would take away his good spirit from me again, so I was in a strait, I was afraid of displeasing God, and afraid of displeasing man, till at last I was charged by the Spirit, with honoring of man more than God, for in my address to God, I did use the plain language, but when I spoke to man or woman I must speak otherwise, or else they would be offended, and some would argue that God Almighty being that only one, that therefore the single language was proper to him alone, and man being made up of compound matter, the plural language was more proper to him, etc.[28] Oh the subtle twistings of proud Lucifer that I have seen, would be too large to insert, but although God Almighty is that only one, yet he is that being of all beings, for in him we live, move and have our being; but let the cover be what it would, I had scripture on my side, which they called their rule, and I knew proud man disdained to receive that language from an inferior, which he gave to the Almighty: So it became a great cross to me, but it was certainly a letting thing in the way of the progress of my soul, until I gave up to the Lord's requirings in this small thing; these things I signify to thee, dear friend, in great simplicity, that thou mayest see, how the Lord leads out of the vain customs that are in the world, not only in what I mentioned, but also in many other things, and hath led in that humble self-denying way, which Christ both taught and practised, when he was visible among men. Christ is the true Christian's pattern, and his spirit their leader, and now I show thee this in truth and sincerity, because I would not be misunderstood by thee, viz., I am a single soul, wholly devoted to the Lord, and so do not plead for a form, for form's sake, neither do I plead for a people as a people, for we are grown to be a mixed multitude, much like the children of Israel when they were in the

27. See Zechariah 4:10.

28. Webb refers here to the Quaker refusal to use specific pronouns (for instance *you* rather than *thee* or *thou*) and bestow honorifics on individuals of high social station or those who held civic office. Quakers used the term *plural language* or sometimes, as in her "Short Account of My Voyage into America," *double language* to condemn those who spoke thus, in what they considered a duplicitous manner.

wilderness,[29] but this I may say to the praise and glory of God, that the principle that we make profession of, is the very truth, viz., Christ in the male and in the female, the hope of glory, and Christ thou knowest is the way, the truth and the life, and none comes to God but by him,[30] so there is a remnant which like Joshua and Caleb of old are true to the Lord, who is their spiritual leader, and follow him faithfully, and they stand clear in their testimonies against all dead formalities, which are but as images, when the vital principle, viz., the divine love is withdrawn, and yet as the spirit of Jesus leads out of all vain customs and traditions, which are in the world, and leads us in the plain, humble, meek, self-denying life and conversation, which Christ walked in while he was visible among men; I could heartily wish all to follow the leadings of his spirit herein, that thereby they may confess Christ before men; but if it please the Almighty to accept of souls, without leading them through such fiery trials, as he brought me through, or without requiring such things of them as he required of me, far be it from me to judge, that such have not known the Lord, or the indwellings of his love, if the fruits of the spirit of Jesus be plain upon them; for every tree is known by its fruits, and to our own master we must stand or fall. But dear friend, as thou well observed, that purification is a gradual work, I may say so by experience, for when the old adversary could no longer draw me out into vain talking, and foolish jesting, then he perplexed me with vain thoughts, some of which were according to my natural disposition, and some of them quite contrary, and Oh! I cried mightily unto the Lord for power over vain thoughts, for they were a great trouble to me, and I stood in great fear lest one day or other, I should fall by the hand of the enemy, but the Lord spake comfortably to my soul, in his own words left upon record, "fear not little flock it is your Father's good pleasure to give you the kingdom,"[31] and the Lord gave me an evidence along with it, that my soul was one of that little flock; another time when I was very low in my mind, these words sprang with life and virtue, viz., "although thou hast lain amongst the pots, yet I will give thee the wings of a dove, covered with silver, and her feathers of yellow gold."[32] Oh! it was wonderfully comfortable to me, when the Holy Ghost did bring a promise

29. See Exodus 12:38; Numbers 11:4.

30. John 14:6.

31. Luke 12:32.

32. Psalm 68:13.

to my remembrance, and gave me an evidence that it was my portion, so I pondered on this, concerning the wings of a dove, and I thought it must needs be the wing of innocency, whereby my soul might ascend unto God by prayer, meditation and divine contemplation, and so I took delight to pray in secret and fast in secret, from the secret outgoings of my mind as well as I could, and my Heavenly Father which seeth and heareth in secret, himself did reward me openly,[33] for then, when I went to meetings, I did not sit in darkness, dryness and barrenness, as I used to do in the times of my disobedience, but I did reap the benefit of the end of the coming of Christ, who said "the thief cometh not but to kill, to steal and to destroy, but I am come that ye might have life, and that you might have it more abundantly."[34] So, the thief had in the time of my disobedience stole my soul from Jesus, who saith, "whoso loveth father or mother, etc., or his own life more than me is not worthy of me,"[35] and so it had been with me, and I missed the benefit of reaping the end of his coming, for several years, but he in mercy being returned, afforded my bowed down soul the enjoyment of his divine presence, and was pleased to cause his love, which is the true life of the soul, to abound in my bosom in meetings, that my cup did overflow, and I was constrained, under a sense of duty, to kneel down in the congregation, and confess to the goodness of God, and pray to him for the continuation of it, and to pray for power whereby I might be enabled to walk worthy of so great a favor, benefit and mercy, that I had received at his bountiful hand; and I remember after I had made public confession to the goodness of God, my soul was as if it had been in another world, it was enlightned and enlivened by the divine love, that I was in love with the whole creation of God, and I saw every thing to be good in its place, and I was showed things ought to be kept in their proper places, the swine ought not to come into the garden, nor the clean beasts ought not to be taken into the bedchamber; and as it was in the outward, so it ought to be in the inward and new creation; so everything began to preach to me, the very fragrant herbs, and beautiful innocent flowers had a speaking voice in them to my soul, and things seemed to have another relish with them than before: The judgments of God were sweet to my soul, and I was made to call to others sometimes, to come and taste and see, how good the Lord is, and to exhort them to prove the Lord, by an

33. See Matthew 6:4, 6, 18.

34. John 10:10.

35. Matthew 10:37.

obedient, humble, innocent walking before him, and then they would see, that he would pour out of his spiritual blessings in so plentiful a manner, that there would not be room enough to contain them, but the overflowings would return to him, who is the fountain, with thanksgivings, etc. And I was made to warn people, that they should not provoke the Lord by disobedience, for although he bears and suffers long, as he did with the rebellious Israelites in the wilderness, yet such shall know him to be a God of justice and judgment, and shall be made to confess one day.

And, thus dear friend, I have given thee a plain but a true account of my qualification, and call to the service of the ministry; but it was several years, before I came to a freed state or even temper of mind, for sometimes clouds would arise and interpose between my soul and the rising sun, and I was brought down into the furnace often, and found by experience that every time my soul was brought down as into the furnace of affliction, that it did still come up more clean and bright, and although the cloud did interpose between me and the rising sun, yet when the sun of righteousness did appear again, he brought healing as under his wings, and was nearer than before.[36] Thus dear friend, I express things in simplicity, as they were represented to me, in the manifestation of them in the morning of my days. So I came to love to dwell with judgment, and used often to pray, saying Oh Lord! Search me and try me, for thou knowest my heart better than I know it, and I pray thee let no deceitfulness of unrighteousness lodge therein, but let thy judgments pass upon every thing that is contrary to thy pure divine nature: thus my soul used to breathe to the Lord continually, and hunger and thirst after a more full enjoyment of his presence, although he is a consuming fire to the corrupt nature of the old man, yet my soul loved to dwell with him, or else I found many sorts of corruptions would be endeavouring to spring up again, and so I resigned up my mind to the Lord, with desires that he would feed me with food convenient for me; and this I can say by experience, that the soul that is born of God, doth breathe to him, as constantly by prayer as the sucking child, when it is born into the world, doth draw in and breathe out the common air; so the child of God doth draw in and breathe forth the breath of life, by which man was made a living soul to God, and this breathing that is pure and divine, all that are in the old man or fallen corrupt nature know nothing of, it is a mystery to them; but a babe in Christ knows it to be true, and although the children in our Father's family are of several ages,

36. See Malachi 4:2.

growths or statures, both in strength and understanding, yet this I have observed in all my travels, that those that live to God, continue in a state of breathing to him while here, and hunger and thirst after a more full enjoyment of his divine presence, that as every day brings us nearer to the grave, so every day the soul may be brought into a more divine union and communion with God; which is a certain sign to me, of the divine life and health of a soul, if I find it sweetly breathing unto the Lord, and hungering and thirsting after his righteousness; and it is very evidently seen, and easily known by the conversation of persons, what manner of spirit doth govern in them, although many will not believe those things if it be declared to them, neither will they try whether it be so or not, but they are satisfied with the husk of religion:[37] Oh! what will they do when the rudiments and beggarly elements of this world fall off, and all our works must pass through the fire; my very soul mourns for them, but we must press forward and leave them if they will not arise out of their false rest.

Dear friend, as thou well observed, it is a great help to the soul to know its own corruptions, and from whence it is fallen, that it may know whither to return. These things are very true, and the knowledge of them hath been a great comfort to me, and so have the experiences of the servants of the Lord, agreeable to the testimonies left on record, which are as waymarks to the spiritual traveler; and we have a great privilege in and by them, but above all Christ our holy pattern and heavenly leader, my soul prizeth the knowledge of his footsteps, the leading of his spirit, the spirit of truth, the Comforter, which the Father hath sent to lead us into all truth, who hath said, "by this I know that I am true, because I seek not mine own honor, but the honor of him that sent me."[38] And Oh! saith my soul, that we may follow the leadings of our unerring guide in all things that he may lead us into, and I have good cause to believe, he will bring through all tribulations to the honor of God and our comfort; for the Lord hath brought my soul through many trials, one after another as he saw meet, some more of which I may give a hint of, viz., after my inward tribulation was abated, then outward trials began, for there were some of no small account, that endeavored with all their might and cunning, to hinder the work from prospering in me, and as Saul hunted David, and sought to take away his natural life, so these hunted my soul to take away its life, which it had in God, but all wrought together for my good.

37. See Luke 15:16.

38. See John 5:23–36.

I have often seen, and therefore may say, the Lord knoweth what is best for his children, better than we know for ourselves, and so my enemies instead of driving my soul away from God, drove it more near to him, for this trial caused me to prove the spirit which had the exercise of my mind, and I found it to be the spirit of truth, which the worldly and self-minded cannot receive, for I found the nature of it to be harmless and holy, and to lead me to love mine enemies, to pity them and pray for them, and this love was my preservation, and as I gave up in obedience to the operation and requiring of this meek spirit, it ministered such peace to my soul, that the world cannot give. But there was a disposition in me, to please all, which I found to be very hard for me to be weaned from, so as to stand single to God, for when I did fear man, I had nothing but anguish and sorrow, and I used often to walk alone and pour out my complaint to the Lord. But after a long time when the Lord had tried my fidelity to him as he saw meet, one day as I was sitting in a meeting in silence, waiting upon the Lord, to know my strength renewed in him and by him. This portion of scripture was given to me, viz., "Comfort ye my people, saith your God, speak comfortably to Jerusalem and cry unto her, that her warfare is accomplished, that her iniquities are pardoned, that she hath received of the Lord's hand double for all her sins."[39] This brought great comfort to my soul, and I treasured it in my heart, and I made this observation, that from that time the Lord gave my soul (as the apostle Peter expresses it) a more abundant entrance into the heavenly kingdom or New Jerusalem, whose walls are salvation and her gates praise, and my mind was brought into more stillness, and troublesome thoughts were in a good degree expelled, and my outward enemies grew weary of their work and failed of their hope. The praise I freely, in great humility, offer up and ascribe to almighty God, for it was his own work to preserve me from many strong temptations. So after I had peace at home every way, I was drawn by the spirit of love, to travel into the north of England, and on my journey my soul had many combats with the evil spirit; when I was asleep he tormented me as long as he could. I have indeed had a long war with the devil many ways, and abundance of courage was given to me to make war with him, and I always gained the victory, when cowardly fearful nature was asleep, which was comfortable to my mind, and I did hope that the Lord would give me perfect victory over the devil when I was awake, as he had let me see it to be so when I was asleep, and the spirit which led me forth, was to me like a needle of a compass, touched with a

39. Isaiah 40:1–2.

lodestone, for so it pointed where I ought to go, and when I came to the far end of the journey. In those days I had certain manifestations of many things in dreams, which did come to pass according to their significations, and I was many times forewarned of enemies, and so was better able to guard against them; I traveled in great fear and humility, and the Lord was with me to his glory and my comfort, and brought me home again, in peace. And in the year 1697, in the sixth month, as I was sitting in a meeting in Gloucester, which was then the place of my abode, my mind was gathered into perfect stillness for some time, and my spirit was as if it had been carried away into America, and after it returned, my heart was as if it had been dissolved with the love of God, and it flowed over the great ocean, and I was constrained to kneel down and pray for the seed of God in America, and the concern never went out of my mind day nor night, until I went to travel there in the love of God, which is so universal that it reaches over sea and land; but when I looked at my concern with an eye of human reason, it seemed to be very strange and hard to me, for I knew not the country, nor any that dwelt therein; and I reasoned much concerning my own unfitness, but when I let in such reasonings, I had nothing but death and darkness, and trouble attended my mind, but when I resigned up my all to the Lord, and gave up in my mind to go, then the divine love did spring up in my heart, and my soul was at liberty to worship the Lord as in the land of the living; thus I tried and proved the concern several times in my own heart, till at last these words ran through my mind with authority, viz., the fearful and unbelieving shall have their portion with the hypocrite in the lake that burns with fire and brimstone; which is the second death; this brought a dread, and I told my husband that I had a concern on my mind to go to America, and asked him if he could give me up. He said he hoped it would not be required of me; but I told him it was, and that I should not go without his free consent, which seemed a little hard to him at first, but a little while after I was taken with a violent fever, which brought me so weak, that all that saw me thought I should not recover. But I thought my day's work was not done, and my chief concern in my sickness was about going to America. But some were troubled that I had made it public, because they thought I should die, and people would speak reproachfully of me, and said, if I did recover, the ship would be ready to sail before I should be fit to go, etc. But I thought if they would but carry me and lay me down in the ship, I should be well, for the Lord was very gracious to my soul in the time of my sickness, and gave me a promise that his presence should go with me; and then my husband was made very willing to give me up, he said if it were for seven years, rather than to have me taken from him forever.[40] So at last all those difficulties passed over, and I sailed from Bristol in the ninth month, 1697, with my companion Mary Rogers. The dangers we were in at sea, and the faith and courage the Lord gave to my soul would be too large here to relate, for I had such an evidence of my being in my proper place, that the fear of death was taken away; Oh! it is good to trust in the Lord and be obedient to him, for his mercies endure forever; so about the middle of the twelfth month, 1697, through the good providence of the Almighty, we arrived in Virginia, and as I traveled along the country from one meeting to another, I observed great numbers of black people, that were in slavery, and they were a strange people to me, and I wanted to know whether the visitation of God was to their souls or not, and I observed their conversation, to see if I could discern any good in them, so after I had traveled about four weeks, as I was in bed one morning in a house in Maryland, after the sun was up and shone into the chamber, I fell into a slumber, and dreamed I was a servant in a great man's house, and that I was drawing water at a well to wash the uppermost rooms of the house, and when I was at the well, a voice came to me, which bid me go and call other servants to help me and I went presently; but as I was going along in a very pleasant green meadow, a great light shined about me, which exceeded the light of the sun, and I walked in the midst, and as I went on in the way, I saw a chariot drawn with horses coming to meet me, and I was in care lest the light that shone about me, should frighten the horses, and cause them to throw down the people which I saw in the chariot; when I came to them, I looked on them, and I knew they were the servants, I was sent to call, and I saw they were both white and black people, and I said unto them, why have you stayed so long? And they said the buckets were frozen, we could come no sooner, so I was satisfied the call of the Lord was unto the black people as well as the white, and, I saw the fulfilling of it in part, before I returned out of America, with many more remarkable things, which would be too tedious here to mention.[41]—But, Oh! great is the condescension and goodness of God to poor mankind, it is a good observation on the tender dealings of our heavenly

40. Richard Webb's willingness to give up his wife "for seven years" was likely meant to echo the biblical account of Jacob, who worked for his wife Rachel seven years before their marriage. See Genesis 29:18.

41. [Author's or publisher's note:] "Ethiopia shall soon stretch out her hands unto God." Psalm 68:31.

Father, "that we may set up our Ebenezer and say Hitherto hath the Lord helped us,"[42] and indeed I may say to his praise, it hath been through many straits and difficulties, more than I can number, and they have all wrought together for the good of my soul, and I have cause to believe, that every son or daughter he receives, he chastens, tries, and proves, and these that do not bear the chastisements of God, do prove bastards and not sons, but I may say as one did of old, "It is good for me that I have been afflicted, etc.,"[43] and it is good to follow the leadings of the Spirit of God, as faithful Abraham did, who was called the friend of God, who did not withhold his only son, when the Lord called for him, and it is my belief the Lord will try his chosen ones as gold is tried, and will yet refine them as gold is refined, and what if he brings us yet down again into the furnace, which way it shall please him, until we are seven times refined. We shall be the better able to bear the impression of his image upon us in all our conversations, and if the day should come, wherein none shall buy nor sell, that have not the mark of the beast, either in their right hand or in their forehead, it is but what hath been told us beforehand,[44] and these that will know an overcoming, it must be by the blood of the Lamb, viz., by abiding in the meek, love, and suffering seed, and by the word of their testimony, and that love not their lives unto death, we may observe that those that had not the mark of the beast in their forehead, if they had in their right hand it would do, they could show it if there was occasion, to keep off a stroke (this I take near home). Oh the mystery of iniquity how secretly it works, we may well say, the testimony that Jesus bore to the young man, that desired to follow him, is very true, "Foxes have holes and fowls of the air have nests, but the Son of man hath not where to lay his head."[45] Oh! Innocent truth, Oh! plain, meek, humble Jesus, where doth he repose, where doth he reign without molestation.

Dear Friend, excuse my freedom with thee, for the love of God constraineth me, and I do believe that the Lord will show thee yet further, what testimony thou must bear for his name, and what thou must suffer for his sake (if faithful), for trying times will come, and offences will be given (and taken) but there is nothing will offend those that love the Lord Jesus above all, for although many murmured and were offended at Jesus when he told

42. 1 Samuel 7:12.

43. Psalm 119:71.

44. See Revelation 13:17.

45. Matthew 8:20.

them the truth, and that which was of absolute necessity for all to know and witness in themselves, as we read in John 6, beginning at the 32nd verse in his answer to the Jews, but by that time he had done, many of his disciples went from him, then said he to the twelve, "Will ye also go away." But Peter said, "whither shall we go, thou hast the words of eternal life, and we believe and are sure, thou art Christ, the son of the living God."[46] So God hath given to the faithful to believe, yea, and we are sure that the spirit of truth is come, that leads the followers of it into all truth, and that Christ who is one with his Spirit, who was once offered, to bear the sins of many, has appeared again the second time without sin unto salvation. Oh! surely the goodness of God hath been very great to the children of men from age to age, and from one generation to another, ever since the fall of our first parents, the more my mind penetrates into it, the more I am like to be swallowed up in admiration of his condescension and goodness through all his dispensations, but above all in the manifestation of Jesus Christ, our holy pattern and heavenly leader. Oh! my soul praise him for whom the knowledge of his holy footsteps, God gave for a light to us gentiles! and to be his salvation to the ends of the earth, and hath given his Spirit to dwell in us, and accepted our souls to dwell in him. Oh admirable goodness! shall we leave him? He is the word of eternal life, and whither shall we go? and so far as any are followers of Jesus, so far I desire to follow them, or to be one with them, and no further, let these do what they will, if any will go back into the sea, out of which the beast ariseth, and receive his mark, our leader is not to be blamed, he holds on his way, and causes his trumpet to be blown in Zion, and an alarm to be beaten in his holy mountain, and whosoever heareth the sound of the trumpet, and taketh not warning if the sword of the Lord do come (in any kind) and take him away, his blood shall be upon his own head. He heard the sound of the trumpet and took not warning, but he that taketh warning shall deliver his own soul. But great is the duty of a watchman, and great is the kindness God expressed in Ezekiel 33. Oh my dear friend, my heart is full of the goodness of the Lord, but I must stop writing lest I should be tedious to thee, and indeed it might be accounted foolishness for me to write after this manner to one in thy station. But I find a constraint thereto and must commit it to thy judgment, be it what it may, but this I will assure thee, my heart is plain, I mean as I speak, and I find it my safest place so to do, and to keep in humble obedience to the Lord, in whatsoever he requires of me, yet I know the wisdom of God,

46. John 6:67–69.

appears to be foolishness in the eyes of the wise men of this world, and we know that the wisdom of this world is foolishness with God, and will prove so in the latter end, to these poor souls, that so mightily esteem of it, but the souls of the righteous are in the hand of the Lord, and there shall no torment touch them, although in the sight of the unwise, both their life and their death is taken for misery, nevertheless they are in peace.

I desire if thou findest anything on thy mind, please to let me have it, etc. So in the love that is pure, doth my soul greet thee and remain

Thy friend in true sincerity, Elizabeth Webb.

THE ANSWER TO THE FOREGOING LETTER

Dear Friend,

I am heartily glad you are come to town again, so that I might have an opportunity of seeing you, before you leave England, your letter hath been read with great satisfaction by myself and many of my friends. But I have not been able to recover it yet out of their hands. Some have even desired to transcribe it for their edification, and this is the reason, I did not send you presently an answer, though it hath been all along upon my mind to express the satisfaction I had at the reading thereof, and to assure how welcome news it is to me whenever I meet with a fellow pilgrim, traveling to the city which is adorned with twelve pearls, to receive all such who have made up the family of God in this wicked generation, and have been presented for his peculiar people in all parts and denominations of Christendom, which now go altogether a whoring after the imaginations of their own heart, I had a mind to have given you at large my thoughts upon your letter, true love being of a universal and overflowing nature, and not easily shut up by names, notions, peculiar modes, forms and hedges of men. And if you'll be pleased to correspond with me, even after your return from America, I shall always be ready to answer your kindness, and to make up again wherein I have been wanting at present, and so recommend you to the infinite favour and protection of the Lord.

I remain in sincerity your friend and servant, Anthony William Boehm

Strand, January 2, 1712.

SOME MEDITATIONS WITH SOME OBSERVATIONS UPON THE REVELATIONS OF JESUS CHRIST

By
Elizabeth Webb

[Webb's fair copy of this undated manuscript is held by Haverford College; an eighteenth-century copy in the hand of Joseph Buffington is held by the Chester County Historical Society. Webb quotes almost the entirety of the King James translation of Revelation in her commentary, reproducing a verse or verses before offering her exegesis on that passage. Because the biblical text is widely available, it has been omitted from this edition; numbers in bold (e.g., **1:1**) indicate the chapter and verse of the biblical text that Webb is discussing.—Eds.]

Some meditations with some observations upon the revelations of Jesus Christ, which God gave to him to shew unto his servants things which must shortly come to pass, which Revelations of Jesus Christ belong to every sincere soul to consider of, because he is a follower of the Lamb, and doth and will [see] the fulfilling of many of these mysteries in himself in his spiritual warfare in his day.[1]

1. Webb clearly regarded the book of Revelation as a guide to contemporary political events and suggests that its prophecies will shortly be fulfilled, during the lifetime of her eighteenth-century readers.

And also he will see the vials of divine vengeance poured out upon Antichrist, for the work of God will be carried on from age to age to the finishing of time here and to the total separation of the tares from the wheat, and then eternity reserves all glory to God in the highest.[2] The secrets of the Lord are with them that fear him and he will shew them his covenant.[3]

I will stand upon my watch, and set me upon the tower and watch to see what he will say unto me and what I shall answer when I am reproved. And the Lord answered me, and said, Write the vision, and make it plain upon tables, that he may run that readeth it. For the vision is yet for an appointed time, but at the end it shall speak, and not lie; though it tarry, wait for it, because it will surely come, it will not tarry. Behold, his soul which is lifted up, is not upright in him; but the just shall live by his faith.[4]

TO THE READER

My friend, or whosoever may read these writings: I tenderly advise thee to peruse them in the fear of the Lord, for in such a state of mind they were written, and they are or will be better understood, being perused in a quiet, retired frame of mind than otherwise. Although they contain great mysteries, yet they are what belongs to our eternal happiness; and as these things were revealed by Jesus Christ, or his angel, to his servant John, who was in the Spirit when he saw and heard these wonderful mysteries, so it is the same Spirit that giveth a right understanding of them. And it is of absolute necessity for every soul to be born of the Spirit that is desirous to see the kingdom of God, according to the testimony of our Lord Jesus to Nicodemus.[5] And also read 1 Corinthians 2 throughout; there the apostle makes use of the testimony of the Prophet Isaiah and says: as it is written eye hath not seen, nor ear heard, neither have entered into the heart of man, the things which God hath prepared for them that love him. But God (says he) hath revealed them to us by his Spirit, for the Spirit searcheth all things; yea, the deep things of God.[6]

2. For the parable of the wheat and the tares, see Matthew 13:24–30.

3. Psalm 25:14.

4. Habakkuk 2:1–4.

5. John 3:1–21.

6. Isaiah 64:4; 1 Corinthians 2:9–10.

And so he proceeds to give convincing arguments or reasons that cannot be gainsaid, which I advise may be read, and considered, in the fear of the Lord and in his pure love. And this I truly testify, that I was very much afraid to write anything concerning these great mysteries, for I have a due regard to the last sentence, given forth, concerning any man that shall add to, or take from, the words of the prophecy of the book [of Revelation].[7] This caused me to be very careful to keep to the true sense of the matter treated on, according to the evidence of the degree of light in my understanding. I also considered my weakness and human frailties, which made me tremble in myself, as Habakkuk did of old when he heard of the work of the Lord, and saw a glimpse of his glory.[8] Yet a concern rested on my mind, day and night, to set down what lived on my mind, or opened in the light of my understanding. Then I thought to set it down for my own satisfaction: I having seen two books that were set forth as expositions on the Revelations, which were not agreeable to my mind; yet it rested with me to believe that these Revelations do belong to all Christians to read and observe, that all may hear the call of Jesus Christ and take notice of it, so as to answer his requirings as much as possible, and the Lord will help those that are willing. And as I gave up to write what opened in my mind, I had great peace.

Blessed be the name of the Lord therefore; for I came to believe it was the mind of the Lord, that I should leave this to the succeeding generations, for the stirring up of the pure mind, that they also may seek the kingdom of God and his righteousness. And those that are desirous so to do must keep low, and near to the spirit of Jesus Christ in their own hearts; for whosoever is truly and fully given up to the guidance of the Holy Ghost hath a true teacher near, that cannot be removed from him, for which we have great cause to praise our gracious God. And this Holy Spirit is the true light and touchstone by which the mysteries of God (or godliness) are manifested, and by which all spirits and testimonies are tried. And none need to wonder that the children of God use not all one phrase or style in speaking or writing. For to everyone is given what he shall open or manifest of the great mysteries of the kingdom of God; but the true spring or fountain from which all true testimonies come is the Spirit of the Son of God, and they are sent in love, and are likened to dew and rain, that when it hath watered the dry and thirsty

7. Revelation 22:18–19.

8. See Habakkuk 3:16.

ground, the overplus returneth into the ocean.[9] Oh! the unfathomable depths of the love and wisdom of God, which he by talents or measures hath revealed to babes and such as fear his name, for so it hath pleased our Heavenly Father, that no flesh may boast, or glory in his presence.[10] So I advise to pure obedience unto God and resignation to his holy will in all things, as they are or shall be made manifest, remembering that the path of the just is as a shining light, that shineth more and more unto the perfect day.[11]

And take heed my children and friends, lest there should be in any of you an evil heart of unbelief in departing from the living God, for we are made partakers of Jesus Christ if we hold fast our faith and love to God, and to one another, to the end. And according to the degrees of growth and faithfulness you are found in, you will see the descendings of the New Jerusalem in her glorious light and will rejoice in the light thereof. For the Lord God and the Lamb is the light of this Holy City, in which there was seen no temple, for the Lord God and the Lamb are the temple of it.[12] So here is the place of divine worship; even to be gathered into the Spirit. God is a spirit, said our dear Lord—likewise here is but one street in this holy city, one river of life, one tree of life, although it bears variety of fruits, and yields its fruits every month.[13] These things are revealed, to set forth the wonderful glory of God, who is king in the New Jerusalem, and the great union and happiness of his people, who walk in this glorious light.

And now I, with many more, do testify that this glorious light is risen, and will arise yet higher and higher, and will shine forth more and more in the hearts and in the understandings of the obedient children of God. And many shall sound forth the praises of God and the Lamb, who hath redeemed them from their vain conversations and from their bondage to the grand enemy and hath brought their souls (in degree) into the holy city. And they will be as trumpets in the angels' hand to call the Lord's people to come out of Babylon: for her fall is nigh at hand.[14] So all that will come may come into the New Jerusalem and lay hold of the tree of life and take of the water of life

9. Ezekiel 19:13, 47:1–8.

10. 1 Corinthians 1:29.

11. Proverbs 4:18.

12. Revelation 21:22.

13. John 4:24; Revelation 22:2.

14. See Revelation 18:4.

freely: for those that will not come out of Babylon will be left without excuse. And I stand in admiration at the mercies of God, and his wonderful patience, and long forbearance.

Oh! saith my soul, that it may lead many to repentance, and that they may be wise, and lay hold of the grace of God in time, for it is by grace that we are saved, through faith, and not of ourselves: it is the gift of God.[15] And as many as do join in their hearts with this wonderful gift of God, they come (through faith, obedience, and perseverance) to be sealed with the Holy Spirit, which is the earnest of the soul's inheritance in the kingdom of heaven forevermore, which the poor may attain unto as well as the rich, and the rich as well as the poor, if they all come to be poor in spirit and put their trust in the Lord alone.[16] Upon such the blessing of God will rest and remain forever; for theirs is the kingdom of heaven, said our dear Lord, who cast up the way that leads thereunto, and is the true guide, and pattern of all his followers. Be ye therefore followers of Jesus Christ, as dear children of God; and walk in love one towards another as Christ also hath loved us, and hath given himself for us, an offering and a sacrifice to God for a sweet smelling savor, etc.[17] And if we are like minded with Jesus Christ, we shall be well-pleasing to God, who loved us when we were his enemies.[18] And the meek Lamb of God exhorted his followers to love their enemies, and he taught resignation to the will of God in all things; and he lived in the practice of it. And those that desire or expect to live with him in his glorious kingdom, must be his followers, bearing the daily cross. And these must be baptized with the baptism he was baptized with, for there is but one way to life eternal, and that is through death, even through the death of the old Adamical will, or the old man with his deeds.[19] And this high way of self-denial and pure resignation our dear Lord cast up, and his Spirit (which God his father—and our father—hath sent into our hearts) leads all his followers, gently along, in the same high way, giving degrees of faith and patience according to the degrees of growth or present wants of his new creature.

15. Ephesians 2:8.

16. Ephesians 1:12–14.

17. Ephesians 5:1–2.

18. See Romans 5:8–10.

19. See Mark 10:38; Colossians 3:9.

Oh! the tender dealings of our merciful Father—how doth it draw the love and obedience of his humble children towards him, even when we consider or meditate on his great love to the whole world of mankind. And such as do so, do really enjoy that great blessing which is made mention of in the first Psalm, saying,

> Blessed is the man that walketh not in the counsel of the ungodly, nor standeth in the way of sinners, nor sitteth in the seat of the scornful. But his delight is in the law of the Lord; and in his law doth he meditate day and night. He shall be like a tree planted by the rivers of water; he bringeth forth his fruit in his season; his leaf also shall not wither; and whatsoever he doeth shall prosper.[20]

Here is great encouragement for the believer that delighteth in the law of the Lord, and believeth in the testimonies of his God, which are many and very true. And this I have found by experience, that the Lord loveth the cheerful giver, even he, or she that give up their hearts willingly and cheerfully to serve their Maker, and to follow their dear Redeemer.[21] But such as read and meditate on the scriptures had need to keep near to the good Spirit in themselves, who alone is the true interpreter of them, and indeed also of all other writings that were given forth by the movings, or dictates of the Holy Ghost. For such as dwell near to or with this Holy Spirit know the work of the new creation carried on themselves gradually, until they come to know the Lord's Sabbath. And such come to cease from their own works, and the good Spirit of God works in them and by them, for the Almighty is become their All in All, and these things are possible with God, i.e., he is able to bring them to pass, and hath promised to make all things new. And it is the believing, resigned soul, that he works in, or upon. The unbeliever will not receive all these testimonies, for he believes it is not possible to live and walk with God while here, or that his will should be done here on earth as it is done in heaven, and so puts the day of the Lord afar off. And there are others, that do and will receive such testimonies, to add to that knowledge which puffs up but will not keep to the grace of God, which only edifies.[22] For neither of those are these writings intended, but for the help of the poor traveler, who is made willing to

20. Psalm 1:1–3.

21. 2 Corinthians 9:7.

22. See 1 Corinthians 8:1.

follow the Holy Lamb of God, in the way of self-denial, bearing the daily cross. These will come to see and know that there is a spiritual as well as a temporal meaning couched in the scriptures of truth. For as all bodies sprang from the Spirit and are nourished in their growth by the universal Spirit of God that fills all things and upholds his whole creation, so these souls that are born from above are fed and nourished by the divine Spirit, from whence they sprung.

The work of God is two-fold, i.e. spiritual and temporal, and likened to a wheel within a wheel, the operation of the spirit of life being the cause of growth and motion in all things according to their kind, which kinds (since the heavy Fall) are so different (in man) that the life of one thing is the death of the other.[23] As, if we live after the flesh, we die to God; but if through the Spirit we mortify the deeds of the body, then we live to God.[24] And so likewise the serpentine fallen wisdom is a different kind or nature from the wisdom of God manifested through Jesus Christ our Lord.[25]

The Apostle Paul would not that the faith of the Christians should stand in the wisdom of men but in the power of God.[26] Yet he spake wisdom among the perfect (or sincere), yet not the wisdom of this world, but the wisdom of God; which none of the princes of this world knew, etc. As it is written (said he), eye hath not seen nor ear heard, neither have entered into the heart of man the things which God hath prepared for them that love him. But God hath revealed them unto us by his Spirit for the Spirit searcheth all things, yea the deep things of God.[27] Read it and peruse the whole chapter (1 Corinthians 2), and bring things home. Deal plainly with thy own soul: the true light will manifest to thee, and in thee, what state of mind thou art

23. Webb's description of a "wheel within a wheel" is an image drawn by prior interpreters from the language of Ezekiel 1:16.

24. Romans 8:13.

25. Webb's distinction between a serpentine wisdom and the wisdom of Jesus Christ was first articulated by George Fox, who framed the struggles of mortality in an Edenic context. Every human choice, for Fox, might be reduced to the alternatives faced by Adam and Eve in the garden, as they decided whether to "Hear him who was the first speaker in paradise" or the "serpent [who] was the second." See George Fox, "Sermon by George Fox Given at a General Meeting, London, April 4, 1674," in Michael P. Graves, *Preaching the Inward Light: Early Quaker Rhetoric* (Waco: Baylor University Press, 2009), 255.

26. 1 Corinthians 2:5.

27. 1 Corinthians 2:9–10.

in. And so I commend thee to the guidance of the grace of God, that is come by Jesus Christ.

Elizabeth Webb

POSTSCRIPT

Caiaphas, the high priest, represented the true high priest under the law whom he imitated by prophecy, but was a real enemy to Jesus Christ, and to his Spirit, whom he rejected and condemned, and so was a lively instance of the spirit of Antichrist and of the false prophets now in the world, who teach people to make imitations of divine things in gay ceremonies and strict observations of outward rules, etc.[28]

But [they] do and will disown and deny the image of life and lamblike spirit Jesus Christ appearing in any that bear their testimony against the lapsed state of their Church: and cannot bow to the golden image they have set up.[29] Thus came in the degeneracy and apostasy upon both Jews and Christians, (to wit) by losing the life of Christ and setting up a lifeless form. If any should be at a loss, by reason of the many lo here's and lo there's, let such look to Jesus, the true light, and be just to God, in giving up to him that part within which he hath reserved for himself.[30] And then they will see that the path of the just is as a burning and shining light, etc.[31]

For there are degrees of light given to mankind. For Christ the true light shines in his sanctuary in man (and elsewhere), and the will of God is the sanctification of his creature. And the more any soul is resigned to the will of his Maker, the more he purgeth it by the workings of his Holy Spirit and so enlargeth the borders of his sanctuary in that creature. And as the soul keep-

28. See John 11:51. Although Caiaphas is reviled for his part in the plot to "take Jesus by subtlety and kill him," John suggests that Caiaphas was nevertheless filled with the true spirit of prophecy because he held the office of high priest (Matthew 26:3–4). Caiaphas represents for Webb the misguided leaders of contemporary religious movements that observe ceremonies (likely a reference to the Catholic Church and Church of England) or enforce strict codes of conduct (likely a reference to the Puritans).

29. See Daniel 3.

30. See Matthew 24:23.

31. John 5:35.

eth watchful and near to the holy meek Spirit, it comes more and more to dwell in the secret place of the Most High, and abideth under the Almighty, and says of God: he is my fortress; my refuge. In him will I trust, and it hath a sweet and quiet habitation and fears the Lord alone, and it is an inward witness of the truth, of abundance of the testimonies left on record in the scriptures of truth. And the delight of this soul is in meditating on the things of God, and [I] have cause to say, with the Psalmist, truly God is good to Israel, even to such as are of a clean heart. And yet his feet were almost gone, his steps had well nigh slipped when he looked out, with an eye of reason, and saw the prosperity of the wicked. Until he went into the sanctuary of God: then he understood their end, etc.[32] So I have often observed, that the spirit of life and light, leads the soul to look through or beyond all worldly enjoyments to the end and adviseth the creature not to fret because of evildoers, neither be envious against the workers of iniquity, for they shall be cut down as the grass, and wither as the green herb.[33] And so, as the soul abideth in the word of patience, the Lord giveth it faith to believe that in the end it shall see the king in his beauty and that it shall behold the land which seems to be very far off and that it shall look upon Zion, the city of the saints' solemnity, and shall see the New Jerusalem, a quiet habitation, a tabernacle that shall not be taken down. And the promise of God is, that the inhabitants of this city shall not say I am sick; for the people that dwell therein, shall be forgiven their iniquities.[34] And the Prophet Ezekiel was told, that the name of the city which he saw, should be Jehovah Shammah: the Lord is there.[35]

A RELATION CONCERNING THE AUTHOR BY A FRIEND

Having been acquainted with the author of the following book for many years and being desired to peruse it, there was something in my heart to impart to the readers concerning the author's life, she being one of them which the almighty Lord in these latter days hath poured out of his Holy Spirit on, as many besides can truly witness, her ministry being sound and

32. Psalm 73:1–3, 17.

33. Psalm 37:1–2.

34. Isaiah 33:24.

35. Ezekiel 48:35.

edifying, being attended with divine life and power.[36] And in her conversation was solid, and discrete, her words few and savory, being seasoned with grace to the hearers.

It was my lot once to cross the sea from America to Europe in company with this servant of Jesus, and her conversation and deportment had a tendency to draw peoples' minds towards God.[37] And heavenly things was her practice to speak, read, and write, so that her conversations seemed to us to be in heaven while she was on earth. I have blessed the Lord that I was acquainted with her, she being like a mother to me in my tender years, and was not only so to me, but was indeed a mother in the house of spiritual Israel.

This good friend of Christ was a great traveler in body as well as in mind, for the promotion of the kingdom of God, and his Christ, and the good of souls. She laboured earnestly for traveling many thousand miles both by sea and land, for no other end. Once when living in Europe, she travelled by sea to America, and visited the provinces of New England, New Jersey, Pennsylvania, Maryland, Virginia [and] Carolina, in which provinces she preached the gospel of God our Saviour, with power and clearness, and much to the satisfaction of the society to whom she belonged and was a member of, as well as many others; diverse being really convinced of the truth of the gospel through her ministry; and went through great hardships often, her sex considered, and returned home in great peace in her soul and true unity with good men and women, as was largely manifested by the testimonials of many pious souls. And after returning home, her husband removed his family to America, and settled in Pennsylvania, in which province for diverse years Elizabeth had good service in the work of the ministry, traveling into diverse provinces in America, the Lord being with her in his work and prospering it in her hand. Blessed be his glorious name, for though she was a good instrument in his hand, the praise is principally due to him that made her so, to God in fullness, and to every good man and woman, according to the measure of grace received.

When she had lived for some years in America, she was drawn in her heart to go and preach the gospel in Europe, of whose services I heard a good account from faithful men and women. Professing godliness, and good

36. See Joel 2:28–29.

37. See Webb's travel journal, on pp. 179–94.

works, she leaving a good savour behind her in many places where she travelled, I observed in her conduct in conversation that if she saw any thing airy or light, she would rather reprove it than join in such communications, according to the apostle's doctrine not to joke or jest but rather to give thanks, which was much practiced by this dear friend.[38]

I have read the ensuing treatise on the revelations of St. John, and it being mystical, the reader, if he or she be acquainted with the mystery of godliness, they may receive instruction and edification. But if the reader be a formal professor only, it's desired that what seems abstruse or obscure may be charitably passed by. And what is plain and easy to be understood may be treasured up in the heart, so that we may lay up something in store for a good foundation for the time to come.

So wisheth and prayeth a lover of Christ and all the souls which he hath made.

Thomas Chalkley

SOME MEDITATIONS AND OBSERVATIONS UPON THE BOOK OF THE REVELATIONS OF JESUS CHRIST

CHAPTER I

1:1. First I observe (with reverence) the pure distinctions that are here made, concerning the distinct operations of the divine being, as of God the Father, and of Jesus Christ his Son, who is the WORD of God, as he is in the bosom of the Father, and how Christ Jesus sent and signified by his angel to his servant John. An angel is a ministering spirit: To which of the angels (said he) at any time, sit on my right hand until I make thine enemies thy foot stool? Are they not all ministering spirits, sent forth to minister for them who shall be heirs of salvation?[39] So Jesus sent his angel to testify unto John these things in great love to the souls of lost mankind. Yet he testifieth in that it is he himself that appeared to John <u>in his glorified humanity</u>.[40] And so I

38. See Ephesians 5:1–5.

39. Hebrews 1:13–14.

40. Revelation 1:17–18.

believe it was; yet it was his own spirit, his angel, that spoke in him, to his servant John: who at other times appeared in another form.[41]

1:2–6. Thus it appears that grace, mercy, and peace was extended to the seven churches (and I have cause to believe to all mankind), from God the Father of spirits, and from Jesus Christ, the only Son of God, and Saviour of souls, who is the faithful witness, and from the seven spirits which are before the throne of the divine majesty of God Almighty. These seven spirits have been seen as seven lamps; the angel told the prophet, saying, they are the eyes of the Lord which run to and fro through the whole earth.[42] Oh! that we may be acquainted with God, and meditate on his goodness, and think upon his loving kindnesses from day to day, even while we have a being here. John also saw seven lamps of fire burning before the throne of God Almighty, which (saith he) are the seven spirits of God.[43] Under the dispensation of the law they had all figures or representations of them.[44] But now the heavenly things themselves are manifested by the Spirit, which appeared to be seven, to manifest the diversity of operations, but are one in union. Thus the beloved apostle seems to endeavor to lead the churches into a divine acquaintance with God the father of their spirits and with Jesus Christ his firstborn son or first begotten of the dead—whom to know is life eternal—and also with the Holy Spirit.[45]

1:7–11. This was the Lord's day of the revelation of the things contained in this book; and John hath now tarried till the Lord is come, as the Lord intimated to Peter.[46] Some have imagined this revelation to be on a first day of the week, but reason itself will tell us that it contained some considerable time more than one day, for John wrote the visions as he saw and heard them, and the Lord's day of revelations and visions continued till he had accomplished them.

41. See Revelation 5:6.

42. Zechariah 4:2, 10.

43. Revelation 4:5.

44. See Exodus 25:37; Numbers 8:2.

45. John 17:3.

46. See John 21:21–22.

1:12–13. Oh! who can read and meditate on these things and not melt and be astonished at the great love of God and his great condescension to the children of men in manifesting himself thus.

1:14–16. The seven stars represent his ministers, that do his pleasure, and are held and supported by the right hand of his power. And the sharp two-edged sword denotes the word of his power and his righteous judgments, and his countenance appearing as the sun shining in his strength. This is to show his great majesty, yea, this is he that the apostle Paul spake of to Timothy, saying, I charge thee in the sight of God who quickeneth all things and before Christ Jesus, who before Pontius Pilate witnessed a good confession that thou keep this commandment without spot unrebukable, until the appearing of our Lord Jesus Christ, which in his times he shall show, who is the blessed and only Potentate, the King of Kings and Lord of Lords, who only hath immortality dwelling in the light which no man can approach, etc.[47]

1:17. Thus this beloved disciple who used to lean on Jesus's breast when he was in his state of humiliation, when he saw him in his glory and exaltation![48]—fell at his feet, as dead, but the Lord comforted him, saying,

1:18–20. Great is the mystery of Godliness: God was manifest in the flesh, justified in the Spirit, seen of angels, preached unto the Gentiles, believed on in the world, received up into glory.[49] To meditate on the mysteries of godliness is very pleasant and profitable to the spiritually-minded.

CHAPTER 2

2:1–3. These good things which the Lord takes notice of in the elders of this church of Ephesus are chiefly those things which Paul left in charge with them the last time they saw his face. He charged them, to take heed to themselves and to all the flock over which the Holy Ghost had made them overseers, and

47. 1 Timothy 6:13–16.

48. See John 13:23.

49. 1 Timothy 3:16.

forewarned them of many things which they seemed to be zealously concerned for, and not to faint.[50]

2:4. By which we may observe that good works that are not done in divine love are defective in the sight of God, for divine love is the golden oil which causeth the lamps to burn and give light.

2:5. The use of the candlestick is to hold up the light, but if the light goes out, the candlestick is of no use. And the Church of God is the light of the world, and that divine love that is in the hearts of the members of it is the golden oil that causeth the light to shine; and a decay in divine love causeth the light to burn dim.[51] And a total fall from divine love is a star fallen from heaven to the earth, which is a woeful state; and yet it is the state of all that love not God Almighty and Jesus Christ his Son above all things in the world.

2:6. What their deeds were was well known to this Church—they being in their day and time—but we may observe that the Lord commends them for hating those deeds which he hates.[52]

2:7. This is a universal call to all the children of men, and every particular soul ought to have a due regard to it, considering from whom it comes and to what it tends. Oh! Gracious promise and sufficient reward for the greatest fight of afflictions that can be endured here.

2:8. The Lord Speaks thus to this Church in a way of comfort, they being under great tribulations and poverty but blameless in the sight of him who seeth in secret.

2:9. Here we may observe that for people to profess to be what they are not in reality is accounted blasphemy with the Lord in a degree, but he saith to the faithful, though poor in their own esteem, or poor in spirit:

2:10. Here we may observe that the Lord suffers his people to be tried by the devil, who is the accuser of mankind. Job was accused by him and tried with

50. See Acts 20:17–38.

51. See Matthew 5:13–15.

52. See Proverbs 8:13; Psalm 97:10.

great tribulations, and Job's belief was that when he had been tried he should come forth as gold.[53] And according to his faith and patience, so it was to him. The apostle James takes notice of it, and said, we count them happy which endure. Ye have heard of the patience of Job and have seen the end of the Lord herein, that the Lord is very pitiful and of tender mercy.[54] And as to their having tribulation ten days, it was to signify to them that their tribulations were bounded, and their adversary, the devil, was limited (and so he is still: glory to God Almighty therefore). And this is encouragement to all tribulated souls, seeing the call is to all, saying:

2:11. And what the second death is, is plainly told: And the sea gave up the dead which were in it, and death and hell delivered up the dead which were in them, and they were judged every man according to their works. And death and hell were cast into the lake of fire; this is the second death. And whosoever was not found written in the book of life was cast into the lake of fire.[55] This will follow the general resurrection, and Jesus Christ foretold of this total separation.[56]

2:12–13. The Lord signifies to this church that he knows and considers their whole state and condition upon all accounts. And by Satan's seat we may understand it was then in the pagan, worldly rulers, for that was the beast that John saw rise out of the sea.[57] And the dragon gave him his power and his seat and great authority. Satan was and is the great adversary of the faithful servants of God and followers of the Lamb and makes use of many wiles and many sorts of instruments, some to kill and slay by, and some to deceive the unwary, who is going Zion-ward. But this was a remarkable time of persecution well known to the Lord and taken notice of by him.

2:14–16. Here we may observe the tender mercies of God in giving time to repent. He is the same God still and calls to all, saying:

53. Job 23:10.

54. James 5:11.

55. Revelation 20:13–15.

56. See Matthew 25:31–46.

57. See Revelation 13:1.

2:17. This hidden manna is the bread of life which Jesus Christ spake of to the Jews.[58] This hidden manna is the daily bread of the faithful followers of the Lamb of God, who hath not only given himself for us, but him hath God the Father sealed and hath given him to us.[59] He also is the white stone that is given to him that overcometh, having a new name written in it which no man knoweth, saving he that receiveth it. Great indeed is the mystery of godliness, not known by the wisdom of this world but revealed to babes.[60]

2:18–19. Here we may observe the exact notice that the Lord takes of the virtues which he seeth in them in the way of well doing, yet saith:

2:20. Thus the Lord compares these false teachers unto Jezebel, that proud idolatrous woman who taught the children of Israel to go from God and to eat things offered to her idols, which became a great snare to Israel and brought sore judgments upon them.[61]

2:21. Here is again a manifestation of the Lord's forbearance, the consideration of which should lead all to repentance, for the Holy Spirit will not always strive with man.[62] For as Jehu was appointed of the Lord to execute judgment on Jezebel in a terrible manner, so the Lord will execute his judgments on the proud in spirit who are departed from him into the love of this world. And yet, they will be sacrificers as Saul the King of Israel was, as also Ahab and Jezebel were; but destruction came on them in due time. So let all hear and fear and repent in time, for the Lord said:

2:22–25. The depths of Satan is the mystery of iniquity, and this Jezebel here spoken of is the mystical harlot, a teacher of false liberty when she herself is in bondage to the God of this world. The Apostle Peter foretold of those in 2 Peter 2, where he largely describeth them, and tells of their destruction. Peruse the whole chapter; here it is set forth under the name of a woman, the weaker part of mankind. But men are concerned in false doctrine as well as

58. See John 6:48–59.

59. John 6:27.

60. 1 Timothy 3:16.

61. See 1 Kings 18–20.

62. See Genesis 6:3.

women—all make up the false church which the Spirit foresaw, and such as did receive such doctrine were called Jezebel's children, which the Lord said he would kill with death.[63] But the faithful he had no other burden laid upon them, but to hold fast till the Lord come. This is a general exhortation to the suffering seed, or children of God, to hold fast their love and integrity to the Lord, their only Savior, till he come for their deliverance. For those that overcome in this spiritual warfare are such as keep the word of patience and wait the Lord's time for their deliverance.

CHAPTER 3

3:1. This is a woeful state indeed, notwithstanding the great name among men, but yet the Lord affords a gracious call, saying:

3:2. This is the searcher of hearts, and trier of reins that giveth this testimony, who hath the fullness of the Spirit, signified by the seven spirits of God. Neither the words spoken nor the works done in the will or by the wisdom of man are found perfect before God. The perfection of a child of God consisteth in perfect obedience and resignation to his will, which cannot be attained unto without perfect love to God. This is the love that casteth out all slavish fear and enableth the soul to trust in the Lord and to resign to his will and to be at his disposal in all things.[64] Into such a soul the kingdom of God is come, and his will is done in that earthen vessel as it is done in heaven, for the man ceaseth from his own will and works, and the Holy Spirit worketh in him, and by him as its instrument to will and to do according to the will of God. And all the works of God do glorify him, and every gift of God is perfect in itself. To be strong in love is the way to be strong in spirit; observe

63. Although Webb alludes to biblical passages that declare women to be the weaker sex (see 1 Peter 3:1, 7), her declaration that "men are concerned in false doctrine as well as women" implicitly suggests that there is no spiritual difference between the sexes. In other words, she, as well as many other Quaker women at the time, did not believe that they were spiritually weaker than or inferior to men. See Rebecca Larson, *Daughters of Light: Quaker Women Preaching and Prophesying in the Colonies and Abroad, 1700–1775* (New York: Knopf, 1999), 19–23; William C. Braithwaite, *The Second Period of Quakerism* (Cambridge: Cambridge University Press, 1961), 269–71.

64. 1 John 4:18.

the worldly lover, how vigorous he is in the pursuit after getting more riches, etc. Many instances might be brought to prove the strength of love!

God Almighty is the fountain of divine love and hath placed a good share of it in the hearts of mankind. But from the fall of Adam to this day, mankind in an unregenerate state, employs this noble faculty wrong and robs God of that which he reserved for himself. A lawyer asked our Lord saying, which is the greatest commandment in the law. Jesus said unto him, thou shalt love the Lord thy God with all thy heart, and with all thy soul, and with all thy mind. This (said our dear Lord) is the first and great commandment, and the second is like unto it: thou shalt love thy neighbor as thyself. On these two commandments hang all the law and the prophets.[65] This is a short testimony, but of large extent. But the way to attain unto power, to enable the soul in the performance of this great duty towards God and man, is by receiving Jesus Christ and loving him above all the world, for as many as received him to them he gave power to become the sons of God, etc.[66] But he that loveth any worldly thing more than the Lord is not found worthy of him, and without him we can do nothing that will find acceptance with God, for this is his only Son in whom he is well pleased; all these things are worthy of consideration.[67]

3:3–5. This is spoken by our sweet Savior to encourage all to make war in righteousness against every appearance of evil in themselves and to persevere in faith, hope, and patience to the end. For he continueth his universal call, saying:

3:6–9. Here I observe that notwithstanding the open door that the Lord Jesus Christ had set before this faithful minister, who had kept his word and had not denied his name, yet there were hypocrites in the church of Philadelphia who did profess to be the people of God yet in reality did belong to the synagogue of Satan. And the searcher of hearts seeth all such now, and in his own time will manifest who are his. Oh! Lord, grant a good portion of the word of thy patience to all thy little ones that thine may be strong in thy love.

65. Matthew 22:35–40.

66. John 1:12.

67. See Matthew 3:17, 17:5.

3:10–11. The crown of all the ministers of Jesus Christ is the love of God moving in their hearts and the light of life shining in their understanding and their being meek and lowly in heart (like to their Master). For though it may appear foolish and contemptible in the eyes of the world, yet is a crown of glory to the soul, given to it from above, in which it shines as a star in the firmament of God's power forever and ever, if kept low and near to the prince of life and light while here.

3:12. These are comfortable promises made by our dear Lord to encourage all souls in their holy warfare. The faithful he will keep in his spirit.

3:13–16. This is a grievous sentence and worthy to be considered by all the lukewarm professors of Christianity, for what will become of my soul, if the Lord will not receive it into his favor? And yet those were high minded, as in verse 17:

3:17. Here I observe and consider the nature of this case. Love to Christ, the true light, was decaying; it was lukewarm. The god of this world, the prince of the power of darkness, was prevailing and so clouded or dimmed the light of life in the understanding. And he, being a proud spirit, he caused them to think they were rich and had need of nothing; he works after the like manner still. But oh! the gracious call and counsel of our dear Lord in verse 18:

3:18. I counsel thee to buy of me gold (saith our Lord) that thou mayest be rich. This gold here spoken of is that precious faith which works by love, which is tried many ways, even by the buffetings of Satan within and by his instruments without. But the more it is tried in the furnace and the oftener it is melted down, the purer and solider it is, and the brighter it shineth to the glory of him who is the giver of it. For true living faith—it is the gift of God, and it becomes a very rich treasure in the creature and makes the soul bold, valiant, and strong in the Lord. For this faith is an invincible shield, and the trial of it is much more precious than that of gold that perisheth.

Those that want further proofs, let them read Hebrews 11 and accept of the counsel of our Lord, as above, and likewise to buy of him that white raiment which is the garment of his salvation, the robe of his own righteousness, which he puts upon that soul that is made willing to be stripped of all its old clothing and washed and made clean by him. Such, when they put off this mortal clothing, shall be clothed upon with their house from heaven, and so the shame of their nakedness will not appear. Oh! The riches of divine bounty in making such offers of love to the children of men.

Thus the Lord Jesus Christ makes use of similitudes, for this eye salve is the unction that all the true believers in Jesus Christ receive from the Holy One, that so enlighteneth their minds in the things of God, that such needeth not the teachings of man.[68]

3:19–20. A gracious and glorious guest indeed—what! The King of Kings and Lord of Lords, and the only ruler of princes, stand at the door of my heart knocking and calling, with all the loving invitations and promises that can be made to any creature. And shall I entertain his and my soul's enemies and keep him out? What? Is there no bowels of compassion in me for my best friend and greatest benefactor, who laid down his own life to redeem me from eternal death and now stands wooing and entreating to accept of him, the Prince of Life? Oh! That all would but weigh and consider the lovingkindness of the Lord and open the door of their heart to him in time. For such as have let him in can say, for the encouragement of others, that he is the best friend that ever was entertained; he brings bread and wine with him. Oh! It is heavenly bread and the new wine of the kingdom of his Heavenly Father: this is a sweet supper indeed. It so quickeneth the spiritual appetite that the soul that hath tasted of this divine food longeth after a more full enjoyment of it. And he hath said, "Blessed are those that hunger and thirst after righteousness, for they shall be filled."[69] Oh! The heighth and depth, the length and breadth of the riches of divine love: who can choose but admire it and blame themselves, for keeping of him out so long, who saith:

3:21–22. Thus we may observe that the Lord Jesus Christ continues his call, even seven times to him that hath an ear to hear, what the Spirit saith unto the churches, so that all will be left without excuse in the great day of account, when all must appear before the terrible majesty of the righteous and just judge to receive the last sentence and final separation of sheep from goats.[70] Those things deserve the best consideration, for the human frame waxeth old as doth a garment, but the soul is of an immortal nature and must live for-

68. See 1 John 2:27.

69. Matthew 5:6.

70. See Matthew 25:31–46.

ever, either in eternal joy and felicity or else in eternal wo and misery, where the worm dieth not, neither is the fire quenched.[71]

CHAPTER 4

4:1–2. This is a plain demonstration that to be taken up into heaven is to be gathered up into the spirit in such a degree as is needful for the service which God Almighty hath for his creature to do. For the good Spirit enlighteneth that soul according to the divine will, and lays hold on all the faculties of the creature, and makes use of them as an instrument in his hand. So this beloved disciple was called up as into heaven, and he, being a resigned soul, was immediately where his Lord would have him to be.

4:2–3. Thus John beheld the glorious similitude of the Almighty as sitting on his glorious throne in great majesty, shining like precious stones. I say similitude because God Almighty, he is possessor of heaven and earth, and the heaven of heavens cannot contain him.

The prophet Ezekiel, he saw such a like vision, and he said this was the appearance of the likeness of the glory of the Lord. And when he saw it, he fell on his face and heard a voice of one that spake.[72]

To read of these and such like manifestations should cause great reverence to be in the minds of them that love and fear God. But how much more to behold the ineffable glory which all souls will assuredly behold, either to their great joy and comfort or else to their terror and amazement. And John saw:

4:4. These twenty-four elders, having crowns of gold on their heads, is to show that they sit with Christ in judgment (having through him gotten the victory).

4:5. These lightnings, thunderings, and voices set forth the dreadful sentences of God's judgments proceeding from the throne of his justice against this wicked world. The Spirit of God is one but is represented here (as also in other places) by the number seven, to set forth the diversity of its

71. Mark 9:44.

72. Ezekiel 1:26–28.

operations.[73] These seven lamps were likewise figured by the seven lamps in the temple which Moses was ordered to make according to the pattern which the Lord had showed him.[74] And the prophet Zachariah—he saw a golden candlestick with a bowl upon the top of it and seven lamps thereon and seven pipes to the seven lamps and two olive trees by it, or olive branches, which the angel told him, saying, these are the two anointed ones that stand by the Lord of the whole Earth.[75] Oh! Glorious Lord God Almighty, great are thy heavenly mysteries that thou hast revealed to the children of men, that we might learn to love thee and to fear, serve, and reverence thee while here, that thou might gather all home into thy heavenly kingdom hereafter. Surely, great is thy love and mercy. Oh! That all may duly consider of it and walk worthy of thy matchless mercies.

4:6–8. The prophet Isaiah, he saw the Lord sitting upon a throne high and lifted up, and his train filled the temple. Above it stood the seraphims; each one had six wings, etc. And one cried unto another and said, holy, holy, holy, is the Lord of Hosts; the whole earth is full of his glory, etc.[76]

These were called seraphims. Them that John saw were called four beasts, but they were seen to be in the like exercise, in giving glory to God. And whereas it is said, they rest not day and night, saying holy, holy, holy Lord, God Almighty, which was, and is, and is to come, some in their reason may think this endless tautologies and tedious work, but oh! No, for it is their life, their breathing, their joy and delight, and how can it be otherwise? For their being represented full of eyes before and behind and within is to signify that they see every way. And these spiritual, angelical creatures—which way soever they look, they see the glory of God.

4:9–11. Thus John saw and heard the heavenly harmony of those whose joy and delight it is to glorify God Almighty and to speak of his wondrous works.

73. Both the number seven and the number three were important to sixteenth- and seventeenth-century Christian mystics, including John Donne, for whom seven represented infinity. See C. A. Patrides, "The Numerological Approach to Cosmic Order during the English Renaissance," *Isis* 49, no. 4 (1958): 391–97.

74. See Numbers 8:2–4.

75. See Zechariah 4.

76. See Isaiah 6:1–3.

5:1. This is to signify that all the mysteries that appertain to the kingdom of heaven are fast sealed up from all those that have not the key of David, which indeed is the spirit of the Son of God who only openeth the seals and that in order.[77]

The prophet Isaiah cried in the word of the Lord, saying the vision of all is become unto you as the words of a book that is sealed.[78]

5:2–6. This is to represent Jesus Christ, as he is the Lamb of God, the only sacrifice for sin, and the seven horns is to signify that all power in heaven and in earth is given to him.[79] And his seven eyes, which are seven spirits sent forth into all the earth, this shows that he hath the fullness of the spirit, and of his fullness have all we received, and grace for grace.[80]

5:7–10. Here we may observe that these that fell down before the Lamb had every one of them harps which were to sound forth his praise, in setting forth his worthiness to take the book and to open the seals thereof. And well they might for he had redeemed them by his blood, and made them kings and priests unto God, and had given them power to reign on the earth. And the viols full of odors are the prayers of saints. This was figured under the law: and the whole multitude of the people were praying without at the time of incense.[81]

5:11–14. This was a ravishing harmonious song which John heard when he was gathered up into the Spirit, by which we may observe what is written: that at the name of Jesus every knee shall bow of things in heaven and things on earth and things under the earth and that every tongue shall confess that Jesus Christ is Lord, to the glory of God the Father.[82]

77. See Isaiah 22:22.

78. Isaiah 29:11.

79. Matthew 28:18.

80. John 1:16.

81. Luke 1:10.

82. Philippians 2:10–11.

6:1–2. In the opening of the first seal is showed [the going] forth of this holy warrior alone, and in Revelation 19:11–14, etc., he was showed to John with his great army that followed him upon white horses. These are they that had returned to him and had given up his enemies in themselves, that would not that he should reign. And he had slain them in them, and they had listed themselves under his banner, to make war in righteousness. And as for the rest, that would not turn to him, he slew them by his sharp sword, and the fowls were invited to eat their flesh, as in Revelation 19:17–18. So he was seen, then, with many crowns, of which more in its proper place. But I say this now, that forever blessed will those be who know or shall know this work of the Lamb of God carried on in themselves. And it is for the promotion of his kingdom and for the encouragement of others, to list themselves under the banner of the Holy Lamb, that I have made some observations on this so necessary a work, according to that light that God Almighty hath granted to me, giving way to a farther manifestation.

6:3–4. This may be said to be the beginning of sorrows among the inhabitants of this wicked world, according to the testimony of our Lord: for nation shall rise against nation, and kingdom against kingdom, and there shall be famines and pestilences and earthquakes in diverse places. All these are the beginning of sorrows.[83]

6:5–6. This is one that is or was sent with a commission or command from the Holy and Just One to see that justice might be done in the earth, for it might be a time of scarcity of corn, for the pale horse followed after. These and such like testimonies left on record are a plain demonstration to every true believer, that the eye of the Almighty is upon them that fear him, and that things are determined in heaven for the punishment of the wicked world. Although God is gracious and bears long with the disobedient in order to win them by his many mercies, yet those that will not do justly, love mercy, nor walk humbly with the Lord, he will humble them by death, as in the opening of the fourth seal will appear. And these and such like things are revealed and published for the good of mankind, that so all might turn to the Lord by a timely repentance.

83. See Matthew 24:7–8.

6:7–8. Thus we may observe, that in the opening of the four seals by the Lamb of God, how God Almighty punisheth the wicked by his four sore judgments when they go in sin, oppression and persecution, as will appear when the fifth seal is opened.

6:9. By this we may observe what the powers of this world had been doing which provoked the Lord to execute those judgments (aforementioned) upon them. For in the opening of the seals by the Lamb of God, the divine light shined, and the divine power wrought effectually in the hearts of those that turned to be followers of the Lamb, by which they were enlightened in their understandings to see into the mysteries that appertains to the kingdom of heaven, which was Christ in them, the hope of glory. And so they were moved by the Holy Spirit in them to call people out of Babylon, that they might not partake with her in her sins, etc. And having received him whose name is called the Word of God, they bore a faithful testimony against the usurpation of the old adversary. This stirred up his rage, and he, being the god of this world, stirred up the worldly powers to persecute the servants of the true God and followers of the Lamb, even to the killing of their bodies; but their souls lived still.

6:10–11. And white robes was given to every one of them: this is the robe of righteousness, the garment of salvation which Jesus Christ gave to every one of them.[84] And it was said that they should rest yet for a little season, until their fellow servants also, and their brethren that should be killed as they were, should be fulfilled. Thus we may observe they were to rest in the will of God and to wait the Lord's time, for both the righteous and the wicked have their time to grow and to ripen in the field of this world, according to the seed received into their hearts.[85] Then comes the harvest and time of separation.

6:12–13. All this is to set forth the dreadful and terrible judgments of God which he is causing to come upon this wicked world in this great and dreadful day of the Lord, wherein all light and joy shall be taken from the wicked.

The like great day of God's wrath was prophesied of by our Savior, to come upon Jerusalem, etc.[86] It is worthy to be perused, for all his promises,

84. See Isaiah 61:10.

85. See Matthew 13:24–30.

86. See Luke 21.

prophecies, and testimonies are faithful and true, for he is the faithful and true witness, and that generation filled up their measure in crucifying the Lord of life and glory, and they said, let his blood be on us and on our children.[87] And so it came to pass, for some of them fell by the sword of the Romans and some by famine in the siege, etc. And the residue were led away captives, and they are scattered into all nations, and Jerusalem shall be trodden down of the Gentiles (said our Lord) until the times of the Gentiles be fulfilled, which we Gentiles are hastening to apace.[88] And we likewise had need take care, lest at any time our hearts be overcharged with surfeiting and drunkenness and the cares of this life, and so the day of the Lord come upon us unawares. For (the Lord said), as a snare shall it come upon all them that dwell on the face of the whole earth. Watch ye, therefore, and pray always, etc.[89]

6:14–17. These testimonies ought to be considered in time by all the children of men, and all should turn to the Lord, by a speedy repentance, that so they may know the work of the Holy Lamb to be carried on in themselves, that the man of sin, the worker of iniquity, may be subdued in themselves. Then such will know the work of the new creation carried on in their own bosoms by him who said, Behold I make all things new and will come to inhabit the New Jerusalem.[90] For the opening of the sixth seal shows a period of time as when a week is ended, as to the six working days; then comes the Sabbath, or as when the corn and tares is ripe, then comes the harvest, etc.[91] These things are often done in the world, as when the iniquity of the Amorites was full—then they were cut off by the Israelites.[92] Then the Israelites, they had their time of proving, and the Lord waited long upon them, to be gracious to them, before he suffered them to be carried captive into Babylon. I have

87. Matthew 27:25. This verse from Matthew provided a pretext for Christian anti-Semitism. The eschatological fervor of the Reformation raised hopes among many Protestants of an imminent mass conversion of Jews, but most English denominations, including Quakers, regarded unconverted Jews with prejudice. See Robert M. Healey, "The Jew in Seventeenth-Century Protestant Thought," *Church History* 46, no. 1 (1977): 63–79.

88. Luke 21:24.

89. Luke 21:36.

90. Revelation 21:5.

91. See Matthew 13:24–30.

92. See Deuteronomy 20:16–18.

admired the loving kindness of the Lord to that people and his long forbearance sending his prophets to warn them before he sent his judgments upon them. Yet they came home upon the disobedient when their iniquities was fully ripe. And I have long admired the kindness of God to us Gentiles, a people professing the name of Christ, yet going on in pride, vanity, and all manner of evils. Surely the Lord will visit for these things, and the vials of his wrath will be poured out on the disobedient when the servants of God are all sealed. For our Heavenly Father and our dear Lord and Savior hath a tender regard to the least that will answer his call and come out of Babylon. All such shall be sealed by the Holy Spirit to the day of their perfect redemption or deliverance.

CHAPTER 7

7:1. Sometimes by the striving or fierce blowing of the winds is represented wars and commotions, as in Daniel: I saw in my vision by night, and behold the four winds of the heavens strove on the great sea, etc.[93] But the moderate or temperate blowing of the winds are the mercies of God, for in it is a secret food of life and the vital spirit of all living creatures. Therefore, the holding of the winds that they might not blow on the earth, nor on the sea, nor on any tree must needs do hurt, but the tender mercies of God were manifested through Jesus Christ, for it is said:

7:2. This is the Sun of Righteousness who ariseth with healing under his wings, having the seal of the living God, for it is he alone that sealeth his followers with his Holy Spirit unto the day of redemption.

7:3–9. The white robe is the robe of righteousness, the beautiful garment of salvation which they ascribe unto God and to the Lamb.

7:10–12. Here we may observe again the heavenly harmony and joy of angels and saints together. What soul can meditate on these things and not long and cry to the Lord to make it worthy to stand amongst this numberless number of the redeemed ones, to sound forth praises to God Almighty and

93. Daniel 7:2.

to the Lamb that died for them and cleansed them by his own blood? Oh! Great love.

7:13–15. (O! Station.)

7:16–17. Here is great encouragement to all believers to persevere and hold on in their way. Though it is a strait and narrow way, our Lord himself hath trodden it before us, and it is he and his followers that shall have the victory, even all those that are willing to follow him to the cross and suffer the old man to be nailed to the cross until it be quite dead, and then to the sepulchre to be buried with him—not regarding a name to live, as among men, if they can but feel their souls to live and breathe to God. To such he will give a part in the first resurrection, and the second death shall have no power over them.

So as we read in the sixth chapter how after the sixth seal was opened, the great day of the wrath of God came upon the wicked in a most terrible manner, so in the seventh chapter we read of the great joy of the saints that had come through many tribulations. So that we may observe that the destruction of the wicked is the work of the Lord, and it is done at the opening of the sixth seal. And as it is in the great world, so it is in every obedient child of God and follower of the Lamb: for the work of Jesus Christ is to destroy the works of the devil and to redeem souls to God.[94] And when a soul comes to a total resignation to the will of God in all things, then the kingdom of God is come into that soul, for the creature hath given up the usurper, and he is cast out, and God Almighty hath taken to himself his great power and ruleth in that earthen vessel. And the creature ceaseth from his own willings and workings, and resteth in the will of God, and his rest is peaceable and glorious, for the will of God is his sanctification, and the Lord worketh in him, for him, and by him according to his own will and heavenly pleasure, until he hath made his creature to be what he would have it to be; and that is and will be such an instrument in his hand as it is capable of being, for it is always God's own work that praiseth him and nothing that man of himself can do.

94. In the eighteenth century, many regarded the human body as a microcosm or "little world," which corresponded to the macrocosm or "great world" in which they lived and moved. Webb regarded Revelation as a guide to both macrocosm and microcosm, a tool for understanding world history and current events as well as an interpretive key unlocking the meaning of significant events in her own life. See John Bernard Bamborough, *The Little World of Man* (London: Longmans, Green, 1952).

CHAPTER 8

8:1. We may observe that at the opening of the first seal there was a stirring of the divine powers, which John (being in the Spirit) heard like the noise of thunder. Then he saw the white horse, and he that sat on him had a bow, and a crown was given unto him, and he went forth conquering and to conquer. So as the divine powers began to stir, and the true light began to arise, and the Spirit of God moved upon the hearts of the people in order to create them anew in Christ Jesus, that the new creation of God might be carried on, etc. So the prince of the powers of darkness raised all his forces to stand in opposition against the prince of life and light and his army which he gathered out of the world. For he was seen at first to go forth alone, and so this mystical war began and was and is carried on at the opening of all the six seals, until this holy warrior had conquered all his enemies.

And then, at the opening of the seventh seal, there was silence in heaven about the space of half an hour, the enemies of God and the enemies of his people being subdued. And the great red dragon got a wounded head, but he found out a way to get his wound healed—by turning professor of Christianity, as will be manifest hereafter, which the Apostle Paul foretold of by the Spirit, saying, now the Spirit speaketh expressly that in the latter times some shall depart from the faith, giving heed to seducing spirits and doctrines of devils, etc.[95]

The Lamb of God having loosed the seven seals, the seven angels receive seven trumpets, and the mystery of God hath been, is, and will be proclaimed by the sound of the trumpets.

8:2. Now it is needful and profitable for all to know God Almighty, who is a spirit and the Father of spirits, and Jesus Christ his only Son, our Lord and Savior, whom to know is life eternal. God is a spirit and fills all things with his power; he is possessor of heaven and earth, and the heaven of heavens cannot contain him, as saith the scriptures.[96] The Psalmist speaketh very excellently of the power and works of God, and among the rest of his notable considerations and expressions he saith, who maketh his angels spirits, his ministers a flame of fire.[97] And he said, bless the Lord, ye his angels that excel

95. 1 Timothy 4:1.

96. 2 Chronicles 2:6.

97. Psalm 104:4.

in strength, that do his commandments, hearkening to the voice of his word; bless the Lord, all ye his hosts, ye ministers of his that do his pleasure.[98]

By these few hints we may consider what the angels of God and his ministers are. Then, if I should call an angel a ministering spirit, I believe I shall not err. Then let us consider the seven angels which stand before God (to whom were given seven trumpets) to be ministering spirits sent of God to influence his servants or minsters in their several dispensations or times of sounding, for considering these things may be beneficial to an honest mind. And we may consider the seven trumpets as dispensations or degrees of the arisings of divine light and manifestations of the divine power as will be made more obvious to the enlightened mind in the perusal of the ensuing part.[99] Moreover, the prophet Isaiah saw to these times by the light or spirit of God, that seeth through all things and times. And he spake, saying, thus saith the Lord God, the Holy One of Israel: in returning and rest ye shall be saved. In quietness and confidence shall be your strength, and ye would not.[100] But to them that would obey, the Lord made very gracious and glorious promises. He saith, moreover, the light of the moon shall be as the light of the sun, and the light of the sun shall be sevenfold, as the light of seven days, in the day that the Lord bindeth up the breach of his people and healeth the stroke of their wound.[101] O glorious day, much to be desired and patiently to be waited for.

98. See Psalm 103:20–21.

99. Here and throughout this passage, Webb employs the notion of dispensationalism. The basic premise of dispensationalism is that God has different intentions and executes different actions with regard to humanity in different time periods. Christians generally accept that Jesus Christ inaugurated the "church" dispensation or the dispensation of the Holy Spirit (so called because Jesus left the Holy Spirit with his disciples in his absence; see John 14:25–26). Many Protestants believed that Catholicism drew that dispensation into apostasy. In the seventeenth and eighteenth centuries, Quakers and other radical Protestants believed in eschatological interpretations of dispensationalism: that is, that in the present day, the church dispensation was wrapping up and God would soon usher in the Millennium. This concluding dispensation would be restorationist in method and involve an undoing of errors in the church. See Melvin B. Endy Jr., *William Penn and Early Quakerism* (Princeton: Princeton University Press, 1973), 38–43, 313–14.

100. Isaiah 30:15.

101. Isaiah 30:26.

8:3. This was the service of the high priest only, under the dispensation of the law, even to offer incense upon the golden altar that [was] before the mercy seat, and doth show that this angel doth represent the Lord Jesus Christ, who is our only high priest, who maketh intercession in us and for us. And there was given unto him much incense, that he should offer it with the prayers of all saints. Yea, he hath an inexhaustible store of incense. Glory to God, the giver of it, for ever and evermore.

8:4. This shows that our advocate, even Jesus Christ the Righteous, presents the prayers of all whom he hath cleansed by his blood or sanctified by the workings of his spirit in them. He causeth the prayers of such to ascend unto his Father as sweet incense and the offering up of their hearts to God to be an acceptable sacrifice.

8:5. Mark, into the earth: the fire of the altar being cast into the earth doth denote God's judgments. And there were voices: this denotes their outcries under a fiery indignation of the Lord. For the day of the Lord was come that the prophet Malachi foretold of, saying, for behold, the day cometh that shall burn as an oven, and all the proud, yea, and all that do wickedly, shall be stubble. And the day cometh that shall burn them up, saith the Lord of Hosts, that it shall leave them neither root nor branch.[102]

The thunderings and lightnings likewise denote the judgments of the Almighty, and the earthquake may denote their trembling under sore judgments. The like judgments was denounced against Jerusalem of old for their sins: Thou shalt be visited of the Lord of Hosts with thunder and with earthquake and great noise, with storm and tempest and the flame of devouring fire.[103] And although many such testimonies are left on record both in the Old and New Testament, yet how few do ponder them or lay them to heart.

8:6. Thus God in his mercies forewarns the children of men that they may fly from the wrath to come and join in with the elect seed in themselves and so come to be gathered to God by the sound of the trumpets. According to the testimony of our Lord Jesus, he shall send his angels with a great sound of a trumpet, and they shall gather together his elect from the four winds, from

102. Malachi 4:1.

103. See Isaiah 29:6.

one end of heaven to the other.[104] Now the elect of God are all those that answer his call and joins in with his Spirit, which is called the seed of the kingdom, which is sown in all hearts.[105]

8:7. As to the year or age of the world wherein the sealed book was opened and the first trumpets were sounded, the knowledge of that not being so essential to salvation (to us and the succeeding generations) as it is to mind the dispensation we are under and to press forward. For notional knowledge puffs up, but the grace of God that edifies the soul humbleth. Therefore, I exhort to faithfulness and a humble walking with God in childlike obedience to his will, even in the day of small things. This is the safe way and the way to grow sound in faith and understanding, for the path of the just is as the shining light that shineth more and more to the perfect day.[106] But this we may safely conclude, that the Lamb of God began to open the sealed book in the days of the Apostles and primitive Christians; and that the trumpets began to sound in their days; and also that the great red dragon wrought mightily in the Roman heathenish emperors, to cause them to persecute the primitive Christians until the time of Constantine, the emperor who received the Christian faith. Then the dragon got a wounded head, of which more in its proper place.

8:8–9. The great fire signifies wrath. Its being cast into the sea signifies its being cast among the multitudes of people which stirred up wrath and sedition among them and broke their peace, so that they killed one another. This seems to be after the opening of the second seal, which may be seen in Revelation 6:3–4, this second trumpet sounding the great day of God's wrath. It might be effected in the overthrow of the heathen empire of Rome by Constantine, and so Christianity came to be established by human laws, and soon after a proud bitter spirit got up among Christians and the apostasy began.[107]

104. Matthew 24:31.

105. See Matthew 13:3–9.

106. Proverbs 4:18.

107. Webb views Constantine's conversion with ambivalence as having destroyed the "great mountain" of heathen, Christian-persecuting Rome at the price of corrupting true Christianity (turning the sea to blood) through admixture with state power. Like William Penn, but unlike some other Quakers, Webb seems to associate the climax of the Christian apostasy with Constantine's conversion, rather than with the immediately post-apostolic era. See Endy, *William Penn and Early Quakerism*, 88, 119.

8:10–11. By the falling of the great star we are to understand the falling of some great minister of the gospel from his meek, humble state of divine love, light, and life (which is the heavenly station of all that are in Christ Jesus who live and walk in the Spirit). But this great star or minister let in a bitter spirit and so fell from the sweet, meek love of Jesus Christ, which is the true Christian's life. And it fell upon the third part of the rivers and fountains of waters: that denotes that a third part of the believers in Christ received or drank in this bitter spirit or doctrine and so died as to their spiritual life, they not being fed nor led by the Holy Lamb who leads his followers unto living fountains of waters, as may be seen in Revelation 7:17 and John. In the last day, that great day of the feast, Jesus stood and cried, saying, if any man thirst, let him come unto me and drink. He that believeth on me, as the scripture hath said, out of his belly shall flow rivers of living waters.[108] But this bitter star corrupted and embittered the third part of those rivers and fountains of waters—that is, this bitter spirit corrupted the wholesome, clean, pure doctrine of the gospel of Jesus Christ, and so as many as drank of it died to God and became dark in their understandings. This spirit of bitterness is a dangerous spirit. The author to the Hebrews warned that people of this danger, saying, lift up the hands that hang down and the feeble knees, and make strait paths for your feet, lest that which is lame be turned out of the way, but let it rather be healed. Follow peace with all men and holiness, without which no man shall see the Lord, looking diligently lest any man fail of the grace of God, lest any root of bitterness springing up trouble you and thereby many be defiled.[109] And thus it was of old, when the shepherds of Israel did backslide.[110]

8:12. Thus it was showed to the beloved apostle after what manner the dark nights of apostasy came on, even by wandering or falling stars that were compared to raging waves of the sea foaming out their own shame, wandering stars to whom is reserved the blackness of darkness forever.[111] Thus it appears that as a third part of the waters were made bitter, which denotes corruption in doctrine and a treasuring up of wrath against the day of wrath, so equally did

108. John 7:37–38.

109. Hebrews 12:12–15.

110. See Ezekiel 34:19.

111. Jude 1:13.

darkness follow, or come over them, and when a total falling away comes, then total darkness will follow, as will appear in the next chapter.

8:13. This angel or ministering spirit was sent of God with that particular message, viz. to make public proclamation before the sounding of these trumpets and to declare that woeful things would follow.

May it be said, for what end? Answer: that all might hear and fear and that as many as did or would believe might retire to the name of the Lord and make it their tower of safety. For a dark and dismal time was coming on, even gross darkness over the Christian churches, darkness that might be felt, as was in Egypt of old. Yet as there was light in Goshen then, so there is a place or state of retirement into the Holy Spirit in the worst of times, where the soul may enjoy divine light and comfort.[112]

CHAPTER 9

9:1. This star doth represent some great minister, and its falling from heaven unto the earth doth show his falling away from a heavenly state to an earthly and carnal state, even a total apostatizing; and to him was given the key of the bottomless pit. The giver of this key is the angel of this pit spoken of in the eleventh verse of this chapter, and his name is Apollyon.

9:2. Here we may observe that while this minister kept his habitation in heaven, he was an instrument in the hand of God for good, but being fallen to the earth he became [an] instrument in the evil spirit for evil works, for he opened the bottomless pit. This smoke is the subtle wiles of Satan, his cunning insinuations cast forth to blind the eyes of the understanding and to cast a veil of darkness over the hearts of the people.

9:3. These locusts do represent the anti-Christian ministry coming out of the smoke of the bottomless pit, and they increased to a multitude in their degrees of canons and church orders and all under pretense of zeal for God and Christ and the holy Catholic Church. And unto them was given power as the scorpions of the earth have power; this is a comparison, for as the

112. See Exodus 8:22, 10:22–23. The Israelites in the land of Goshen were exempt from the effects of the ten plagues.

scorpions of the earth do give a deadly wound to the body, so these scorpions in spirit wounded many a poor soul that came under their power. And they received their power (in this respect) from that old serpent, who with his lies beguiled our mother Eve and so brought death and darkness upon all the posterity of old Adam.[113] These are those that our Lord and Savior foretold of, saying beware of false prophets that come to you in sheep's clothing but inwardly they are ravening wolves, etc.[114]

9:4. This showeth that they were not common locusts, for it is their nature to hurt the trees and almost every green thing, but the Spirit of God makes use of these sort of vermin to represent the numberless multitude and mischievous nature of Antichrist by. But these are limited; they had no power or allowance to hurt anything but only those men which had not the seal of God, by which we may observe to our comfort, that Apollyon and all his army are limited. The sense of which makes the souls of the followers of the Lamb to rejoice in hope of a perfect deliverance and praise the Lord daily for his present mercies, which indeed are very many.

9:5. Here we may observe again that the evil spirit is limited, which if it were not so, he would make this world to be hell upon earth, which if people did but rightly understand and consider they would be always inwardly thankful to God Almighty for every mercy they did receive. For all good comes from God; it is he that sends rain and fruitful seasons, yea it is in him that we live, move, and have our being.[115]

And their torment was as the torment of a scorpion when he striketh a man; thus the oppressions of those false teachers are set forth. Yea, they are grievous tormentors, all the time of their continuance. They bring people into a miserable state of perplexity, for they cannot direct people or load them into the way of peace because they are not acquainted with it in themselves, but these, like their forerunners, which the prophet Micah spoke of, build up Zion with blood, and Jerusalem with iniquity. The heads thereof

113. Both Webb's vilification of the Catholic Church and her characterization of the end times as a continuation of religious conflict begun in Genesis are typical of Protestant interpretive traditions. However, Webb would likely include most Protestant sects, which sought to restore the church to its ancient purity, in this condemnation. See, for example, her commentary on Revelation 16:19 or 11:10.

114. Matthew 7:15.

115. Acts 14:17, 17:28.

judge for reward, and the priests thereof teach for hire, and the prophets thereof divine for money, yet will they lean upon the Lord, and say, is not the Lord amongst us? None evil can come upon us.[116] So mystery Babylon said, she should see no sorrow, but there is a just God that beholds all things as they are and will render recompense to his enemies.[117]

9:6. Thus are they distressed with fears and torments, so that death is chosen rather than life in the days of apostasy, for they cannot die to sin under that doctrine which teacheth that there is no freedom from sin on this side the grave.[118] Also, they are terrified with the fear of God's wrath and eternal judgment, so there is no peace to the wicked, as saith the scriptures.[119]

9:7. This shows that they are warriors under the banner of their Apollyon, and they had crowns like gold. This shows their grandeur in the world, and the faces of these locusts were as the faces of men.

9:8. Thus they appeared to John in the vision. Thus the Spirit shews their form according to their nature.

9:9. Which may denote that they are or were substantially harnessed, armed with hardness of heart, and the powers of this world, to go forth to make war against Christ and his followers.

9:10. Thus the Spirit shows them according to their inward form and nature.

9:11. This was a very sorrowful time with the faithful followers of Jesus Christ, so that now they prophesied in sackcloth, and they received power to con-

116. Micah 3:10–11.

117. See Revelation 17:5. Mystical or mystery Babylon seems to represent the Catholic Church for Webb; see her commentary on Revelation 9:12–14.

118. Quakers sought for the infallible guidance of the Holy Spirit in their lives and believed in the possibility of achieving perfection while in mortality. Webb's suggestion here, that perfection or "freedom from sin" might be possible "on this side the grave," exemplifies that position, which was often a target of attack for the Society's detractors. See Carole Dale Spencer, *Holiness: The Soul of Quakerism* (Milton Keynes, UK: Paternoster, 2007); Hugh Barbour, *The Quakers in Puritan England* (New Haven: Yale University Press, 1964), 149.

119. See Isaiah 48:22, among others.

tinue in their testimony until Antichrist got to such a head that the two witnesses were slain by them, but they would keep up their dead bodies, and not suffer them to be buried—of which more in its proper place.

9:12–14. This voice, which spoke to the angel which had the sixth trumpet, came from the four horns of the golden altar. Now we may observe that under the dispensation of the law, atonement was wont to be made on the four horns of the golden altar by the blood of the sin offering, which things under the law were types and figures of heavenly things.[120] But we may likewise observe that these things revealed in this book to the beloved disciple John are the heavenly things themselves. Therefore, this was the voice of our high priest, the Lord Jesus Christ, who had been making atonement upon the four horns of this altar which is before God, for no man was to be in the temple when the high priest was within making atonement.[121] And we may observe that the voice that came forth from the four horns of this golden altar was a word of command to the angel which had sounded the sixth trumpet to loose the four angels that were bound in the great river Euphrates.

Now it is necessary to consider what is intended by the great river Euphrates, for this Revelation is manifested and delivered by similitudes. Euphrates then was a river that did belong to old Babylon, as may be seen [in] Jeremiah Chapter 41. The whole chapter is a prophecy concerning the fall of old Babylon, where many of the Lord's servants were in captivity under a strange king and hath a near resemblance with the fall of mystical Babylon. The four angels then being bound in the great river Euphrates doth denote that they were bound under the power and dominion of mystical Babylon.

But after the angel had sounded the sixth trumpet, which was to give notice what was to follow, notwithstanding it was in the time when mystery Babylon was in her great glory and had gotten great dominion, yet the command of the Lord and the word of his power was obeyed. This was the time of the first Reformers.[122]

120. See Leviticus 4:24–25.

121. See Leviticus 6:17–18.

122. Webb locates this sounding of the sixth trumpet in the sixteenth century, with the efforts of reformers such as Martin Luther and John Calvin curtailing the power and spread of mystical Babylon, or the Catholic Church.

9:15. Here we may observe that angels are spirits. And these four angels, being bound under the power of mystery Babylon, do signify that the spirits of God's servants were bound down under oppression. God Almighty suffered it to be so for a season, and Antichrist reigned and made merry over God's faithful witnesses, but now the four angels or ministering spirits are loosed. That is thus to be understood: the good spirits that before did sigh and cry is now set at liberty and brought up into a good degree of dominion, so that they in whom it dwells stand in a readiness to bear their testimony when they shall be called unto it. For they are prepared for the destruction of a third part of the mystical Babylon, being an army gathered and disciplined by the Lord Jesus to fight a spiritual battle with mystery Babylon, by bearing testimony against all her idolatries.[123]

9:16–17. Their breastplates of fire and jacinth and brimstone shows their armor, that they were armed with zeal for God and holiness, for jacinth is a precious stone, an emblem of light and purity. And the heads of their horses were as the heads of lions: this is to demonstrate by whose power these warriors were bore up, even by the power of him who is called the Lion of the tribe of Judah, the Root of David.[124] And out of the mouth of the horses issued fire, smoke and brimstone: this may signify the power of God did go before them and was as a wall of fire for their defense.

9:18. This signifies the wrath of God was kindled against those locusts, and those warriors were as Jeremiah was of old, even God's battle ax and weapons of war, for with them will he break in pieces the nations, and with them will he destroy kingdoms, etc.[125] Yet they lift up no sword, for the weapons of their warfare are not carnal.

9:19. All these are mystical things and are not to be understood after a carnal manner, for whereas it is said their power is in their mouth, this is no new thing but what hath been of old, as is testified in the scriptures of truth. Therefore (said the Lord) I have hewed them by the prophets, I have slain

123. Webb suggests that the testimony of the first Protestant reformers drew away a third part of mystical Babylon, or the Catholic Church; this battle for converts is a form of spiritual warfare between Christ and Antichrist.

124. Revelation 5:5; see Hosea 5:14; Isaiah 11:10.

125. Jeremiah 51:20–21.

them by the words of my mouth.[126] And Jeremiah was the Lord's battle ax, and yet we do not read that he did fight with carnal weapons. But the prophets of old and also these spiritual warriors that John saw in this vision—they overcame their enemies, those that were within, by the blood of Lamb that cleanseth from all sin. And those that were without that were instruments of Satan—those they overcame by the word of their testimony. And they loved not their lives unto death, for they are made to pronounce the judgments of God (against those that oppress the seed of God and keep it in bondage) even before judgment is executed on them, as Moses and many of the prophets did of old. And the execution followed as the tail, and death and sore judgments to the wicked hath a terrible sting in it; so the sting is in the tail, for the wicked that are hardened do not regard the testimony of truth at all, and were it not for the sting of death that comes after, they would vaunt over it forever. Yet it is deemed as if they were slain by that which issued out of the mouths of this select army, because by it they were hewed or wounded, and their resting in opposition against it did procure to them what followed as the tail.[127]

9:20–21. These were hardened sinners, for as they repented not of their idolatries, so they repented not of their murders, for they killed the servants of God for bearing their testimony to the truth and against their idolatry and evil ways. And they repented not of their sorceries: that may be meant their false doctrine, whereby they bewitched the people that they should not obey the truth, although it were set forth evidently before their eyes, as the Galatians were.[128] Very many are the wiles and cunning devices of Satan to keep poor souls in bondage. Neither repented they of their fornication: that may be meant spiritual as well as natural, even in departing from Jesus Christ. Neither repented they of their theft, for though the Saints took patiently the spoiling of their goods, knowing in themselves that they have in heaven a better and an enduring substance, yet that did not excuse the others who took their goods from them. But the Lord Jesus said to his kinsmen after the flesh, who believed not in him, the world cannot hate you, but me it hateth

126. Hosea 6:5.

127. Here the destructive power of God is compared to the tail of a snake. Webb explains that the fulfillment of prophetic decrees announcing the future chastisement of the wicked is sure and inevitable, just as the tail of a serpent surely and inevitably follows its mouth as the serpent moves forward.

128. Galatians 3:1.

because I testify of it that the works thereof are evil.[129] And as the world hated our Lord, so also it hateth his followers and believers in him for the same reasons, which thing our Lord foretold his disciples of as may be seen, saying, if the world hate you, you know that it hated me before it hated you. If ye were of the world, the world would love his own, but because ye are not of the world, but I have chosen you out of the world, therefore the world hateth you. Remember the word that I said unto you, the servant is not greater than his Lord: if they have persecuted me they will also persecute you; if they have kept my sayings, they will keep yours also. But all these things will they do unto you for my names sake because they know not him that sent me.[130] Oh! The tender care and concern that our dear Lord showed to his followers when he was about to leave this world, as to his personal appearance in it, and to go away, as to that appearance or dispensation, that the Comforter, the Holy Ghost might come, as he plainly told his disciples.[131] Oh! The comfortable promises that he made to his followers and the many things that he foretold should come to pass shows plainly that he is the Son of God, the true Light, the Divine Wisdom, and that he saw through all time, from the beginning of it to the end thereof. This is our Lord; we have waited for him. This is the Lamb of God that taketh away the sins of the world. Glory to God forevermore. This is the faithful and true witness that hath revealed these things unto his followers.

CHAPTER 10

10:1. This is the messenger of the covenant of grace, light, and life that God the Father hath made with his people, as the rainbow was a token of God's covenant made with Noah.[132] And his face was [as] it were the sun: this was to manifest the brightness of his glorious light, who is arisen with healing virtue as under his wings and his feet as pillars of fire, whereby he will tread his enemies, and they shall be ashes under his feet.[133] I observe that when he

129. John 7:7.

130. John 15:18–21.

131. See John 16:7.

132. See Genesis 9:23.

133. Malachi 4:2–3.

took the sealed book out of his Father's hand in order to open the seven seals thereof, he then appeared as a Lamb Slain, but now he appeareth in great glory, having finished that great mystical work which none else was found worthy to do. And being now ascended on high, he is come to lead captivity captive and to give gifts to men.[134]

10:2. This doth plainly show that all things are put under his feet, for he must reign till he hath put all enemies under his feet. The last enemies that shall be destroyed is death.[135]

10:3–4. Thus John is forbidden that which the seven thunders uttered, which doubtless were the secret judgments of God. These things followed the second wo trumpet, and we may safely observe that the judgments are set forth in the scriptures in many places by thunders. The Lord thundered from heaven, and the Most High uttered his voice.[136] He sent out arrows and scattered them, etc. And thou shalt be visited of the Lord with thunder and with earthquake, etc.[137] This was part of the great judgments of God which he denounced against Jerusalem of old, also when the angel that offered the incense with the prayers of all Saints had filled the golden censor with fire of the altar and cast it into the earth, there were voices and thunder and an earthquake.[138] And this mighty angel cried with a loud voice, as when a Lion roareth: thus the Lord did of old, when he had a controversy with the nations. The Lord shall roar from on high and utter his voice from his holy habitation. He shall mightily roar upon his habitation; he shall give a shout as they that tread the grapes, against all the inhabitants of the earth.[139] The Lord also shall roar out of Zion and utter his voice from Jerusalem, and the heavens and the earth shall shake, but the Lord is the hope of his people.[140] Thus the voice of God's anger is set forth by the prophets, which comes suddenly many times

134. Ephesians 4:8.

135. 1 Corinthians 15:25–26.

136. 2 Samuel 22:14–15.

137. Isaiah 29:6.

138. Revelation 8:5.

139. Jeremiah 25:30.

140. Joel 3:16.

on the wicked, even as a snare or as a thief in the night. But the Lord is the hope of his people.

10:5–7. Here this mighty angel gives testimony to what was declared by the prophets, and indeed I have found such a harmony and agreement between the testimonies of the prophets and the things revealed to the Apostle John in this book that I have admired at it, even at the continued harmony of the Holy Spirit. Oh! It is good to have some time of retirement to look into the things of God before the soul is separated from the body, that so by having familiar conversation with the Holy Spirit, the soul may be made acquainted with heavenly things and learn here by the Spirit how to behave in the divine presence in Eternity and also to be fitted to stand upon the sea of glass mingled with fire. All the works of man must be tried by fire.[141] Observe the seventh angel hath the finishing or last trumpet and is the finishing prophecy or testimony of all things, as may be seen: and the seventh angel sounded, and there were great voices in heaven, saying, the kingdoms of this world are become the kingdoms of our Lord and of his Christ, and he shall reign forever and ever.[142]

10:8–10. This signifieth that the apostle was inspired and filled with the divine word, having received command by a voice from heaven to take the book. And being commanded (by the messenger of the covenant) to eat it up, he received commission from God to go forth in his future service. Likewise, the prophet Ezekiel was commanded to eat a roll of a book, which was written within and without, and there was written therein lamentations and mourning and wo. Then he was to go speak unto the House of Israel.[143]

10:11. It is comfortable to observe the agreement of the testimonies given forth under the openings of the seven seals and sounding the seven trumpets and the pouring out of the seven vials of the wrath of God, for they are the dispensations of God to mankind or the proclamation of things that are revealed by Jesus Christ to his followers, that all may hear and fear and turn to the Lord before the vials of his wrath be poured out on them. For the seven vials are said to be full of the wrath of God, and as the seals are opened by

141. See 1 Corinthians 3:13.

142. Revelation 11:15.

143. See Ezekiel 2:9–10.

Christ, the true light, so the trumpets sound according to the dispensations of God, and the pouring out of the vials follow.[144]

CHAPTER 11

11:1. By this is intended the real temple of God, that Solomon's temple was a figure of. The temple that Solomon built was in Jerusalem, that is from beneath, that is in bondage with her children. But Jerusalem that is from above is the mother of the faithful, and the city of the great king, and there was seen no temple therein, for the Lord God and the Lamb are the temple of it. Therefore it is those that worship God in his own spirit and in the spirit of Christ Jesus, who is the truth and the life, that are within the measuring line and notice of the Almighty God, and such are to be squared and polished by his Holy Spirit. If at any time anything that is superfluous or unclean should grow upon them, these things are known by experience. And as to the altar, that is the spirit of Jesus Christ, and he is the pattern that all are to be measured and squared by.

11:2. Here the name of the true worshipers is derived from the Jews because they were God's people under the first covenant, and the name of the nominal Christians, who worship in the form without the life and power of Godliness, are distinguished by the name Gentiles. And such, in the black and dark night of apostasy, trod the holy city under foot for a long time, which the Spirit calls forty and two months measured by the moon, which rules the night because those apostatized Christians were children of the night governed by the prince of the powers of darkness.

11:3. We may here observe that God Almighty had his true and faithful witnesses on the earth in these dark times, though they were in a very mournful state because Antichrist reigned, and who these two witnesses are will be manifested by scripture.

11:4. The church of God under the dispensation of the Law was represented by and called a candlestick and an olive tree: the Lord called thy name a green olive tree, fair and of goodly fruit.[145] And, for if thou wert cut out of the olive

144. See Revelation 15:7.

145. Jeremiah 11:16.

tree, which is wild by nature, and wert grafted in contrary to nature, into a good olive tree, how much more shall these which be the natural branches be grafted into their own olive tree?[146] And, I have looked and behold a candlestick all of gold with a bowl upon the top of it, and his seven lamps thereon, and seven pipes to the seven lamps, and what are these two olive trees upon the right side of the candlestick, and upon the left side thereof, etc. And, what be these two olive branches, which through the two golden pipes empty the golden oil out of themselves? Then said the angel, these are the two anointed ones that stand by the God of the whole earth.[147]

Christ Jesus is that olive tree that the apostle, speaking to the Gentiles converts, told them that they were grafted into. And he is the fountain of that golden oil which indeed is the love of God, that nourishing divine principle which is the food and life of all the faithful souls and hath been so in all generations and will be to the end of time. And the second olive branches, which through the two golden pipes empty the golden oil out of themselves, these are God's instruments under both testaments, that he makes use of to convey the heavenly oil through to the thirsty soul that is not yet come into a very near acquaintance with himself. So Jesus Christ is the root and stock, and those that have received and shall receive the unction from the Holy One, both under the dispensation of the Law and Gospel, are the two anointed ones and the two witnesses that stand before the God of the whole earth: Thou hast loved righteousness and hated iniquity; therefore God, even thy God, hath anointed thee with the oil of gladness above thy fellows.[148] This is meant: as Christ is the anointed of God in his human nature, thus the Spirit and the Bride are called two olive trees and two candlesticks, because under two ministrations. There are abundance more scripture testimonies might be produced to prove that the spirit of Christ and the Bride (i.e., his Church) are the two witnesses that stand before the God of the whole earth and are calling to the children of men to come out of Babylon and to come and be reconciled to God, for the word of reconciliation is sent into the world. Yet it is said,

11:5. This denotes that what [when] the Lord hath strove long, and people will not be reconciled to his ways, his vials of wrath will be poured out on

146. Romans 11:24.

147. Zechariah 4:2, 11–12, 14.

148. Hebrews 1:9.

them at last, which are generally proclaimed by the mouth of the witnesses, and so it is rendered as if they had done it.

11:6. This doth hold forth a mystery in it, although it is set forth in a similitude of that judgment executed upon the idolatrous Israelites in the days of Ahab, pronounced by the mouth of Elijah: and Elijah said to Ahab, as the Lord God of Israel liveth there shall not be dew nor rain these years but according to my word.[149] So as the outward showers were withheld in the days of Jezebel, that idolatrous woman, so the heavenly showers of spiritual doctrine was withheld from the people in the days of idolatrous mystery Babylon, and there was a famine of the divine word. For the heavenly showers that causeth the heart of man to be fruitful to God is distilled into it by the faithful and true witnesses, and many times through his instruments he causeth his doctrine to drop as the dew and distill as the rain on the tender plants of his own right hand planting.[150]

This prophecy is to show that God is ready to execute his judgments on them that hurt his witnesses, as if it were done at their will: but their will is totally resigned to the will of God.[151] And whereas it is said these have power over waters to turn them into blood, this doth speak a mystery, for the doctrine of the two witnesses, which is the word of their testimony, doth not only denounce judgments but also doth teach love, patience, and self-denial: to love enemies, to do good to them that hate us and so to be followers of the Lamb of God; also declaring to those apostatized Christians what would be the effects of their apostasy if they did not return, repent, etc. Now, though these and such testimonies were born in love and good will yet it being contrary to the proud spirit of Antichrist, it stirred up his choler and a murderous spirit in him and his people, and so they taught that it was good service to kill heretics. And so it is said they drank the blood of the saints, and afterwards their waters were turned into blood, as may be seen when the third vial of the

149. 1 Kings 17:1.

150. Deuteronomy 32:2.

151. This sentence is drawn from the Buffington manuscript because the sentence in Webb's hand is incomplete and requires reconstruction: "This prophecy is to show that God is ready to execute his judgments on them that hurt his witnesses, as if it were done at their will is too [large blank space] resigned to the will of God."

wrath of God was poured out upon their rivers and fountains of waters—then they became blood.[152]

11:7. Now the time was fully come, that the apostle told Timothy of when he exhorted him, saying, preach the word; be instant in season, out of season; reprove, rebuke, exhort with all longsuffering and doctrine, for the time will come, when they will not endure sound doctrine; but after their own lusts shall they heap to themselves teachers, having itching ears; and they shall turn away their ears from the truth and shall be turned unto fables.[153]

Now such apostatized Christians, hearing the testimony of the two faithful witnesses (which is Christ in his followers, the hope of their glory), they make war against them and overcome them and kill them, when they had finished their testimony.

11:8–9. This shows plainly that the great city, which spiritually is called Sodom and Egypt, doth not denote a city builded in particular country or place but doth intend mystery Babylon the great, in all places of her dominions, which was so large as that it contained all the locusts that came out of the bottomless pit, or all those that trod the Holy City under foot. As for the time that the bodies of these two witnesses lay quite dead in those large dominions, [it] is said to be three days and a half. How many months or years the Spirit measures by that is not made known to me, but doubtless it intends all the time, wherein there was no living testimony born publicly, against their dead formality. For,

11:10. Now we are to inquire what the dead bodies of these two prophets are, that while they were living tormented them that dwell on the earth. Answer: while they were living among men they were the Spirit and the Bride who were calling to the children of men to come to God, to come out of Babylon, etc., which did break the peace and torment the earthly-minded.

But what are their dead bodies? I take it, in short, to be, in short, a dead formality of Christianity without the life and power thereof. But for the sake of some, I shall explain it a little more, according to that light, that it hath pleased God to give to me. We read that the letter killeth, but the Spirit giveth life; and the same apostle said that their sufficiency was of God, who

152. Revelation 16:5–6.

153. 2 Timothy 4:2–4.

also had made them able ministers of the New Testament—not of the letter but of the Spirit.[154] But those apostate Christians had banished the Spirit from among them.

For the child that the woman brought forth, the great red dragon could not devour him, for he was caught up to God and to his throne. And the woman (viz., the true church) was fled into a wilderness, and the remnant of her seed they had persecuted and put to silence. So, now, what had they but the dead bodies of the witnesses, which I take to be their last will and testaments left behind them, which contain abundance of ordinances, testimonies, and instructions in religious matters. But the Spirit being withdrawn, they are called a dead letter, and those formalists, not having the Spirit in themselves, by which they were given forth, did wrest them to their own outward advantage, though to their own inward (and outward) destruction too, at last. And they rejoiced over them and made merry and sent gifts one to another, and the dead letter did not torment them for their making merry over the witnesses for the eye of their understanding was darkened, and their hearts hardened, so that they did not understand the scriptures, neither the power of God. And it is so still with all those that are in Babel—i.e., in the confusion of languages, in which is couched a great mystery.[155] These dead bodies they could see, but not the bodies of the saints whose blood they had spilt, for they had mangled their bodies with many sorts of tortures, so that it was not desirable to keep them above ground. Thus the false church got the upper hand, and they were very merry on their holy days and festival days, of which they had many, which they called saints' days or the feast of such a saint.[156] And they sent gifts to one another when the true and faithful witnesses

154. See 2 Corinthians 3:5–6.

155. The Quakers participated in a seventeenth-century debate over how best to recover the *lingua humana*, or Adamic tongue that was spoken before Babel's fall, but insisted that such efforts could only be successful with the guidance of the Spirit—and not through the scholastic efforts of individuals learned in Hebrew, Greek, Latin, and other ancient languages. Webb here participates in a long Quaker tradition of condemning those who rely on university training in biblical languages as formalists, students of a "dead letter." See George Fox, John Stubs, and Benjamin Furley, *A Battle-Door for Teachers & Professors to Learn Singular and Plural* (London: Robert Wilson, 1660); Zachary McLeod Hutchins, *Inventing Eden: Primitivism, Millennialism, and the Making of New England* (New York: Oxford University Press, 2014), 172–75.

156. These holy days originated in the Roman Catholic Church but continued in the Church of England; the Society of Friends, like other Protestant sects, including the Puritans, rejected holy days and feast days as a form of idolatry.

lay slain, even the slain Lamb and his followers, who had long prophesied in sackcloth. But their dead bodies were kept up and made so merry with, that they did sing the Lord's prayer and their *te deum* and chant to the sound of their organs and call it worship and say they sung to the praise and glory of God. They had their singing men and their singing boys to raise the voice higher or lower according to the sounding of their organs. These, and such-like things too tedious to enumerate, they called divine service. I have been an ear witness to many such things, being bred up and educated among the great mother's daughters and living nigh to one of her great cathedrals in my youthful days.[157] Oh, the abundance of images and idolatry that I have seen: but I grow weary of this strain and want to come to speak of the arising of the witnesses, for that is abundantly more pleasant than all the glorious trumpery of mystery Babylon, although indeed her colleges and all her ministers and attendance were richly furnished and arrayed to the great sorrow and slavery of the poor lay people.[158]

11:11. Three days and a half measures the whole time wherein there was no living testimony born publicly among Christians so called, but now the spirit of life from God entered the witnesses, and they stood upon their feet. The spirit of life from God did not enter into the written or printed word or testaments, that the faithful have left behind them, but the same Spirit by which they were given forth entered into as many as would receive it, in the day of the first reformers, and raised up an army for the Lord. And they, being instructed and disciplined by the heavenly teacher in the heavenly university, were as the scribe instructed to the kingdom of heaven, which our Lord compared to an householder which bringeth forth of his things new and old.[159] So the Holy Spirit, we know by experience, lays hold on the testimonies left on record in the scriptures of truth and is the alone true interpreter of them, because by him they were given forth. For as no man knows the

157. Here and elsewhere, Webb refers to the Church of England as a "daughter" of the apostate Catholic Church, implying that it is different in name but not in substance.

158. Webb characterizes the state-mandated financial support for the Church of England as a kind of slavery, a monetary burden that was exacerbated for early Quakers, who could be fined, imprisoned, and in rare cases transported for failing to attend services or contribute to the living of a local clergyman.

159. Matthew 13:52.

things of a man save the spirit of a man that is in him, so no man knows the things of God but the Spirit of God. So the faithful witnesses in all ages have received a measure of the Spirit of God, that they might know the things that are freely given to them of God, which things also they speak, but not in words which man's wisdom teacheth, but which the Holy Ghost teacheth—comparing spiritual things with spiritual. But the natural man receiveth not the things of the Spirit of God, for they are foolishness to him, neither can he know them because they are spiritually discerned.[160] This was a great day of salvation and a mighty visitation of God to the children of men after a great time of darkness and treading underfoot, but now the witnesses are risen, and it is said great fear fell on them that saw them.

11:12. Thus their comforts increase. They are not only set upon their feet by the spirit of life from God entering into them, but are also called up into heaven, out of the reach of their enemies spiritually understood. And after this they are making war in their heavenly stations under the banner of their heavenly prince, and the weapons of their warfare were not carnal but spiritual and mighty through God. And now great Babylon begins to shake.

11:13. Here we may observe that the same hour that the two witnesses ascended into heaven there was a great earthquake, and the tenth part of the city fell. This was the beginning of the fall of Babylon, and this earthquake was not a common earthquake, for we do not understand that the bodies of men were slain thereby, but their names were slain. That is, they had gotten names of blasphemy put on them by the beast and the false prophet. For men were not only called master one of another, which was forbidden by our Lord because, said he, one is your master, even Christ, and all ye are brethren, but they were called your majesty, your lordship, your worship, reverend fathers, and many such titles that belongeth to God alone.[161] So those men which the power of God laid hold on, and his spirit rested on, it shook their human frame and cast confused self down (on which foundation Babel is built) and in the earthquake their names of blasphemy were slain, their spiritual eye

160. 1 Corinthians 2:11–14.

161. Matthew 23:8. Quakers spoke to one another—and, more problematically, to civic and ecclesiastical officials—using the familiar pronouns *thee* and *thou*, in order to avoid elevating men with honorific titles that they believed should only be used in reference to God.

opened, and they were converted to God like Saul when he was going to Damascus.[162]

Here we may observe that at the first earthquake, it was but a tenth part of Babel that fell. But another woe trumpet being ready to sound, we shall understand thereby a further carrying on of the work of God.

11:14–15. Now we are come near even to the dispensation we are under, wherein there are many voices in heaven praising God and saying as above, in the spirit of faith, seeing and feeling that the work of conversion is begun, which God Almighty will carry on until he brings kings to be nursing fathers, and their queens nursing mothers to the babe of grace.[163] And they shall take Babylon's brats and cast them away. There are many voices in heaven praising God, in a sense that this great work is begun and in believing that the Lord will carry it on to perfection. Now if any should say where is heaven, is it not above the stars, etc., I answer such and say that the kingdom of heaven is everywhere where the Holy Spirit rules or where God Almighty is obeyed. And our Lord Jesus told the Jews that the kingdom of heaven did not come with observations to say lo here or lo there is the kingdom; for behold the kingdom of God is within you.[164] But we may observe he did not tell the Pharisees that they were in the kingdom, for the kingdom of heaven sometimes suffers, and the meek king of it also, but now he is about to take to himself his great power which causeth such great joy in all the heavenly host.

11:16. These twenty four elders are as representatives of the churches of God both under the Law and Gospel. Twelve of them doth represent twelve tribes of the children of Israel or sons of Jacob, and the other twelve doth represent the twelve apostles of the Lamb. The names of these twenty-four elders are written on the twelve gates and on the twelve foundations of the holy city, the New Jerusalem.

11:17–18. Observe: and the nations were angry. Who were they angry with? They were angry with the faithful witnesses of God and put them to death, and now God is angry with them. I do not understand this here spoken of to be the last and general judgment, but a time of the wrath of God is come

162. See Acts 9:1–8.

163. Isaiah 49:23.

164. Luke 17:21.

upon those that are dead in sin and have hardened their hearts and defiled their hands with the blood of saints. This answers to the cry of those souls that were seen under the altar in Revelation 6:9–11. Now the time is come that their cry should be answered, and those should be destroyed that destroy the earth. Those that destroy the earth are the locusts that come out of the smoke of the bottomless pit, whose king in the Hebrew tongue is called Abbadon, but in the Greek tongue hath his name Apollyon, that is a destroyer, a destroyer indeed, and were he not limited by the Holy One, mankind would feel more of his rage.

11:19. Observe: and the temple of God was opened in heaven and there was seen in his temple the ark of his testament. This is a farther manifestation of the antitype of that ark that was in the temple at Jerusalem. This is a great token of the favor of God to his people to open his temple thus to them, even to the very oracle, the most holy place. For when Solomon had finished the temple that he built, the priests brought in the Ark of the Covenant of the Lord into his place, into the oracle of the house to the next holy place, even under the wings of the Cherubims, as may be seen at the dedication of that temple.[165] But we are come to the antitype, the substance, for which favor and great mercy let all that are believers in Jesus Christ, with glad and thankful hearts, bow in reverence before the Almighty for his great benefits that he hath bestowed upon us under this great and glorious dispensation. For the Ark of God's testament, now even the New Testament, or Covenant, is the spirit of Christ dwelling in his people, who are his temple. For it is the indwelling of the spirit of Christ that makes the body God's temple, for herein is the place of divine worship, and the testament here spoken of is the law of the spirit of life in Christ Jesus, which sets the true Christian free from the law of sin and death. So, then, the body is the temple of God, the heart the holy place, where the soul retires to speak with God. The Lord Jesus Christ is the Ark, the law of the spirit of life. In him is the New Testament (or Covenant) which the Lord promised in his mercy by the mouth of his servant Jeremiah.[166]

We may observe by the text, that after the temple in heaven was opened, etc., that there were lightnings and voices and thunderings and an earthquake and great hail. Those things show that the great power of God was at work among men, for the enlightening of those that were willing to receive him,

165. See 1 Kings 8.

166. See Jeremiah 31:31–33, 32:40.

who said, as the lightning ariseth in the east and shineth to the west, even so shall the coming of the Son of man be.[167] The voices might be of several significations: some, it may be, praising God for his mercies; others, crying out under a sense of his judgments, for there was thunderings and an earthquake and great hails, which denote judgments upon the man of sin, the worker of iniquity—yea, even in those that are saved. And the great hail denotes a sweeping judgment, not only to sweep away the refuge of lies, but also to sweep away those that make lies their refuge and trust in falsehood.[168] For the Lord will go through with his work in unfolding the mysteries of his kingdom and the utter overthrow of Babylon, even under the sound of the seventh trumpet, according to the testimony of that mighty angel that came down from heaven, who was clothed with a cloud and had a rainbow on his head, etc.[169] He testified that in the days of the voice of the seventh angel, when he shall begin to sound, the mystery of God should be finished, as he hath declared to his servants the prophets. And we have cause to believe that this angel knew the mind of God, and it would be well for all people to read and observe these Revelations and to be more spiritually minded, for time in this world is short and very uncertain, and eternity is our long home. And the call of the Lord is going to the very end of the earth. [He] that hath an ear may hear what the Spirit saith to the churches.

What have we to do then but to watch and pray to the Lord that his kingdom may come into us more and more, that he will take to himself his great power and reign in my heart and help me his poor creature, that I may be able to keep my heart with all diligence, seeing out of it proceeds the issues of life. For without the continual assistance of the Prince of Life, I can do nothing that will find acceptance with thee, Oh! my God. Let every poor soul say, and lift up the heart continually to God, and he will carry on his own work in it.

167. Matthew 24:27.

168. See Isaiah 28:15.

169. See Revelation 10:1.

CHAPTER 12

12:1. This woman represents the true church, and her being clothed with the sun doth signify that she is clothed with the garment of salvation, even with the robe of righteousness of Jesus Christ, in which she shines as the light of the world.[170] She being clothed with the sun of righteousness, which rules the day and swallows up the light of the moon that rules the night. The sun being so much more excellent in brightness that the moon is said to be under her feet as useless, or she treads on these sublunary things. The crown of twelve stars may represent the twelve elders of the twelve tribes of Israel or sons of Jacob (or the twelve apostles of the Lamb).

12:2. This woman being with child cried, travailing in birth and pained to be delivered. Here is a great mystery presented to our view, for the church under the law did not only travail in birth that Christ might be brought forth, but also the Christian church. Yea, every true Christian in their own particulars do travail in pain that Christ may be formed within and may be brought up into dominion within themselves and others. The faithful among the Jews, from Abraham to the Prophet Malachi, saw in and according to the measure of the Spirit which each one received of God, which Spirit seeth from the beginning to the end of time. By this divine light they saw to the day of Christ and were in great hope and expectation of his outward or personal appearance, so that very plain and punctual prophecies were given forth concerning him, which would be too long and indeed needless to relate. But when the fulness of time came, God sent forth his Son, made of a woman, made under the Law, etc.[171] Well then, Christ was brought forth, offered up, arisen and ascended into his glory, before the same apostle said, my little children, of whom I travail in birth again until Christ may be formed in you.[172] And Christ himself signified that whosoever doth the will of his Heavenly Father, the same is his brother, sister, and mother.[173] These things are worthy of consideration, that all may inwardly travail, though it may be in pain, till Christ be brought forth in them, to rule over the man of sin, the

170. See Isaiah 61:10.

171. Galatians 4:4.

172. Galatians 4:19.

173. Matthew 12:50.

worker of iniquity. That so every one may say unto me, and so being united to the true church together may say, unto us a child is born, unto us a son is given, and the government shall be upon his shoulders: and his name shall be called wonderful, counselor, the Mighty God, the Everlasting Father, the Prince of Peace. Of the increase of his government and peace there shall be no end.[174] Oh happy soul, happy people that experienceth but the beginning of this day and puts up a resolution that he shall govern in the inward man. And now I shall say without hesitation that whosoever hath put off their own righteousness, and have been washed from unrighteousness by the blood of the Lamb that cleanses from all sin, and have put on the Lord Jesus and are following of him in the way of self-denial, bearing the daily cross—such are under this glorious, holy clothing, for it is the garment of salvation. And they are true and living members of this woman who was seen in such bright clothing, let them be Jews or Gentiles. And the day will come, when Wo will be to all that are covered and not with the garment of salvation, the robe of the righteousness of the Son of God.

12:3. The dragon's station was an usurped station that he got when he deceived our first parents, even a rule and dominion in the hearts of the children of men, where God Almighty only ought to rule and reign. And his appearing in a red color shews his murderous spirit. Our Lord said he was a murderer from the beginning and abode not in the truth.[175] And his seven heads denote the great dominions he hath in this world, which he showed and offered unto our Savior, if he would but fall down and worship him. But our Lord rejected his offer, for which we have cause to bless God forever, who upheld his Son by his own power. But the worldly rulers received power from him, viz. the dragon, and great authority and power were seen like a scarlet-colored beast. After that, having seven heads and ten horns, like the dragon, and it is worth our while to observe how things are seen by the eye of the Lord, which is the divine light, that sees all things as they are. And they were represented to John according to their inward form, which is according to their natures, or the predominate principle that rules within men.

12:4. By his tail drawing a third of the stars of heaven is intended his allurements and enticements, drawing the minds of those who were once heavenly-

174. Isaiah 9:6–7.

175. John 8:44.

minded into a desire after the riches, honors, and pleasures of this world, who, by giving way thereto did apostatize and fall away from their heavenly station into an earthly and carnal state, and so the devil is going about yet with his subtle temptations, seeking whom he may ensnare. And the dragon stood before the woman to devour her child as soon as it was born. The dragon had such a prevalence over our first parents, and since prevailed to draw so many stars from heaven to the earth, that he attempted to devour the Son of God not only in or by Herod the King, but also by his temptations and insinuations. He sought to draw the second Adam, the Lord, from heaven to the earth; yea, he is an unwearied adversary, and all had need to watch. For he came to our Lord near the time that he was to be offered up, as may be seen: hereafter I will not talk much with you (said Jesus Christ) for the prince of this world cometh, and hath nothing in me.[176] Oh, happy state! Oh, that we could say so too; for if our adversary the devil could find nothing of worldly- or earthly-mindedness within, then he would have nothing to lay hold of. And that soul that is wholly given up into the hand of God to be disposed of according to his will is at rest, for it resteth in the will of God, and no torment can touch it. For such do believe that all things as tribulations, reproaches, persecutions, and buffetings of Satan shall all work together for good if the soul can but abide in the love and fear of God, as our holy pattern continued in resignation to the very last, saying to his Heavenly Father, Not my will but thine be done.[177]

12:5. He was found worthy to be taken up unto God and to his throne because of his faithfulness in all his testimonies and sufferings, for he took human nature upon him, that through death he might destroy him that had the power of death—that is the devil—and deliver them who through fear of death were all their lifetime subject to bondage.[178] And having overcome, he is set down with his Father in his throne, and now we may say as it is said: God, who at sundry times and in divers manners spake in times past unto the fathers by the prophets, hath in these last days spoken to us by his Son, whom he hath appointed heir of all things, by whom also he hath made the worlds. Who, being the brightness of his glory and the express image of his person (but truly translated of his substance) and upholding all things by the

176. John 14:30.

177. See Luke 22:42.

178. Hebrews 2:14–15.

word of his power when he had by himself purged our sins, sat down on the right hand of the majesty on high.[179]

12:6. This is the time spoken of in Revelation 11:2–3: even wherein the holy city is trodden under foot, and the witnesses prophesied in sackcloth one thousand two hundred and sixty days. This was a mournful, solitary time with the true lovers of truth and righteousness but a time of great mirth and idolatry with the worldly-minded, for they then had their day.

12:7. This war here spoken of I take to be great contention among ministers, for ministers are called angels, as may be seen in Revelation 1:20. This Michael here spoken of I take to be our Lord Jesus; and his angels to be the faithful ministers who bore a faithful testimony, for the truth is the life of it and abode in meekness and patience, and so they gave up their lives for their holy cause.[180] And the angels of the dragon we may believe were tinctured with his nature and were the ministers of Antichrist. And the war being seen to be in heaven was because it was in the Christian Church, before there was a clear separation. And whereas it is said only thus, Michael and his angels fought against the dragon, by this we may observe that they only made war against the man of sin, the worker of iniquity, and not against the lives of men, whom Jesus Christ came not to destroy but to save.[181]

12:8. i.e. the dragon prevailed not, so they lost the spirit of Christ, which makes the heavenly places or stations in men, and the dragon had drawn those down into the earth in such a great degree that their place was found no more in heaven.

12:9. For when and wheresoever the meek, divine love and life of Jesus prevaileth, then and there Satan falleth. As our dear Lord said to the seventy disciples that he had sent forth to preach, when they returned with joy, they said, Lord, even the devils are subject to us through thy name. Jesus said unto them, I behold Satan as lightning fall from heaven. Behold, I give unto you power to tread upon serpents and scorpions and over all the powers of the

179. Hebrews 1:1–3.

180. Webb's equation of Michael with the pre-incarnate Christ is consistent with early Protestant views, which is perhaps why she seems to take the assertion for granted.

181. See Luke 9:56.

enemy, and nothing shall by any means hurt you. Notwithstanding, in this rejoice not, that the spirits are subject unto you; but rather rejoice because your names are written in heaven.[182] Now these things are spiritually to be understood.

12:10. Here is great cause of joy indeed, for when the devil is cast by the power of God, and the spirit of his only Son is received into any poor soul, then it finds by an inward breathing and touch of divine love that (instead of an accuser) it hath an advocate with the Father, even Jesus Christ the Righteous, who washeth the sinner by his own blood and reconcileth the soul to its Heavenly Father.

12:11. Here is an account of the faithfulness and dear love of the children of God to him through Jesus Christ. Oh! That all may come to witness this inwardly carried on by degrees, that they may come to rejoice in their heavenly places in and with Christ Jesus our Lord, by overcoming the enemy within.

12:12. The inhabiters of the earth and sea are such as have their minds centered here or have their chief treasure here on earth, so the dragon is very busy with those and very wroth with these whose treasure is in heaven. And he is doing all the hurt he can, for he knoweth he hath but a short time before he must be chained up.

12:13–14. This is spiritually to be understood. The true church was not visibly among men but had allowance to retire and eat her morsel alone, yet she was mixed among the other people as to the outward, where she did mourn to see the idolatries of those times. For the Lord had his people in Babylon.[183]

12:15. This was doubtless by priestcraft and deceit, pretending a religious concern and a design for the good of souls. And those that saw their hypocrisy and could not join in many things but followed the advice of Jesus, who said, by their fruits ye shall know them, such they branded with the name of heretics, etc., also using many flatteries to draw them forth after worldly honors,

182. Luke 10:17–20.

183. See Revelation 18:4.

profits, and pleasures, etc., that he might cause the true in heart to be carried away from God by such wiles.[184]

12:16. By the earth doubtless is intended the earthly-minded, for the waters which the serpent cast out of his mouth as a flood are pleasant doctrines to those that would willingly enjoy heaven and eternal happiness so they may but enjoy the treasures and pleasures of this world, also which we know that Antichrist alloweth of. So this sort of school divinity and cunning doctrine, delivered by the ministers of Satan under his transformations, was all swallowed up by worldly-minded people, but the woman, i.e., the true Church, was not carried away with it but escaped to her place of retirement, which is spiritually to be understood.

12:17. By this is manifest that the dragon discovered some of the Lord's faithful ones, notwithstanding their quiet disposition of mind, and he grew very angry with them.

CHAPTER 13

13:1. This was the Roman pagan beast, for he arose out of the sea, which in many places of the scriptures signifieth multitudes of people, and the seven heads signify the dominions of this world, and the ten horns signify kings or powers derived from the beast, or set up by him. And the name of blasphemy doth show the powers of this world, both heathen and anti-Christian, are wont to blaspheme God and his tabernacle and them that dwell in heaven.

13:2. This is a fearful, strange figure for a man or men to be represented by, but it is according to the nature that is predominant in them and according to the form that such stand or appear in, in the eye of the Spirit, who seeth all things as they are in their nature or inward idea or form, and so they were showed to John in the vision. There are rulers in the world that have received their powers from God, and such are not a terror to good, but to evil works. And those that do good shall have praise of the same, for the apostle said, for he is a minister of God to thee for good, but if thou do that which is evil, be afraid; for he beareth not the sword in vain. For he is a minister of God, a

184. Matthew 7:20.

revenger to execute wrath upon him that doeth evil.[185] But the power derived from the dragon is quite contrary to nature.

13:3. This wound was given him by the glorious light of the gospel after the resurrection and ascension of Jesus Christ, it being spread among the Gentiles even until Constantine the Emperor received the Christian faith. And so an end was put to that persecuting power thereby for some time, but the healing of his wound was by the apostatizing of the Christians and the arising of Antichrist, for then the false church had dominion and was upheld by worldly power. And a persecuting spirit soon got the upper hand, and that pleased the dragon and healed his instruments, and all the world wondered after the beast, for the dragon (who had given power to the beast)—he deceiveth the whole world.

13:4. For now all the worldly minded, whose spiritual eye was blinded by the god of the world—they concluded it was a Christian power that ruled. And so they said, who is like unto the beast? Who is able to make war with him? As if they should say, who is like unto the emperor, king, or pope? And who are so wise as the ministers, both of church and state? Thus the dragon and the beast could keep in subjection the whole world under false worship, they not knowing the only true God by all their wisdom, who only is to be worshipped in spirit and in truth.[186]

13:5. These great things and blasphemies were spoken against God and against all those that would not be subject to the ordinances of men. For their fear towards God was not taught by the precepts of men; therefore, they would obey God rather than men. And power was given to him to continue forty-two months: here we may observe his time was limited and expressed by forty-two months, but I think it too great an undertaking for mankind to calculate these times and seasons and to pretend to know them, which God the Father hath put in his own power.[187] But the promise of Christ is sufficient for his followers: but ye shall receive power after that the Holy Ghost is come upon you, and ye shall be witnesses unto me, etc.[188] But this we may

185. Romans 13:4.

186. See John 4:24.

187. Acts 1:7.

188. Acts 1:8.

observe, that these forty-two agree with the time spoken of concerning the holy city being trodden under foot of the gentiles, and the two witnesses prophesying in sackcloth, etc.[189] And it is good to observe the harmony and agreement of the testimonies all along through these revelations, although delivered under diverse similitudes as they were revealed: to make known to the children of men the actions and transactions that have been, are, and shall be carried on in the world even to the end, which I take to be revealed in great love and mercy to the children of men, that all may hear and learn to love and fear the Lord and follow the leadings of his good spirit, though it be through many troubles. For the recompense of reward will out-balance it all, and indeed, to be spiritually-minded is life and peace.[190]

13:6. His tabernacle here below is with men, yea, in men. A tabernacle signifieth a dwelling place, as may be seen in many places in scripture, and them that dwell in heaven or earth is where the Lord rules in the heart.[191] And that soul that hath its constant conversation with the good spirit within and liveth in the love and fear of God may be said to dwell in heaven. Such are reproached by the beast and his adherents.

13:7. This was a time when paganism was in great pomp and did persecute the saints and did overcome their bodies and kill them. For they loved not their lives unto the death, and so the holy city was trodden under foot, and power was given him over all kindreds, tongues, and nations. This was a woeful time of slavery and torment, like that spoke of under the sound of the fifth trumpet, where it is said, men shall seek death, etc.[192]

13:8. Those that have their names written in the book of life of the Lamb slain from the foundation of the world are such who have given up their will to the will of God and their hearts and their names to serve him. And the Lamb of God hath taken away their sins and given them an evidence of it in themselves, the Holy Spirit bearing witness within that they are born of God and reconciled to him by the blood of the Lamb. And their peace is made with the Lord; and the life they now live is by truth in the Son of God. And they

189. See Revelation 11.

190. Romans 8:6.

191. See, for example, Revelation 21:3.

192. See Revelation 9:6.

die daily, and Jesus Christ lives and reigns in them. And the Lamb being said to be slain from the foundation of the world is spiritually to be understood, as he is the suffering seed of God, who suffers under the man of sin. But the usurper will be cast out: first out of particulars, and after in a more general manner, for, the Lamb and his followers shall have the victory in the latter end.

13:9. Here is manifested the universal love of God, again, to the children of men, in this, his universal [call] for attention, that people might understand the determinations of the Almighty and be made partakers of the divine nature of the Lamb of God, who takes away the sins of those that come to him and learn of him.[193]

13:10. For the saints do not only profess to be Christians but are made partakers of the divine nature and are daily learning of their Lord and Master, who said, take my yoke upon you and learn of me, for I am meek and lowly in heart, and ye shall find rest unto your souls. And he also said, for my yoke is easy and my burden is light.[194] Yea, it is so to the divine loves who love their Lord above their own life. To such the Lord makes hard things easy, by the increase of his love and by the word of his patience—for which we have cause to bless his holy name.

13:11. Doubtless this is the same Antichrist that came out of the smoke of the bottomless pit, but we may observe the cunning workings of Satan to heal his wounded head. For although he speaks as a dragon and received his authority from the dragon, yet he appears like a lamb as much as he can to deceive the simple. He would be thought to act for Christ and be his vicar on earth; but the divine eye saw him in his native form as he was of his father the devil and let his beloved servant John see his arising to be out of the earth. This seems to be the first setting up of popes, but it will be profitable for all to observe the saying of our Lord: no man hath ascended up but he that came down from heaven, even the Son of Man which is in heaven.[195] We may take notice: he was in heaven while on earth, even when he called himself the Son of Man, as being partaker of human nature. Meditate on these things, and if thy

193. See 2 Peter 1:4.

194. Matthew 11:29–30.

195. John 3:13.

old man die daily, and Christ come to live in thee, thou wilt have some knowledge of a heavenly frame of mind and what it is to have thy conversation in heaven while on earth.

13:12. The first beast was the pagan powers, but now it is thought to be a Christian government, both in state and church. And this beast that arose out of the earth, that put on sheep's clothing, is the false prophet, and is inwardly a ravening wolf, as we shall hear more of him hereafter.[196] For the arising and fall of Antichrist showed to the Apostle under or by diverse similitudes, as first of locusts; then of a beast something resembling a lamb; also in similitude of a great woman and a great city; a false prophet, etc. In or by all which is set forth the wily workings of the serpent and his enmity against the true church, or faithful spouse of Christ and her seed, and also the great power of God by which they are limited and at last shall be cast into the bottomless pit.

13:13–14. These wonders that the false prophet did were done by the power of the evil spirit, as his brethren did in Egypt, before pharaoh of old.[197] Likewise Simon the sorcerer bewitched the people of Samaria, giving out that himself was some great one insomuch that they said, this man is the great power of God.[198] And like Balaam, he loved the wages of unrighteousness but was limited by the power of God, yet he (viz. Balaam) taught Balak to cast a stumbling block before the children of Israel: to eat things sacrificed to idols, and to commit fornication.[199] This doctrine of Baalam was held by some in the Church of Pergamus in early days.[200] So they that had their dwelling on earth were ordered that they should make an image to the beast that had a wound by a sword and did live. This was a church order, and it was a setting up images and idolatry to please the rulers of this world. For the worship that was performed in Babylon and all her suburbs was a strange mixture of heathenish idolatry and Jewish ceremonies, under a pretense of Christian liberties, and finding out in the wisdom of man fine ways to please God: as witness

196. See Matthew 7:15.

197. See Exodus 7:10–12.

198. See Acts 8:9–10.

199. See Numbers 22.

200. See Revelation 2:12–17.

the sumptuous buildings of their churches; their inscriptions over the doors (viz., how dreadful is this place; this is none other but the house of God; and this is the gate of heaven—these words were set over the doors of their churches, so called, in great capital letters); and within, all adorned with images, pictures, organs, altars with vessels of gold and silver to perform their sacraments in, with priests, surplices, and abundance of such embellishments to dazzle the eyes of the beholders, to cause them to fall down and worship the beast, and his image.[201]

13:15. This was the idolatrous worship joined in with the pomps and vanities of this world, and the whole nest of locusts were the limb and members of the said image. And some of them were the mouth, and others had other offices, and they could both speak and inform the beast that such an one would not worship the image that was set up by his approbation and authority. And then such a one, if he will not conform in such a time, must be killed. Now the animal life that the members of the said image had, they received that from the universal Spirit and Providence of God, as all other animals do. But the power they had to persecute and kill, that they received from the great beast to whom the dragon gave his seat and great authority, that had a wound by the sword of the Spirit, i.e., the word of God—but now this deadly wound was healed, and the dragon's persecuting power got up into great dominion.[202] So that:

13:16–17. This doth show that judgment without mercy was to be executed on them that had not one of those three characters on them. Some of his marks might be the different dresses, of which there were abundance which did belong to the clergy, to distinguish them in their degrees of school divinity (so called) and to discriminate them from the laity. This was a public mark

201. Before the 1689 Acts of Toleration, most Quakers could not legally build a public meeting house in which to worship, and often met in barns or in the open air. When they did begin to erect places of worship, which were devoid of ornamentation, Quakers strove for an aesthetic of plainness. For a study of some of the meeting houses in which Elizabeth Webb worshipped during her time in North America, see Catherine C. Lavoie, "Quaker Beliefs and Practices and the Eighteenth-Century Development of the Friends Meeting House in the Delaware Valley," in *Quaker Aesthetics: Reflections on a Quaker Ethic in American Design and Consumption*, ed. Emma Jones Lapsansky and Anne A. Verplanck (Philadelphia: University of Pennsylvania Press, 2003), 156–87.

202. See Ephesians 6:17; Hebrews 4:12.

and therefore might be termed as in the forehead. The mark in the right hand was more private and might be seen by the many flattering titles that they did give to each other, together with their bowings in doing reverence (as they called it) to their betters.[203] These things the true servants of God and followers of the Lamb could not do; it was and is contrary to their Master's precepts. Also, we may read of a young man that feared God and was moved by the Spirit to stand up and answer Job and his friends. He said, let me not, I pray you, accept any man's person, neither let me give flattering titles unto man. For I know not to give flattering titles; in so doing, my maker would soon take me away.[204] But to receive the number of his name: this must be counted a great title and may denote an observer of all his institutions and orders in matters and forms of worship, even in the whole number of them, which never brought any poor soul to rest.

13:18. Here is wisdom indeed. For it must be counted by the wisdom or Spirit of God, and none but such as Jesus Christ enlighteneth (who alone is the true light) can count the number of the beast. Notwithstanding, it is the number of a man, for it is concerning worship, and that soul that is gathered into the true spirit, or spirit of truth, and in it performs worship and duty to Almighty God—such an one, being taught of the Lord, is able to distinguish and number the worship of the beast in all its ceremonies from the true worship of God. And it is called the number of a man because their doctrines and precepts and their fear toward God is taught by the commandments of man. And it being an image or dead form of worship set up by carnal, bestial man, it is called the beast and his image. And the many ceremonies therein used being set up in the name of the beast and by his authority, it is called the number of his name, and it is the number of a man (and so not of God).

And this is a mystical way of numbering, even according to the nature of the thing treated on. The number is a certain number, but the ordinances of men are very uncertain, for they are sometimes abundance of them and sometimes fewer, even according as the will of man is, for to set them up or

203. In addition to addressing civic and ecclesiastical officials using the informal pronouns *thee* and *thou*, eschewing honorific titles, Quakers also refused to observe common social customs, such as bowing to or removing one's hat in the presence of a magistrate. This refusal to recognize the authority or social station of officials provoked punishment; magistrates at Massachusetts Bay sentenced William Leddra to death in 1660 for refusing to remove his hat in court.

204. Job 32:21–22.

pull them down. But they are numbered by sixes because they never bring a soul to the true sabbath of rest which is only in God, and he that is entered into his rest hath ceased from his own works and from his own will. And God is in him, his all in all, working in and by his creature to will and do according to his own good will and heavenly pleasure. And so the soul, being in the hand of God and resting in his will, there is no torment can touch it. The dragon and his instruments may afflict the body and put it to death, and in the sight of the unwise they seem to die, and their departure is taken for misery, but they are in peace. And we may observe that the number seven signifieth a complete number, or the whole of what it treats on, in several places in this book, as the seven spirits of God, the seven stars, the seven candlesticks, seven seals, seven trumpets, seven vials, etc.

These signify the complete or perfect number of what is treated on under those heads. So those sixes: they signify a coming short of perfection, notwithstanding all their toil. The innocent life of the lily of the valley is wanting, for they have no rest day nor night who worship the beast and his image and receive the mark of his name.[205] Thus it appears plain to be an enlightened mind, that the number of the beast and his image was seen fittest by the Spirit to be numbered by sixes: If they are hundreds they are numbered by six, if they are tens they are numbered by sixes, and if they are units they are six, for they never come to the number seven, which signifies perfection and rest.

We may observe that the arising and fall of Antichrist was showed to the Apostle John under diverse similitudes as in the forepart of this book have been demonstrated. And now we are come to hear the preaching of the everlasting gospel, which will sound forth the downfall of Babylon to her utter destruction and the restoration of Zion, the city of the saints' solemnity.

CHAPTER 14

14:1. This is the spiritual Mount Zion, where the city of the great king is.[206] And saith the Psalmist, they that trust in the Lord shall be as Mount Zion,

205. See Revelation 14:11.

206. Psalm 48:2. Mount Zion is the highest point in ancient Jerusalem, a broad hill south of the Old City's Armenian Quarter. In the Bible, Mount Zion serves as a metaphoric symbol for heaven or the promised land.

which cannot be removed, but abideth forever.[207] Thus he speaks of them that come to God by faith and so stand by the supporting power of the divine arm, only and alone. We may observe that in this book of the Revelations the Spirit makes use of similitudes of the figures under the first Testament, to express spiritual things by which they figured.[208] These 144,000 sealed ones were spoken of, and they were of the twelve tribes of the children of Israel.[209] And John saw a great multitude, which no man could number, of all nations, etc.[210] They were sealed after the Lamb had opened the sixth seal. And now the Lord is gathering the numberless number out of all nations, kindreds, tongues, and peoples, etc., by the sound of the everlasting gospel. And some of them are already gathered, and their voices are heard in their heavenly places, and more will be gathered and added to them. But John being in the Spirit, which seeth from the beginning to the end of time, he saw and heard many things, as if they were present before him. As in the second verse:

14:2–3. This is to set forth the thanksgivings of this heavenly host, praising God with innumerable voices for the great deliverances that he had wrought for them. So it is called a new song, as being the song of the redeemed by the blood of the Lamb under the new covenant. But those that were redeemed out of the twelve tribes of Israel, that were the first fruits unto God and to the Lamb, they had a right understanding of this new song.

14:4–5. These here spoken of are they that were gathered to God under the first covenant and are called the first fruits unto God and to the Lamb.

14:6. Observe in the time of the false church's glory: there was false and fruitless doctrine preached by the beast that arose out of the earth with two

207. Psalm 125:1.

208. The First Testament refers to the Old Testament. Webb is engaging in typology, reading the narrative of the Old Testament as expressive of spiritual truths revealed more fully in the New Testament or in contemporary and future events prefigured by the Old Testament. For an overview of this interpretive tradition in the colonial period, see Mason I. Lowance, *The Language of Canaan: Metaphor and Symbol in New England from the Puritans to the Transcendentalists* (Cambridge: Harvard University Press, 1980); *Typology in Early American Literature*, ed. Sacvan Bercovitch (Amherst: University of Massachusetts Press, 1972).

209. Revelation 7:4.

210. Revelation 7:9.

horns like a Lamb, which was the head of the false prophets. But now we are come to see and hear a glorious dispensation of the true God and Jesus Christ, whom he hath sent. For this angel that is flying in the midst of heaven is the angel of Jesus Christ, and he is a ministering spirit, by which the true ministers are moved to preach the gospel of God openly, as our Lord commanded his disciples: what I tell you in darkness that speak ye in light—that is, dark sayings or parables lost [on] record which the future dispensations of the Spirit were to explain—and what ye hear in the ear, that preach upon the housetops, and fear not them which kill the body but are not able to kill the soul, but rather fear him which is able to destroy both soul and body in hell.[211] Now this everlasting gospel is to be preached to them that dwell on the earth and to every kindred and tongue and people. This work is begun, and the Lord will carry it on to the perfection of it. For the angel that flies in the midst of heaven is a heavenly spirit, a messenger of Jesus Christ. And he can inspire men, in all nations and of all languages, and spirit them or raise them up when the time of their visitation is come and cause them to sound forth the everlasting gospel among their own people. As well as he raised up able ministers of the gospel in the morning of this dispensation and sent them forth as sheep among wolves, in and amongst the natives of Old England; and sent them also to New England, and to other lands.[212] Now here is the foundation of the everlasting gospel which the angel proclaimed,

14:7. This is the true and living God, who will be worshiped in the spirit and in the truth (and blessed be his holy name), who hath made us witnesses that God the Father of our spirits is seeking such to worship him. God is a spirit (saith our Lord), and they that worship him must worship him in spirit and in Truth.[213]

14:8. Here we may observe what followeth the preaching of the everlasting gospel, even the fall of Babylon, whose situation is among all nations. And the reason of her fall is rendered to be, because she made all nations drink of the wine of the wrath of her fornication. This is to be understood spiritually for the nations, by drinking in of her false doctrine, they departed from the

211. Matthew 10:27–28.

212. Anne Austin and Mary Fisher arrived in New England in 1656. Quaker missionaries who traveled during the 1650s were honored as the First Publishers of Truth.

213. See John 4:21–24.

love and fear of God and from the covenant they made with him in their baptismal vows, and also in [times] of distress. And so by the enticing allurements of the God of this world were drawn after many worldly lovers, which was and is called spiritual fornication, which draws down the wrath of God upon the worldly and carnal minded, that keeps not in covenant with God.

14:9–10. Thus the merciful God and Father of the spirits of all flesh, who willeth not the death of him that dies, sends forth his angels with loud voices, to proclaim his determinations on Babylon, that all that will come out of her may have timely notice to leave off worshiping the beast and his image and return to the Lord by a timely repentance. And such as answer the heavenly call find mercy and escape eternal punishment: which, that all may do, is the intent of the labor of love that is bestowed among the children of men from time to time. But how shall that be understood, that he shall be tormented in the presence of the holy angels and in the presence of the Lamb? Shall he, or they, be in heaven? This is a mystery, indeed, that is hid from the wise and prudent of this world, and revealed to babes, for so it hath pleased our Heavenly Father, that so proud man might not glory in his presence but that the praise of his own works may be rendered unto him, who is alone worthy to receive honor and glory forever and forever more.[214]

Now, that the Lamb of God and the holy angels are in heaven, is very true. And that the wicked shall be tormented in their presence: this is not to be understood by thinking, lo here or lo there is heaven, or hell; for wheresoever the Lamb of God is, he is in the bosom of his father, and wherever the holy angels are, they are in heaven. For to be short and as intelligible as I can, I say that the love and favor of God, his glorious light and the meek spirit of his Son, is the life of the good angels, and the souls of the regenerate have a portion of the same, and it dwells in them. And they live in the love and meekness of God, which is a heavenly, paradisiacal life. And on the contrary the devils and the souls of mankind that have sinned out their day, they having despised meekness, humility, mercifulness, and divine love, they are shut up in darkness and horror in themselves, filled with anger and rage in themselves, and acting in confusion one among another, for they are shut up in that principle. And the wrath of God is compared to a stream of brimstone that kindles their rage, for they are at enmity with Christ, and so they are in hell fire, wherever they are, and cannot get out of it, for it is in them. And as

214. See 1 Corinthians 1:29.

the good angels stand in readiness to be sent on God's errands of love, mercy, etc., so the devils are very ready, if they may be allowed to do hurt to mankind, as witness the case of Job, that perfect and upright man, and also the case of Ahab, one of the Kings of Israel, a man that had sinned out his days.[215] The whole of 1 Kings 22 is very well worth the perusal of the most enlightened mind, for there is an account of the transactions of spirits in the court of heaven, and there we may also observe how the prophets that were time-servers, and man-pleasers were blinded, though they thought themselves prophets of the Lord, the God of Israel, of which there were about four hundred men. But we read there but of one true prophet, and the idolatrous king hated him, and the false prophets vaunted over him, etc. But he had the greatest privilege by having his eye single to the Lord alone, for he saw the lying spirit present himself in the divine presence and heard him make an offer to be a lying spirit in the mouth of all the king's prophets, etc.

Thus the devil and his angels and the souls of unregenerate people may be in the presence of God and in the presence of the holy angels and yet be in torments in themselves, and it may aggravate their torments to see the joy of the saints.

14:11. I take the smoke of their torment to be their hideous yelling and miserable outcries, together with their blasphemous oaths, cursings, etc., as being at enmity with God, and all his redeemed ones. As sometimes here is seen a small resemblance of heaven and hell upon earth, of which I could say something more by my own experience and observations but am desirous to be brief and let others observe the different conversations of the children of men and also look into themselves, to see the different operations of the two spirits within. And I advise thee, love the light of Christ Jesus above all worldly things, and he will teach thee and lead thee gently on and will enlighten thy understanding gradually and grant thee a portion of the word of his patience. Yea, he is our Emmanuel, a present helper in the times of trouble.

14:12–13. This last verse signifies what will be the effects of the patient suffering of the saints and of them that keep the commandments of God and the faith of Jesus.

215. See 1 Kings 22:21–22.

14:14. This is the time that our Lord foretold of: and it is set forth after the similitude of a harvest, and after that a vintage.[216] But our Lord said concerning that prophecy, verily I say unto you, this generation shall not pass away till all be fulfilled, etc.[217] Which testimony of our Lord hath caused great thoughtfulness to be on my mind formerly, not understanding, or not considering, that all things and people have their time to ripen, or come to perfection, before they are gathered in and separated according to the parable of the tares.[218] So, in this consideration, we may read of many harvests in this world, for we do believe that when God made this world by Jesus Christ that he sowed good seed in it. For he beheld all his works to be very good, but the enemy came and sowed tares, and we may take notice what a plentiful crop the tares brought forth, so that the earth was soon filled with violence, and the thoughts and imaginations of men's hearts were only evil continually.[219] Then the good seed was gathered into the ark; then came the deluge. After that, the Lord God Almighty did choose himself another man in the world, even Abraham, whom he called from his father's house and from his kindred, to follow him according to his leadings in that dispensation. And Abraham was obedient to the heavenly call, and after it had pleased God to prove him in the beginning and found him faithful in the day of small things, he made a covenant with him, which covenant the Lord renewed diverse times. And at length it pleased the Lord to prove him with the nearest trial that can be, even by calling to him to offer up his only son whom he loved!

Abraham knew the voice of God and was obedient thereunto, believing in his word and in his power who is able to raise the dead. Then the Lord established his covenant with Abraham and with his seed after him, and so this good householder sowed good seed in his field again, and the busy enemy, he came and sowed tares amongst Abraham's seed, and the tares grew up and almost choked the good seed. Then it pleased God (after he had borne long with them, and they had crucified his only son) to make a separation of the good seed from the tares amongst them, and those that would

216. See Matthew 13:24; Luke 21:27.

217. Luke 21:32.

218. See Matthew 13:24–30.

219. Genesis 6:5.

receive the Lord Jesus were gathered to him, as into an ark of safety.[220] Then came the destruction of old Jerusalem and the end, or abolishing, of the old covenant and the dispersing of the remnant of the Jews, which was a dismal time to them.

Even as our Lord Jesus set it forth in the chapters before mentioned, which came to pass in that generation and was a great harvest, or separation, between the good seed and the evil seed. Now we are come to and under the new covenant which the Lord promised to make with his people, which was taken notice of by the author to the Hebrews.[221] If any should say, that belongs to the Jews only, I say I believe it belongs to both Jews and Gentiles, for Jesus Christ is the mediator of it. And let all observe the exhortation of the apostle: See that ye refuse not him that speaketh; for if they escaped not who refused him that speak on earth, much more shall we not escape, if we turn away from him that speaketh from heaven, whose voice then shook the earth. But now he hath promised, saying, yet once more, I shake not the earth only but also heaven, etc.[222] And now, again, the good husbandman hath sowed the good seed of his kingdom plentifully in the field of this world, which seed is the grace of God that bringeth salvation, that hath appeared and doth appear to all men and will appear to the succeeding generations. And in the night while men slept, and still in the night men sleep or are off the watch, the busy enemy hath sowed and is sowing tares, and another separating time is near which is compared to a harvest, and afterward to a vintage, as we shall hear. And the Son of Man, whom John saw sitting on the cloud, is sending forth his angels, according to his promise: and they are gathering out of his kingdom all things that offend and them which do iniquity and shall cast them into a furnace of fire. There shall be wailing and gnashing of teeth: then (said our Lord) shall the righteous shine forth as the sun in the kingdom of their Father. Who hath ears to hear, let him hear.[223]

220. Webb is comparing God's decision to save Noah and his family from the mass of wicked humanity to the extraction of Jewish Christians from a corrupted Jewish religion—in turn a fulfillment of Jesus's parable of the wheat being sorted from the tares.

221. See Jeremiah 31:34; Hebrews 8, 12.

222. Hebrews 12:25–26.

223. Matthew 13:41–43.

14:15. This was a prevailing cry that came from the angel that came out of the temple, or out of the true church. For although the Lord knows when is the best time to work deliverance for his people and stands in readiness to do it, yet he will be sought unto, and now the loud intercession of the angel prevails with the Lord.

14:16–17. This is an angel of our Lord Jesus Christ and came out of the temple which is in heaven, where the throne of God and the Lamb is; and his sharp sickle is to gather the clusters of the vine of the earth. This is the time that the Lord foretold of after he had been speaking of great tribulations, and then (said he) shall appear the sign of the Son of man in heaven; and then shall all the tribes of the earth mourn, and they shall see the Son of man coming in the clouds of heaven, with powers and great glory.[224]

And he shall send his angels with a great sound of a trumpet, and they shall gather together his elect from the four winds, from one end of heaven to the other. These things are spiritually to be understood and not to look out to the clouds that arise out of the earth and sea in order to see the Lord. For he comes in the clouds of heaven, even in clouds of witnesses that are raised by the heavenly wind or breath of the Almighty, that are sent forth as clouds full of rain. In these clouds the Lord appears, with power and great glory and will yet appear more and more and make the place of his feet glorious. And his trumpets shall be sounded more and more, by the angel of his divine presence, and many shall be gathered out of Babylon, and shall come to the New Jerusalem. These things I write in full assurance of faith and in as much brevity as I can.

14:18. This angel, that had power over fire, did minister at or about the holy altar and was seen by the apostle with a golden censer. And to him was given much incense, and he offered it, with the prayers of all saints, upon the golden altar which was before the throne. And the angel, after that, took the censer and filled it with fire off the altar and cast it into the earth.[225] And now he calls for judgment to be executed upon the vine of the earth, and sayeth her grapes are fully ripe.

224. Matthew 24:30–31.

225. See Revelation 8:3–5.

14:19–20. Thus the great effusion of blood is set forth by the similitude of red wine that cometh out of a wine-press and seems to denote wars and the treading of horses in a war-like posture. The prophet Isaiah, he saw almost such a like vision when he cried, who is this that cometh from Edom, with dyed garments, from Bozrah? This that is glorious in his apparel, travailing in the greatness of his strength? I that speak in righteousness, mighty to save. Wherefore art thou red in thine apparel and thy garments like him that treadeth in the wine-fat? I have trodden the wine press alone, and of the people, there was none with me, etc.[226] Thus, by many testimonies left upon record in the scriptures of truth, we may observe and believe that the rod of the wicked shall not always rest on the back of the Lord's servants, but the day of their deliverance will come. Now we may observe that as in this chapter, the judgments of God upon the hardened sinners that were ripe in sin hath been represented by a harvest and a vintage, so, in Revelation 16, it will be represented by the pouring out of the seven vials of the wrath of God; and in Revelation 18 by the burning of a great city; and in Revelation 19 by open war to her utter destruction. And the Lamb and his followers will have the victory. To understand these things is encouragement to all that believe in our Lord Jesus and do love him and follow him, bearing the daily cross.

CHAPTER 15

15:1. These seven angels appear to be those that poureth out the wrath of God—after the trumpets have sounded and after the elect are gathered in every dispensation, as our Lord testified.[227] The apostle John calleth this vision a sign, great and marvelous. A sign is a representation of something that may reach to or lay hold on a human capacity or understanding, and indeed, all the visions that John saw were marvelous representations of the things of God and concerning the destruction of his enemies, which are sounded by the seven angels that have the seven trumpets. For the angels are ministering spirits, and the trumpets that they speak through are human organs and capacities, which capacities are very different. And so were the trumpets under the dispensation of the law, for there were silver trumpets in the camp, and there were trumpets

226. See Isaiah 63:1–3.

227. See Matthew 24:31.

of rams' horns, and all had their times of service, according to the appointment of the Lord. So they were made use of, and to good purpose, for the walls of Jericho fell down at or before the sounding of the trumpets of rams' horns.[228] And indeed, great and marvelous are all the works of God, and many signs and wonders he doth in heaven above and in the earth beneath. And John, being taken up into the Spirit, he saw these angels in heaven, which is the place or rather station of their habitation. For they are always in the divine presence, beholding the glory of God and hearing the voice of his word, and are in readiness to go at his command. And wheresoever they are, they are in heaven. Yea, the divine power fills them, for the name of God Almighty is in them.

15:2. This may be called a sign great and marvelous also, for who can stand on a sea of glass? Surely those only that are born up by the Holy Spirit and who can stand among fire; surely none but such as are purified by the baptism of the Holy Ghost and the fire of God's judgments. Many people think, and some say, if they can but get within the gate of heaven, all is well enough—not considering that God Almighty is a consuming fire to all the works of iniquity and that the inhabitants of the holy city are redeemed through judgment. And in meditating on the sea of glass mingled with fire, to be the place or state of the standing of the redeemed ones, hath brought into my mind many times the solid answer of our Lord to two of his disciples, when they, or their mother in their behalf, requested of their Lord that one of them might sit on his right hand and the other on his left in his kingdom. But Jesus answered and said, ye know not what ye ask; are ye able to drink of the cup that I shall drink of and be baptized with the baptism that I am baptized with? They say unto him, we are able. He saith unto them, ye shall indeed drink of my cup and be baptized with the baptism that I am baptized with, but to sit on my right hand and on my left is not mine to give, but it shall be given to them for whom it is prepared of my Father.[229] By which I do observe that those that desire a place in the kingdom of heaven must expect to go through the baptism of Jesus Christ and to drink of the cup of sufferings, for that was the cup of the meek Lamb slain from the foundation of the world. Being the suffering seed, that suffered in the world and in the servants of God—in their afflictions he was afflicted, and the angel

228. See Joshua 6:20.

229. Matthew 20:20–23.

of his presence preserved them. And I also observe that Jesus taught his disciples to resign to the will of God when they had gone through all their sufferings, and who is it that thinks to go to heaven any easier way than by following our Lord? These things deserve the most serious thoughts and the best considerations, for to be deprived of heaven and happiness at last will be the greatest of disappointments, the consideration of which hath caused me to be the more particular in these observations.

15:3–4. Thus they that had gotten the victory over the beast and his image, etc., are heard to sing the song of Moses and the song of the Lamb, attributing all the praise to God Almighty and all the holiness to him, saying, for thou only art holy. Here is nothing taken to self, but they stand clear and upright-hearted to God in their worship, adoration, and praise, singing of the judgments and mercies of God in abundance of joy, for their deliverance, as Moses and the children of Israel sung a song of praise upon the banks of the Red Sea after they had seen the mighty hand and outstretched arm of God's power in many signs and works of wonder wrought for their deliverance.[230] So the Lamb of God, he had washed those that were and are saved, by and under the new covenant, by his own blood, and had wrought great deliverance in them and for them. And he have gotten victory over him that had the power of death, and it is by him and through him that these came to get the victory over all their enemies. And therefore they have great cause to sing a new song of praise to God and the Lamb.

15:5. John saw the temple of the tabernacle opened in heaven. This is the temple of God, the tabernacle or dwelling place of the Most High, which the tabernacle that Moses erected in the wilderness was a figure of. But now Christ being come, an high priest of good things to come, by a greater and more perfect tabernacle not made with hands, etc.[231] And Jesus Christ [is] the minister of the sanctuary and of the true tabernacle, which God hath pitched and not man. So these things here spoken of are the heavenly things themselves; and the days are come which the Lord promised by the Prophet Jeremiah.

But this shall be the covenant, said he, that I will make with the House of Israel. After those days, saith the Lord, I will put my law in their inward

230. See Exodus 15.

231. Hebrews 9:11.

parts and write it in their hearts and will be their God, and they shall be my people. And they shall teach no more every man his neighbor and every man his brother, saying know the Lord, for they shall all know me, from the least of them unto the greatest of them, saith the Lord. For I will forgive their iniquity, and I will remember their sin no more.[232] Now as many as receive Jesus Christ, the mediator of this new covenant, hath a right to this heavenly, gracious promise and do know him to be that teacher that cannot be removed into a corner. For now the days draw near that were prophesied of by Isaiah: and it shall come to pass in the last days, that the mountain of the Lord's house shall be established in the top of the mountains and shall be exalted above the hills, and all nations shall flow unto it. And many people shall go and say, come ye let us go up to the mountain of the Lord, to the house of the God of Jacob. And he will teach us of his ways, and we will walk in his paths, for out of Zion shall go forth the law, and the word of the Lord from Jerusalem. And he shall judge among the nations and shall rebuke many people, and they shall beat their swords into plowshares and their spears into pruning hooks. Nation shall not lift up sword against nation; neither shall they learn war any more.[233]

My soul rejoiceth and praiseth God in a sight and divine sense of this peaceable and glorious day that is to come, to some already, and will be offered to all. But there are many that, like potsherds of the earth, will be dashed to pieces, one against another. For the Lord will judge among the nations, and as many as will let his judgments pass upon the man of sin in themselves, and with the whole heart turn to the Lord, they shall know his sweet peaceable government and divine teachings. And under their own heavenly vine they shall sit, and the droppings down of the new wine of the kingdom into their hearts will be sweet.[234] This hint I gave by way of invitation to all, to come, taste, and see how good the Lord is. The Lord hath afforded many calls and loving invitations to the children of men, to come home to him, from whom we have gone astray.

15:6. These seven angels may represent the seven spirits of God sent forth into all the earth, which was revealed to the apostle. And I beheld (said he), and

232. Jeremiah 31:33–34.

233. Isaiah 2:2–4.

234. Micah 4:4.

lo, in the midst of the throne and of the four beasts, and in the midst of the elders, stood a Lamb as it had been slain, having seven horns and seven eyes, which are the seven spirits of God sent forth into all the earth.[235] The seven horns signify all power is given to the Lamb, and the seven eyes signify the fullness of the Spirit and divine life and light. So in the Holy Lamb dwells the fullness of the Godhead, in power and life, light and perfection. And the seven spirits of God sent forth into all the earth are here represented to John as seven angels. As the psalmist saith, who maketh his angels spirits, his ministers a flaming fire.[236] The number seven includes all, as the seven stars and the seven candlesticks intended, all the ministers and all the churches of the Christians before the apostasy.

And although the Spirit of God is one and undivided, yet manifold in its degrees of operation, and therefore represented as seven, a measure of which is given to every man to profit withal. And a measure is given to all true ministers, to enlighten and enliven them in their ministry, for the movings of which all ought to wait and to speak by the dictates of it, as it gives utterance. For as our Lord told his disciples, it is no more ye that speak, but the Spirit of my Father, that speaketh in you.[237] Then the will and wisdom of man must be silent, and all the organs and faculties of the creature must be given up to God. I do not speak, or write these things without some experience, having an evidence in my spirit of the truth of them.

15:7–8. This here spoken of is the true temple of the tabernacle of testimony, even the antitype of that testimony written on stone; even the testimony of the Son of God, in his people, by his Holy Spirit, not now written on tables of stone but in the fleshy tables of the heart, with the Spirit of the Living God.[238] And the temple being filled with smoke from the glory of God and from his power is a token of God's powerful presence with his church, as may be seen in in the figure when Moses had reared up the tabernacle in the wilderness and had finished the work. Then a cloud covered the tent of the congregation, and the glory of the Lord filled the tabernacle, and Moses was not able to enter into the tent of the congregation because the cloud abode

235. Revelation 5:6.

236. Psalm 104:4.

237. Matthew 10:20.

238. See 2 Corinthians 3:3.

thereon, and the glory of the Lord filled the tabernacle.[239] And likewise, when Solomon dedicated the temple which he built, it came to pass when the priests were come out of the holy place that the cloud filled the house of the Lord so that the priests could not stand to minister, because of the cloud. For the glory of the Lord had filled the house of the Lord.[240]

From hence we may observe that the apostle had the true temple of the tabernacle of testimony set before him by the figure that was under the first testament. And this is a token of God's divine presence with his people. While the seven angels are pouring out the vials of his wrath upon their enemies, and as the enemies fall by degrees, so the true church will be advanced after so long a time of her being trod under foot of the gentiles, or apostate Christians.

CHAPTER 16

16:1. This voice must needs be the voice of God, seeing no man was able to enter into the temple, and the voice came with authority, saying go your ways, etc.

16:2. This plague seems to resemble one of the plagues of Egypt: and they took ashes of the furnace, and they stood before Pharaoh, and Moses sprinkled it up toward heaven, and it became a boil, breaking forth with blains upon man and beast.[241] And afterwards, when Israel revolted, the prophet Isaiah cried, saying, from the sole of the foot even to the head, there is no soundness in it but wounds and bruises and putrefying, sores, etc. Your country is desolate, your cities are burnt with fire, and so the prophet goeth on, sounding forth the judgments of God that were coming on the revolters, and says, except the Lord of Hosts had left unto us a very small remnant, we should have been as Sodom, and we should been like unto Gomorrah.[242] Thus sin and iniquity draws down the judgments of God upon the inhabitants of the earth, to the laying waste kingdoms and countries, oftentimes in the world.

239. Exodus 40:34–35.

240. 1 Kings 8:10–11.

241. Exodus 9:10.

242. Isaiah 1:6–9.

16:3. The first vial of the wrath of God carried in it a torture of the body with noisome and grievous sores. But the people not repenting of their sins, nor forsaking their idolatrous worship, this second vial seems to carry in it great mortality or effusion of blood. The sea, or many waters, signifies multitudes of people.

16:4. By these rivers and fountains of waters is intended Antichrist's blood doctrine, which doctrine was that as many as would not worship the image of the beast, i.e., a dead form of worship set up by human invention, should be killed. But now a vial of God's wrath being poured upon these rivers and fountains of waters, and they became blood, and mystery Babylon herself is made to drink of it—now is come to pass what was written: he that killeth with the sword must be killed with the sword, after the faith and patience of the saints have been tried.[243] And John saw her drunken with the blood of the saints and martyrs of Jesus, but now blood is given to them to drink, as will appear in the next verses.

16:5–7. And well might this angel out of the altar acknowledge the righteous judgments of God Almighty upon that blood-thirsty generation, for he had been witness to the loud cries of the souls under the altar that were slain for the word of God and for the testimony which they held.[244]

16:8–9. This is a day of horror and amazement to the wicked, and the more so because of the strangeness of God's salvation to them that fear him, for these things are revealed by way of similitudes.

And the prophet Malachi foretold of such a day, saying, for behold the day cometh, that shall burn as an oven, and all the proud, yea, and all that do wickedly shall be as stubble. And the day cometh that shall burn them up, saith the Lord of Hosts, that it shall leave them neither root, nor branch, but unto you that fear my name shall the Son of Righteousness arise with healing in his wings, etc.[245] And men were scorched with great heat and blasphemed the name of God, etc. These were hardened sinners, such as would not give up the man of sin to be consumed by this glorious breaking forth of divine light, which discovers unto mankind their folly, madness, and misery and

243. Matthew 26:52.

244. See Revelation 6:9–10.

245. Malachi 4:1–2.

shows them the way of self-denial and the daily cross, even the Lord's way home to the Father. But proud mortals, disliking the way, they grow angry with God and with those that fear him, and so they treasure up wrath against the day of wrath. For that spirit that a soul entertains and loves to be conversant with, while here, is its treasure and will be its companion hereafter, forevermore. And therefore our dear Lord and loving master, Jesus Christ, advised all to lay up treasure in heaven: for where your treasure is, there will your heart be also (saith he).[246] And the apostle witnessed that their conversation was in heaven.[247]

This is an inward conversation with the Holy Ghost, the Comforter, who dwells in the bosoms of all that love God above this world. These are they that shall hunger no more, neither thirst any more, neither shall the sun light on them, nor any heat. For the Lamb that is in the midst of the throne shall feed them and shall lead them unto living fountains of waters, and God shall wipe away all tears, etc.[248] This is the same living spring or fountain that our Lord spoke of to the woman of Samaria and the same living bread or food that he told the Jews of.[249] And it is given daily to all true believers and followers of the Lamb, for the nourishment of their souls, even while here. But they shall be taken into a more full enjoyment of the divine fullness hereafter, which is the recompense of reward, that all whose treasure is in heaven are, with patience, and hope, and a steady faith, waiting for. Such go through great tribulation in this world, of one kind or other, and have their robes washed in the blood of the Lamb. But these give up God's enemies in themselves to the judgment, and their soul enters into the word of his patience, into the meek, Lamb-like spirit of their Lord, and are saved or preserved out of wrath, and so out of torment and out of murmurings that many fall into—some into a greater degree of it than others. But the least degree of murmuring offends God; therefore, beware of murmuring in times of trials, and remember the children of Israel when in the wilderness, what great plagues and sore judgments the murmurers brought on that congregation, many times. But honest Joshua and Caleb lived still, being men of true hearts to God.[250]

246. Matthew 6:21.

247. Philippians 3:20.

248. Revelation 7:16–17.

249. On the Samaritan woman, see John 4:13–14; on the living bread, see John 6.

250. See Numbers 14:6–9.

16:10. The seat of the beast is the place where the anti-Christian powers of this world sit as judges in religious matters, condemning all that will not conform to their way. And the kingdom of the beast is large; even wherever the prince of the power of darkness, the god of this world, rules, for the dragon gave him his power and his seat and great authority, as may be seen.[251] But now, the prince of light and life, who is the true and right heir, being upon returning to his kingdom, the usurper is brought to judgment, and a vial of the wrath of God is poured out upon his seat, and his kingdom is full of darkness. This is a spiritual darkness that brings with it such horror and terror that none can imagine but those that have felt something of it. When the beast and the man of sin have been brought to judgment in themselves; and this work of God can be read in the line of experience by all those that turn to God with the whole heart and do or shall give up the man of sin to the righteous judgments of God in themselves and let the enemies of his son Jesus Christ be slain by his sharp, two-edged sword (to wit) his divine word—these do and will find mercy and be supported by the word of faith and patience and comfort by the Holy Ghost. I write these things, and leave them as a testimony of experience, and do say the Lord is on his way, going on conquering and to conquer. And blessed will all be, who turn to be his faithful followers, and them that will not turn to God and acknowledge his judgments to be just and righteous altogether, they will get into utter enmity, and do as it is said in the next verse.

16:11. The work of God is twofold, i.e., spiritual and temporal. And here we may observe that neither mercies nor judgments will bring some people to repentance. I have seen people professing Christianity that, when things have gone smooth and well on their side, then oh! How vain, how airy they will be, which shows great folly. And if things go hard a little while, then there is murmurings and anger and sometimes breaks out into rage. So there are degrees of blasphemy. But Job said in answer to his wife, shall we receive good at the hand of God, and shall we not receive evil?[252] And so Job retained his integrity to the end, and all that love and fear God, they follow the Lamb in his leadings although it be through many tribulations, believing that the Lamb and his followers shall have the victory.

251. See Revelation 13:2.

252. Job 2:10.

16:12. This is an allegory and hath a mystical meaning belonging to it: the river Euphrates was a river that belonged to old Babylon, as may be seen [in Jeremiah] 51. The whole chapter is worthy of perusal in this case, for it treats of the fall of old Babylon, the place of Israel's captivity. And Jeremiah said to Seraiah, when thou comest to Babylon and shalt see and read all these words, etc., and hast made an end of reading this book, thou shalt bind a stone to it and cast it into the midst of Euphrates. And thou shalt say, thus shall Babylon sink, etc., which was accomplished in the Lord's due and appointed time by drying up the river Euphrates, by the hands of the Medes: and they came in upon Babylon as a thief in the night, even when they were at their banqueting.[253] The prophet Daniel, he saw the accomplishment of that which the prophet Jeremiah foretold of. The city was taken at one end, and the passages were stopped, and the reeds were burnt with fire, and the men of war were affrighted, indeed; for in that night when the handwriting came forth was Belshazzar the King of the Chaldeans slain, and Darius the Median king took the kingdom, and soon after the Lord wrought deliverance for his people Israel.

I have often observed the concurrence and agreement that there is between the Old Testament and the New, only that was the figure or type, this the substance or antitype, and the great harvest of God Almighty in this world, wherein the tares will be severed from the wheat. And all in the end, will be gathered home into their proper places.

Now, as touching mystical Babylon it is said, and the sixth angel poured out his vial upon the great river Euphrates, and the waters thereof was dried up: by which is intended her defense is taken away, alluding from what was done of old by drying up the river Euphrates, by which means old Babylon's defense was gone, so that the kings of the east came into the city suddenly and took it. And they were an army prepared by the Lord, as may be seen by many prophecies in the Old Testament.[254] And as the Lord did prepare an army beforehand, for the destruction of Babylon, so we find in the prophecy of this book that an army is prepared to be in readiness to make war against mystical Babylon, which before the sounding of the sixth trumpet were bound under her power—mentioned by the similitude of being bound, in the river Euphrates.[255] But we must observe this difference between that army under the first covenant, or dispensation of the law, and this of the new, viz., that the weapons of these last

253. Jeremiah 51:61–64.

254. See Isaiah 45:1; Jeremiah 51:28.

255. Revelation 9:13–15.

are not carnal but spiritual. For it is the word of their testimony that, like fire and smoke, issued out of their mouths, or out of the mouths of the horses that carried them, which signifies the powers that bears them up.[256]

And here we may observe with the eye of the mind what agreement there is between the sounding of the trumpets and the pouring out of the vials of God's wrath. For the trumpets sounded, or the ministers declared the will and counsel of God, according to the dispensation they were under, and those that would not receive the counsel of God, nor answer his will and requirings in their time, or dispensation of light—they were ripe in iniquity and fell under the wrath of the Almighty. As in this, so in all the rest of the trumpets and vials. For the pouring out of the vial appears to me to be the finishing work of the particular dispensation. And the angels of God are the reapers, or executioners, as King David saw an angel of the Lord stand between the earth and the heaven, having a drawn sword in his hand, stretched out over Jerusalem. That was when David had offended the Lord by causing Joab to number the people.[257] So the destroying angel that slew the first-born in the land of Egypt was not suffered to enter into any house where the blood of the paschal lamb was sprinkled on the two outside posts and on the lintel of the door.[258] Oh! That all could read this in the mystery of it in themselves; then they would see how the Lord knows and preserves his people. But I have digressed from the present subject. And the sixth angel sounded, and I heard a voice (said John) from the four horns of the golden altar which is before God, saying to the sixth angel which had the trumpet, loose the four angels which are bound in the great river Euphrates. And the four angels were loosed which were prepared, for an hour and a day and a month and a year for to slay the third part of men. (But four angels yet.) And the number of the army of the horsemen were two hundred thousand thousand, and I heard the number of them. And he saw the horses in the vision and them that sat on them, having breast-plates of fire, etc.[259] Thus the army was prepared by the loosing of the four angels which before were bound under the power of mystical Babylon. And now they stand in readiness, waiting upon the Lord, to go at his command. For the waters will be dried up; the defense of mystical Babylon will be taken away; and the way of the kings and people of the East

256. Revelation 9:17.

257. See Chronicles 4:16.

258. See Exodus 12.

259. Revelation 9:13–17.

shall be prepared, or opened, that they that will come forth may come to New Jerusalem and drink of the water of life freely, which runs as a river through the midst of the street thereof, and not drink of the bitter and bloody waters of Babylon any more.

16:13–14. So the unclean spirits were represented to the apostle like frogs upon the drying up of the great river Euphrates, and they are the spirits of devils. But they were represented thus to show what was in the inside of the dragon, and in the inside of the beast, and in the inside of the false prophet; for all the world worshiped the dragon, thinking him to be the true God.

And the beast or power of Antichrist invested in the magistrates to be the power set up by God, to establish his worship. And the world takes the false prophets to be the true ministers of Christ, for they are of the world, and the world heareth them because they speak of the world and make sermons to please great men, for their own advantage. But at the downfall of Babylon it will appear what was and yet is in the inside of these three impostors all the time of their fair pretenses of religious worship and care over souls, and yet all carried on by the [X] spirits of devils, working miracles. And they are called three frogs, or spirits (though but one in nature), in respect of the three operations of its workings, viz. in the dragon, and in the beast, and in the false prophet or prophets. And these are the spirits that go forth unto the kings of the earth and of the whole world, to gather them to the battle of the great day of their own destruction, by their making war against him that sits on the white horse and against his army. Here we may observe that this great battle was stirred up by the spirits of devils, working miracles to deceive the kings of the earth and of the whole world, viz., all worldly-minded people, to gather them to the battle of the great day of God Almighty, which will prove their utter overthrow and the final end of mystery Babylon.

16:15. This is good counsel indeed. But is there no human creature that hath not done something whereof he or she may be ashamed? May not some few stand before the Lord in their own righteousness? Let the witness of God answer to that in each particular, and let all have a care of boasting, for the apostle testifieth that all have sinned and come short of the glory of God. But all are justified freely by his grace, through the redemption that is in Jesus Christ.[260] What is the garment then that we are to watch and keep? Why, it

260. Romans 3:23–24.

is the garment of God's salvation, the robe of his righteousness. For the day is coming upon all in which wo will be to the soul that is covered and not with the Spirit of God.

But blessed is the man whose sin is covered and to whom the Lord imputeth not iniquity. Therefore, it is good that a man should both hope and quietly wait for the salvation of God. And it is good for a man that he bear the yoke in his youth.

16:16–17. This voice speaking from the throne is the voice of Almighty God, saying it is done.

16:18. And well may these things be, when the wrath of the Almighty God is poured out into this noble climate, i.e. the air, wherein is the vital spirit of every living creature or thing. For what is there in this low world that can live without the refreshing breezes of an wholesome air? And also thunderings and lightnings are many times very dreadful and hurtful, and such a great earthquake doth not only set forth the shaking of the fabric of the great world but also the trembling of the people under a sense of the great judgments of God Almighty. They being unwilling to meet the Lord in the way of his judgments, and this causeth voices which may signify great outcries among the people.

16:19. And the great city was divided into three parts: it is probable that one part might turn to God and another part might be outrageous and blasphemous, as we shall hear in verse 21. And a third part might be as neuters or as a sort of quiet animals. And the cities of the nations fell: these I take to be the national churches, that are the daughters of the great Babylon that is called the Mother of Harlots, that is the mother of all them that go from God in their love and receive other lovers.[261]

16:20. i.e., the high places of the earth fled away, which signify the great men of the earth, of which more may be seen by perusing and meditating on what followed, the opening of the sixth seal.[262]

261. Webb regularly experienced the opposition of these "national churches"—including the Church of England and the Congregational churches of New England—during her labors as a missionary and eagerly anticipated their downfall.

262. See Revelation 6:12–17.

16:21. These are such as made lies their refuge; but now, judgment being laid to the line and righteousness to the plummet, and the hail having swept away their refuge of lies, they are angry, though they were told that it should be so by Isaiah.[263] Then judgment shall dwell in the wilderness: it was in the wilderness where John saw mystery Babylon the great, mounted on her scarlet-colored beast in her rich attire. And now the day is come that was promised, i.e. the Spirit is poured out from on high, and judgment doth dwell in the wilderness. And righteousness doth and shall remain in the fruitful field, and the work of righteousness shall be peace, and the effect of righteousness quietness and assurance forever. And my people (saith the Lord) shall dwell in a peaceable habitation and in sure dwellings and in quiet resting places when it shall hail, coming down in the forests, etc.[264] So herein is the safety of them that love and fear God. His name is their strong tower, wherein they trust, and his holy will is their resting place. And such have this witness in themselves, that if the outward man should fall in times of common calamities, the soul shall rest in that mansion that is prepared for it in our Father's house.

Now what we shall farther read of in this book concerning mystery Babylon, the beast, and the false prophet etc., relating to their final end, is the effects of the pouring out of the seven last vials of God's wrath, expressed by other similitudes. And the seven vials, they follow the sounding of the seven trumpets, for when the seventh angel sounded, there were great voices in heaven, saying, the kingdoms of this world are become the kingdoms of our Lord and of his Christ, and he shall reign forever and ever. And there followed great joy, with praise and thanksgiving.[265] And when the seventh angel had poured out his vial, there was a great voice heard that came from the throne, saying, it is done.[266] And it is worthy the best observation to see and to consider that there was nothing of these mysteries of God opened or sounded in the world but as the Lamb of God opened the seals in order. And so one dispensation of light, grace, and truth came after another, and so the work of God is carried on orderly and gradually in the new creation, as it was in the old. And this mysterious work of God is known to be carried on in the little world, viz. man, as well as in the great world.

263. See Isaiah 28:17.

264. Isaiah 32:15–19.

265. See Revelation 11:15–17.

266. See verse 17, above.

And before the Lamb took the book in order to open the seals, the vision of all was as the words of a book that is sealed, which neither the learned, nor the unlearned could read.[267] And so it is still with those that have not received the Lamb of God into their hearts, in order that he may carry on his great work within, but entertains his grand enemy, even the God of this world, the prince of the power of darkness. These are they on whom the great and terrible day of the Lord will come as a thief in the night.[268] And it is worthy of observation to see and consider the great work of God carried on under the opening of the sixth seal.[269] There is finishing work, and when the seventh seal was opened there was silence in heaven for a season, for he that went forth conquering and to conquer had done his work, which may be compared to the six days' work, and had arrived at the Sabbath of rest. And there was no enemy to rise up against him, for all his enemies were fled to hide themselves in the dens and in the rocks of the mountains and said to the rocks and to the mountains, fall on us, and hide us from the face of him that sitteth on the throne and from the wrath of the Lamb. For the great day of his wrath is come, and who shall be able to stand?[270] Likewise in the time of the sounding of the sixth trumpet, what great works of God are wrought in the world? Even finishing works, in order to bring souls (that love the operation of the Spirit of his son in their hearts), to bring such to the sabbath of rest and for the cutting of all those enemies within that stand in opposition. Even so be it, saith my soul. Carry on thy work, O Lord, inwardly and outwardly, and gather out of thy kingdom all things that offend thee or that do iniquity, that thy people may dwell in a quiet habitation and in sure resting places wherein they may worship, reverence, and praise thee for ever more. Amen.

CHAPTER 17

17:1–2. By the wine of her fornication is intended her false doctrine and all other allurements by which the love of the soul is drawn from her maker. For this Christian Church knew the day wherein her maker was her husband,

267. See Isaiah 29:11–12.

268. See 2 Peter 3:10.

269. See Revelation 7, 6:12–17.

270. Revelation 6:16–17.

and her Redeemer was the holy one of Israel, the God of the whole earth. And because of her apostatizing from the love of God to the love of this present evil world, therefore is she called a harlot. And because she calls herself the mother Church, she is termed the mother of harlots, i.e., of all those that forsake their first love, or new covenant, that all souls in the day of their visitation or convincement make with the Lord when they see the want of a Savior or Deliverer.[271] For such days many have known, wherein they have made great covenants with the Lord, to love him forever if he would but deliver them from the bondage of sin and Satan.

But the subtle wiles and snares of Satan are very many; therefore, it is of absolute necessity that all walk and pray continually and keep low and near to Jesus Christ, the true light and only Savior of all souls that come to the Father by him. But those that depart from the Lord are like Israel of old, that changed their glory for that which did not profit them: Be astonished, O! Ye heavens, at this, and be ye horribly afraid; be ye very desolate, saith the Lord. For my people have committed two evils, they have forsaken me, the fountain of living waters, and have hewed them out cisterns, broken cisterns that can hold no water.[272] Such are they that think to worship God by a form of godliness but denying the power thereof. These are the perilous times that were foretold of, wherein men should be lovers of themselves, covetous, boasters, proud, blasphemers, etc., traitors, heady, high-minded, lovers of pleasures more than lovers of God, having a form of godliness but denying the power thereof: from such turn away.[273] For these know not the quickening virtue or powerful operation of the Spirit of God which worketh mightily in the humble, meek followers of Jesus Christ, strengthening them with might in the inner man, by whom their prayers are presented—or ascend to the Lord, God Almighty—as incense.[274] And the offering up of their whole heart is accepted as the morning and evening sacrifice, yea these are temple worshippers and go no more out but worship God in the Spirit night and

271. Quakers often used the term *convincement* to describe their conversion, as they came to a knowledge of divine truth through the justifying and sanctifying power of the Holy Ghost or Light of Christ. For an overview of common themes or patterns in convincement narratives, see Nikki Coffey Tousley, "Sin, Convincement, Purity, and Perfection," in *The Oxford Handbook of Quaker Studies*, ed. Stephen W. Angell and Pink Dandelion (New York: Oxford University Press, 2013), 172–86.

272. Jeremiah 2:12–13.

273. 2 Timothy 3:1–5.

274. See Ephesians 3:16.

day.[275] And such is God the Father seeking to worship him, and they that are already gathered into his Holy Spirit—their worship finds acceptance with him, and he affords them the lights of his gracious countenance, which maketh their hearts more glad than the increase of corn, wine, or any worldly treasure.

17:3. From hence we may observe that mystery Babylon is in a wilderness, or in a bewildered estate of mind. And the scarlet-colored beast that she sits upon signifies the persecuting powers of this world, which persecuting spirit and power the beast received from the dragon.[276] There is a description of this beast in his native form, before he became red and before he bore so much of the image of the dragon as now he is seen to bear.

17:4. Her sitting upon the beast doth show that she had the rule over the kings and governors of this world, as indeed she had—and kept them all in awe, with pretending to have the keys of the kingdom, etc. So all, both high and low, are compelled on pain of excommunication to attend on her at all her solemn meetings and to observe all her holy days (so called) and all her saints' days: both fasting days and festival days, which she had invented in abundance, with all her many prayers, and her gospel ordinances (so called). Thus she gloriously appeared with all her rich attire, and her golden cup in her hand, which even the wise men of this world thought to be full of the wine of the kingdom of heaven. But they were mistaken, as may be seen in the second verse: they being made drunk with the wine of her fornication. And so their spiritual eye was blinded by the god of this world, and they were allured by her golden cup, i.e. her glorious pretenses to holiness, to drink in of her false and bloody doctrine to that degree that they were mad with zeal against all that did or should bear any testimony against it. For her prophets, or preachers, are of the world, and the world heareth them.[277] And the beginning of this apostasy, was even in the apostles' days, and so proceeded to a great degree of darkness, and wickedness.[278] But this is the joy of this, and will be the joy of future generations, that the darkness is past and the true light now shineth in the little world (viz.) man. Then spoke Jesus again unto

275. Revelation 3:12.

276. See Revelation 13:1–7.

277. 1 John 4:5.

278. See 1 John 4:1–3.

them, saying, I am the light of the world: he that followeth me shall not walk in darkness but shall have the light of life.[279] And now the day is come and coming that the Lord promised: In that day shall the deaf hear the words of the book, and the eyes of the blind shall see out of obscurity and out of darkness. The meek also shall increase their joy in the Lord, and the poor among men shall rejoice in the Holy One of Israel. For the terrible one is brought to nought, and the scorner is consumed, and all that watch for iniquity are cut off.[280] This is very comfortable and is made sure in and unto all that follow Jesus Christ, who, in the days of his humiliation, was meek and lowly in heart, and so are his true followers.

17:5–8. Thus far, this showeth the rising and fall of Antichrist, which rose out of the bottomless pit and got into union with the kings of the earth. For the first beast that rose out of the sea and received power from the dragon was to maintain the heathenish worshiping of idols, but the pure life and spiritual worship of Christ and his apostles and the rest of his faithful followers gave the first beast a deadly wound. But that wound was healed, by the rising up of the second beast that rose out of the earth with two horns like a Lamb but spake like a dragon, who exercised all the powers of the first beast. For the subtle dragon caused the beast that rose out of the earth to make or cause an image to be made to the beast that had a wound by a sword and did live. The deadly wound was given by the sword of the Spirit, and the wound was healed by the apostatizing of the Christian Church, for the second beast spake like a dragon and exercised all the power of the first beast before him.[281] Thus the deadly wound was healed by the rising up of Antichrist and their images and idolatry instead of heathenism. And so, carrying on persecution against the true followers of Jesus Christ as the pagans or heathens had done before—for the beast that rose out of the bottomless pit or out of the earth joined in with the kingly powers of this world, both receiving power from the dragon—became one persecuting power, in union together until the pouring out of the seven vials of God's wrath shall be accomplished, to the final overthrow of Antichrist. And then it is that the beast that did ascend out of the bottomless pit is gone into perdition, but the civil power will yet remain, only deprived of the dragon's power or persecuting spirit. So it may be said

279. John 8:12.

280. Isaiah 29:18–20.

281. See Revelation 13:12–15.

(and yet is), for though the persecuting power is not, yet the kingly power is yet remaining, for that is ordained of God.

17:9. The seven heads of the beast, or the seven heads of the dragon, or of both in union, is said to be seven mountains on which the woman sitteth. This includes the whole dominion of the dragon's usurped power over the whole world, and it also includes the whole dominion of the powers of this world. And this woman, or false church, is upheld and supported wholly by that power derived from the dragon, in the hands of the kings and judges of the earth, who are ordained of God only to be ministers of the law, to punish evil doers, etc. But the dragon have given an opposite power, for he is an opposite spirit, even an enemy to all good, and the dragon gave to the first beast his power, and his seat, and great authority.[282]

17:10. The seventh or last king was not then come, and when he came he was to continue a short space. Here we may observe that all things are seen, yea, and foreseen by the divine eye and also that the evil powers are limited. For I do believe that these seven kings do include all the kings that received power from the dragon. And the seventh king here spoken of may signify the last persecuting power that shall appear for to uphold mystery Babylon.

17:11. This I take to be the Antichristian beast that rose out of the earth with two horns like a lamb. For the false prophets were to come in sheep's clothing (said our dear Lord) but inwardly, they are ravening.[283] So this beast is counted as the eighth king, to distinguish it from the other seven kings because they were powers ordained of God before they received power from the dragon. But the beast that did ascend out of the bottomless pit, or rose out of the earth (which I count one and the same beast), he is wholly an usurper and a cheat, having gotten into the worldly government wholly by the subtlety of the dragon. But this beast shall go into perdition, and it is reckoned to be of the seven kings only because of the union that was between this and the first beast, by reason of the dragon's power and persecuting spirit, whereby they were united in their idolatrous worship and in persecuting all that would not worship their image, or prescribed form of godliness, that they had set up.

282. See Revelation 13:2; see also Luke 4:5–7.

283. See Matthew 7:15.

17:12–13. These ten kings I take to be the kings of the national churches that are separated from the mother church and yet are her daughters.[284] For they shall make war with the Lamb and yet hate the whore. They shall give their power and strength to the beast, viz., to worldly government and grandeur, with the bestial properties of fallen nature. For,

17:14. These kings, who seem to me to be in our day the persecuting power, were evidently seen and felt in the morning of this present dispensation, not yet out of remembrance—both in Old England, and in New England, which will stand on record in ages to come together with the faithfulness of the sufferers.

17:15. So here we may observe the largeness of her dominions; for not only kings and the rulers have been deceived by her, but also the inhabitants of the earth are made drunk with the wine that she holds forth to them in her golden cups.

17:16–17. These ten kings are instruments in the hand of God, the just and righteous judge, to execute judgment on mystery Babylon, as Darius, King of the Medes, was instrumental in the hand of God to bring down the loftiness and pride of Belshazzar and the inhabitants of old Babylon, who kept Israel in captivity. And by the hand of Darius and Cyrus was deliverance wrought for the Lord's people, in the Lord's due and appointed time. And although Darius was a friend to Israel by God's decree, yet the subtle serpent wrought so cunningly by his instruments, that they prevailed so on the king, that he signed an idolatrous decree. And the prophet Daniel was cast into the lions' den because he did not obey the idolatrous decree, which proved a trial of Daniel's faith and resignation and tended to the glory of God, in his manifesting his powers over the hungry lions and preserving his servant that trusted in him.[285]

284. Webb never clarifies which ten sovereigns, nations, and national churches she is speaking of (or anticipating). During her lifetime, there were never ten Protestant nations in Europe. However, she may be referring to smaller regions within a larger state, such as the Lutheran portions of eighteenth-century Prussia, including Swedish Pomerania and the Duchy of Prussia. In her commentary on verse 14, she characterizes New England (presumably the Massachusetts Bay colony) as one of the ten nations, but gives no indication who the "king of the national church" of New England might be.

285. See Daniel 6.

These observations I set down to encourage to faithfulness in the true worship of the living God and in the words of the testimony of truth, whatever it may please God to suffer to come for a trial. For there is grown abundance of chaff among our wheat, and I do fully believe that a winnowing and trying day will come; and many in such a day will turn to the national churches. But the cities of the national will fall, when the seventh vial of God's wrath shall be poured out and the great city will be divided into three parts. This we may observe and be sensible of, that in those days wherein the seventh vial will be poured out into the air, that there will be great searchings of heart, and divisions, and many voices, and great commotions in the world, and among men—signified by thunders and lightnings and a great earthquake.[286] But let the center of thy mind be in this, viz., be thou a follower of the Lamb in love, faith, and patience, for those that make war with or against the Lamb: he shall overcome them. For he is Lord of Lords, and King of Kings, and they that are with him are called and chosen and faithful.

17:18. This great city was spoken of in Revelation 11:8 and is spiritually called Sodom and Egypt. And she is said to reign over the kings of the earth because they, being deceived by her false prophets, are made to stand in awe of her for fear of being excommunicated out of the church. And, so, shut out of the kingdom of heaven by her pretended key keeper. But these ten kings here spoken of, they have no such fear upon them, for they are so furious in their zeal against her that they are for making of her desolate and naked, and eating her flesh, and at last will burn her with fire, i.e. they shall strip her of her jewels of silver and gold, precious stones and pearls, and riches, and shall eat her flesh. I do understand this to be by taking away her college lands, abbey lands, and other revenues given to her in the dark night of Apostasy for praying of souls out of purgatory, and for absolutions, etc.[287] For the church called Catholic is very rich, made so by such wiles, by which a great swarm of church officers (called by the spirit locusts) were maintained in idleness.[288] Now these kings, they have already begun to eat these fat benefits, whereby

286. See Revelation 16.

287. This reading suggests that Henry VIII, who stripped the Catholic church of property between 1534 and 1540 when he established the Church of England as an ecclesiastical body separate from the Roman Catholic Church, might be one of the ten monarchs Webb is thinking of.

288. The locust imagery that Webb calls on here is drawn from Revelation 6:2.

these idle crew were fed fat. This I take to be meant by eating her flesh, and her being burnt with fire we shall have an account of in the next chapter. For God hath put it into their hearts to fulfill his will on mystery Babylon, and yet they agree to give their kingdom unto the beast and do not follow the Lamb, but on the contrary, make war with him. These things are worthy of consideration and observation that so, all that will come, may come out of Babylon and also out of the national churches which are her daughters, and may follow the Lamb of God, in and by the leadings of his spirit, that they may come to be fellow citizens together, in the New Jerusalem which we shall read of in the twenty-first chapter, into which holy city there shall in no wise enter anything that defileth, neither whosoever worketh abominations or maketh a lie.[289]

CHAPTER 18

18:1. This is an angel of him who said, I am the true light; he that followeth me shall not walk in darkness but shall have the light of life.[290] This angel, or messenger, is now come, and the earthly hearts of as many as do receive him in are enlightened with his glorious light. And such hear his voice spiritually as they are gathered into the Spirit in this, the Lord's day of visitation unto the children of men.

18:2. She was the habitation of devils before, for she was full of swarms of the locusts that came out of the smoke of the bottomless pit, whose king is called Abaddon, and Apollyon.[291] But now, by this glorious, bright light, it is manifested what is within: the inhabiters of Babylon the great, mystery of iniquity.

18:3. Here the reason is given of her fall by the Just and Holy One.

18:4. By this we may observe that there is a people in Babylon that are not got into enmity against God. These the Lord calls his people, and his call is to them to come out of her. The reasons are given above.

289. Revelation 21:27.

290. John 8:12.

291. See Revelation 9.

18:5–6. This judgment is begun and will be accomplished by the pouring out of the seventh and last vial of the wrath of the Almighty. Then what measure people will mete, it will be measured to them again. And then the merciful will receive the blessing, for they shall obtain mercy.[292] Therefore, have a care, and do not treasure up wrath against the day of wrath and perdition of ungodly men, which will certainly come.

18:7–8. And thus it will be to all that will not obey the voice of the Holy Spirit, who calls, saying: come out of her my people, and be not partakers of her sins, etc.

18:9–11. By the kings of the earth and merchants of the earth is intended earthly-minded men, who have their portion in this life and glory in the pomps and vanities of this world and live deliciously with mystery Babylon. Such bewail the loss of her profits and pleasures, set forth by a similitude, for the woman and the city are called mystery Babylon.[293]

18:12–13. These last are such as the apostle Peter prophesied of: but there were false prophets also among the people, even as there shall be false teachers among you who privily shall bring in damnable heresies, etc.[294] First they did it privily, but soon after many followed their pernicious ways, by reason of whom the way of truth shall be evil spoken of and through covetousness shall they with feigned words make merchandize of you, whose judgment now of a long time lingereth not.

Babylon's teachers have abundance of sermons and prayers to sell, of different degrees in value, so that according to the pay so is the prayer or sermon, which if that way would please God and cause him to receive souls into his favor, then the rich had an advantage over the poor. But God the Father of our spirits said all souls are mine—as the soul of the father, so also the soul of the son is mine. The soul that sinneth, it shall die, (that is) the soul that sinneth must die to sin, or else it shall die in sin and for sin.[295] And if any die in sin, the second death will follow, which by timely repentance may be prevented. For the purgation of the soul is on this side the grave, but

292. Matthew 7:2, 5:7.

293. See Revelation 17:12.

294. 2 Peter 2:1.

295. Ezekiel 18:4.

Babylon's merchants made and yet makes people believe other ways and so made slaves of the people and merchandize of the souls of men.

But the just and merciful God hath testified, saying: when the wicked man turneth away from his wickedness that he hath committed and doeth that which is lawful and right, he shall save his soul alive. Because he considereth and turneth away from all his transgression that he hath committed he shall surely live; he shall not die. Oh! Merciful God and Gracious Father. And yet the house of Israel said his ways are not equal.[296] Consider it well. Oh! The justice and equity of Almighty God. And yet his long forbearance and fatherly kindness, it hath been admirable to me, and there is a cloud of witnesses that hath borne testimony to the same from age to age, to the praise and glory of God. And it is left on record for the encouragement of succeeding generations to draw nigh to their Heavenly Father and put away the evil of their doings in time, that so they many not fall with mystery Babylon.

18:14–17. (This shows that God Almighty is able to bring to nought the pomp and pride of the greatest in world, and that he will do it.) Therefore, blessed are the meek and lowly in heart, for they shall rejoice in the Lord, even when all this weeping and wailing shall be in the world.

18:17–19. Thus we have a large account of the great lamentation of the kings of the earth, and the merchants of the earth, and of as many as traded by sea. In their beholding the destruction of mystery Babylon the great, the mother of harlots, i.e. the mother of all that depart from God in their love and obedience and set their love on things that appertain to this low world, such will be brought to nought except they speedily return to God with the whole heart and repent.

18:20. This is a day of great joy to the dwellers in heaven. We read of the like joy in heaven when the great dragon was cast out, that old serpent called the devil and Satan.[297] So at the fall of Babylon, there is and will be great joy in and among the inhabitants of the Holy City, New Jerusalem, whom they of mystery Babylon used to tread underfoot and not allow them to buy nor sell among them because they had not on them the mark of the beast.[298]

296. See Ezekiel 18:25–32.

297. See Revelation 12:9–12.

298. See Revelation 13:17.

18:21–23. Sorceries is a sort of witchcraft, which I take here to intend false doctrine and cunning devices to bewitch people that they should not obey the truth. But according to the prophecy of the apostle Peter, the overthrow of those false teachers is come, which he begins to set forth by taking notice how God spared not the angels that sinned but cast them down to hell and delivered them into chains of darkness, to be reserved unto judgment; and how God spared not the old world but saved Noah, etc., and turned the cities of Sodom and Gomorrah into ashes, etc., and delivered just Lot, etc.[299] Here we may observe the just judgments of God, and the harmony of the scripture testimonies, and also how the servants of God did make observations on the dealings of God from age to age, to see how he punished the wicked and saved those that trusted in him. And I may say, such meditations and contemplations are very sweet and profitable to the soul that loves and fears God.

18:24. By this we may understand that it is not the city of Rome only, for they were not all slain in that city that were slain upon the earth, but in this mystical city was found the blood of all that were slain upon the earth. For this city is so large that every unregenerate soul is an inhabitant in it, and the Lord in his great love and tender mercy is calling to all to come out of her, i.e. out of mystery Babylon, out of all known sin, out of all strife and confusion, and to follow the leadings of the grace of God that brings salvation, which will teach all that love it and obey the dictates of it, as it did teach the apostles and primitive Christians, that denying all ungodliness and worldly lusts, they did live soberly, righteously, and God-likely in this present world, etc.[300] And so both Jews and Gentiles come to be fellow citizens with the saints, and of the household of God. See Ephesians 2—peruse the whole chapter.

CHAPTER 19

19:1. Here we may observe that John heard the voice of much people in heaven. Is it queried, how came the people into heaven, or where is heaven? As to the last, Christ said it is not to say, lo here or lo there is the kingdom,

299. 2 Peter 2:4–7.

300. Titus 2:11–12.

for the kingdom of God is within you.[301] The kingdom of God cometh not with observation or outward show, but the kingdom of God is known in every heart that is wholly given up to God, that he may sit therein as judge and lawgiver. And the creature is a loving and loyal subject to him, being willing to obey the voice of his word, which word is Christ, who is always in the bosom of the Father and sits with him in his throne.

And how came so many people into heaven, seeing no unclean thing can enter thereinto? The apostle John declared that God is light, and in him is no darkness at all. If we say we have fellowship with him and walk in darkness, we lie, and do not the truth. But if we walk in the light (i.e., in Christ), we have fellowship one with another, and the blood of Jesus Christ, the Son of God, cleanseth us from all sin. If we say we have no sin, we deceive ourselves, and the truth is not in us. If we confess our sins, he is faithful and just to forgive us our sins and to cleanse us from all unrighteousness.[302] Thus it is the work of God, in and by the spirit of his son (that he hath sent into our hearts) to sanctify, cleanse, and save the souls of the children of men that receive him and love him above all the world. To such he giveth power to become the sons of God.[303] And if thou read with understanding thou may find who are the children of God and of the household of faith and fellow citizens in the new Jerusalem, which is called the mother of the faithful who dwell in Christ and walk in his spirit (and are making war in righteousness against every appearance of evil in themselves; these are the armies that John saw in heaven in verse 14 following), and they praise God, saying:

19:2–3. It seems plain to me that the joy of the saints is and will be an aggravation to the torment of the wicked; yea, I have seen something of it in envious people. It is hard to say how the mercies of God to others have pinched their minds; therefore, people have need to look well into themselves, to see what manner of spirit ruleth within. For as the kingdom of God is within the saints and the joy of his salvation causeth them to sing praises to his powerful name, so the kingdom of darkness and the hell of the wicked is in themselves, because the prince of power of darkness ruleth in them, and they are at enmity against the meekness of divine love. For Lucifer is a proud spirit, but Christ and his angels are so meek that they do not bring railing

301. Luke 17:21.

302. 1 John 1:5–9.

303. See John 1:11–14.

accusations against the devil; but an angel said, the Lord rebuke thee, O Satan, even the Lord that hath chosen Jerusalem rebuke thee—is not this a brand plucked out of the fire?[304] See Zachariah Chapter 3; there it may be seen how Satan did endeavor to resist the work of God when he was about to cleanse Joshua the high priest. The serious perusal of this chapter hath done me good under diverse considerations that are therein, so I recommend it to thee and say again that the torment or tormentor of the wicked is chiefly within—for a further confirmation of which, see Revelation 14:9–11. There it is proclaimed by an angel, if any man worship the beast and his image, etc., the same shall drink of the wine of the wrath of God, etc. And he shall be tormented with fire and brimstone in the presence of the holy angels and in the presence of the Lamb. Now this we believe: that the Lamb of God and the holy angels are in heaven. And I believe heaven to be a holy and glorious station and that in heaven there are degrees of glory to be understood by an outward resemblance. It is compared to the stars that differ in brightness.[305] This resemblance is used to inform the natural man, but the spiritual man believeth it to be an inward, spiritual brightness in the meek love and inward, exulting joy of the divine life. Therefore, strive to live near the Lord while here, for he is the fountain of divine light and life, and such a state cannot want a place. For wherever such a creature is, it is in its heavenly station and is filled with love, light, life and heavenly joy, according to its capacity to receive it. The believers in Christ in the days of the apostles—they tasted of this good word of life and the powers of the world to come. And there have been some that in this life have tasted of the wrath of God and of the terrors and anguish of the dark world. Those things are spiritually discerned and so: as, while a soul is at home in the body it is not in the full enjoyment of its Lord. And so, although it may taste of the good word of life, etc., yet the body is a hindrance to the soul in many respects and keeps it back from the clear sight and enjoyment of heavenly objects.

So, on the contrary, while the wicked are at home in the body, the pleasures of the body and the joys of this life are a mitigation of the black, dark thoughts that they are sometimes troubled with. But I have seen some few that have fallen into despair and have been like as in hell while they have been in the body, but the body cannot subsist long under such a state of mind but is (as it were) burnt up with the inward anguish of the soul. Oh! take care of

304. Zecharaiah 3:2.

305. See 1 Corinthians 15:41.

thy immortal part in time, for God Almighty said (concerning the Old World), my spirit shall not always strive with man.[306]

I have felt this sort of inward burning anguish and horror of spirit; it is caused by the prince of the power of darkness. He, entering in, brings unbelief, hardness of heart, and doubtings and reasonings, and brings the soul to question the truth of all things. This is a horrible state; it is darkness that may be felt indeed. But in that time, my soul did cry continually night and day, saying, O Lord give me faith, O Lord, give me faith. For all the faith that I had received by education and tradition was overthrown in this dismal condition my soul was for several months, in which time I walked much alone. And one day, when I was alone, crying to God after my wanted manner, I felt the divine love to spring in my heart, and the divine light shined in my understanding. And the power from on high overshadowed my soul, and the prince of the power of darkness fled before it, and the power of God took place in my heart. And then I could see and believe in the power and operation of the divine word, both in the outward or visible creation and also in the invisible or inward work of God in the regeneration of the soul. So I do leave this as a testimony to succeeding generations and say, this indeed is the work of God, that ye believe on him whom God hath sent. And true saving, living faith, it is the gift of God. And those that want it may have this special gift of faith given to them for asking for it and waiting the Lord's time. And it was by faith that all God's servants know an overcoming of their enemies in all ages—see Hebrews 11; there is a large account given of it. All those there testified of are gathered home to God and to Jesus Christ, their bridegroom, and are among the heavenly host whom the apostle John heard saying Allelujah. And the smoke of the torment of the wicked arose up forever and ever.

19:4–6. This is a mighty heavenly harmony ascribing praise to God Almighty for his righteous judgments upon the false church who had reigned so long over the true, yea, and also over the kings of the earth.[307] But now the Lord God Omnipotent reigneth; therefore, all that love and fear him praise his

306. Genesis 6:3. By "the Old World," Webb seems to mean the antediluvian earth and, more broadly, the wicked threatened with destruction at the Second Coming. But Webb's accounts of immigrating from England to North America suggest that she also considered Europe a place of questionable spiritual values.

307. See Revelation 17:18.

holy name, according as they were commanded by a voice that came out of the throne.

19:7. This is the joy of the great multitude of all them that fear God, both small and great, which the apostle John heard as the voice of many waters and as the voice of mighty thunderings, etc., which signifies the mighty gatherings that will be after the fall of Babylon. For the voice that followed the angel who came down from heaven, having great power, and the earth enlightened with his glory.[308] This angel is now in his ministry giving notice of the fall of Babylon and manifesting by the glorious light that she is the habitation of devils, etc., and calling the Lord's people to come out of her, etc. This is the present dispensation of God to the children of men. But the judgments of God will increase in the world, and happy will that soul be that can say as the prophet Habakkuk did.

When I heard, my belly trembled; my lips quivered at the voice, rottenness entered into my bones, and I trembled in myself, that I might rest in the day of trouble. When he cometh up unto the people, he will invade them with his troops.[309] I observe the cause of the prophet's trembling, viz., he heard and he believed. And mark the effects: although (said he) the fig tree shall not blossom, neither shall fruit be in the vines, the labor of the olive shall fail, and the fields shall yield no meat. The flock shall be cut off from the fold, and there shall be no herd in the stall. Yet I will rejoice in the Lord; I will joy in the God of my salvation. The Lord is my strength, and he will make my feet like hinds' feet, etc.[310] Thus the Lord God, he was and is and will be the joy and strength of his [people] in all generations, even of these that tremble at his word. Such will have a hiding place in the day of trouble and will have on the wedding garment when they are called in unto the marriage supper of the Lamb.[311]

19:8. Here I observe, and to her was granted, etc.—this shows that the righteousness of saints is not their own righteousness, but it is granted or given to them by their dear Lord and Bridegroom, who hath so loved the children of men that he gave himself for them, that he might sanctify and cleanse his

308. See Revelation 18:1–4.

309. Habakkuk 3:16.

310. Habakkuk 3:17–19.

311. See Matthew 22:1–13.

church (that is) as many as do and will receive him with the washing of water by the word, that he might present it unto himself a glorious Church, not having spot or wrinkle or any such thing but that it should be holy and without blemish.[312]

19:9. And blessed be God: his call is to all, even to the ends of the earth, to look unto him and be saved. But it concerns each particular soul to come to Christ to be washed with the water of regeneration and to be clothed with the garment or robe of his righteousness, lest the soul should receive that sentence that is mentioned in Matthew 22:13. Oh! That all would hear and believe and fear the Lord and not make light of his call, as our Lord said they did that were called to the marriage supper of the king's son. And they went their ways, one to his farm, another to his merchandise, and the residue took the servants (that were sent in love to call them) and entreated them spitefully and slew them. But when the king heard thereof he was wroth and sent forth his armies and destroyed those murderers and burnt up their city.[313] The Lord foresaw these days, and he spake many things in parables concerning the kingdom of God that is come and coming. The angel testified saying, these are the true sayings of God and, I say, therefore worthy of our observation and meditation. And indeed, the meditations on them hath been sweet to my soul.

19:10. Here we may observe the meekness and humility of this angel of Jesus Christ and how he declares himself to be the apostle's fellow servant and of his brethren, etc. This may be a word of encouragement to all faithful servants of Jesus Christ, to believe and consider that where our Lord is, there are his servants also. This is an angel of Jesus: I Jesus have sent mine angel, to testify unto you these things in the churches, etc.[314] For the testimony of Jesus is the spirit of prophecy, and prophecy comes by revelation or inspiration of the Holy Ghost. The apostle to the Corinthians said, no man can say that Jesus is the Lord but by the Holy Ghost.[315] And indeed I may say so too, under diverse considerations, and first as touching his holy conception in the virgin's womb. There is no mortal can pry into that mystery that is revealed

312. Ephesians 5:26–27.

313. Matthew 22:1–7.

314. Revelation 22:16.

315. 1 Corinthians 12:3.

by the Holy Ghost, even in the time of its overshadowing the soul. And secondly, as touching his government, how can any soul call Jesus my Lord without he feel the Holy Ghost to rule and govern him inwardly in all things? Which, to go into particulars of his leadings and movings would be too large. But when the Lord was personally present among men, he asked his disciples, saying, who do men say that I, the Son of Man, am? And they said, some say that thou art John the Baptist, some Elias, and others Jeremias or one of the prophets. He saith unto them, but whom say ye that I am? And Simon Peter answered and said, thou art Christ, the Son of the living God. And Jesus answered and said unto him, blessed art thou, Simon Bar-jona, for flesh and blood hath not revealed [it] unto thee but my Father which is in heaven, and I say unto thee that thou art Peter, and upon this rock will I build my church, and the gates of hell shall not prevail against it.[316] I take the Rock to be the Father, revealing his Son in us for a foundation, a chief cornerstone. For there is no man can come to Christ except the Father draw him; every man that heard and hath learned of the Father cometh to Christ the Anointed, not that any man hath seen the Father save he which is of God. He hath seen the Father, which is Christ, the Son of God, unto whom all things are delivered by or of the Father. And no man knoweth the Son but the Father, neither knoweth any man the Father save the Son and he to whomsoever the Son will reveal him.[317] So herein consisteth the mystery of godliness and the foundation of the true Church and every member of it in particular, viz., the Father is revealing the Son in us and the Son is revealing the Father. And the faithful, not consulting with flesh and blood, give up to the heavenly manifestation to be as instruments in the divine hand, and so the work of God is carried on by his own power, light, life, and wisdom, according to the degrees of his manifestations in the world and in the creature. For God in himself is the fountain and fullness of all light, life, wisdom, and power, and all good. And our Lord said, there is none good but one, that is God.[318] And so here God is exalted and man debased until God Almighty become our all in all and the soul know an overcoming of all its enemies by following Jesus Christ, who hath promised, saying, to him that overcometh will I grant to sit with me in my throne even as I also overcame and am set

316. Matthew 16:13–18.

317. Matthew 11:27.

318. Matthew 19:17.

down with my Father in his throne. He that hath an ear, let him hear (saith our Lord) what the Spirit saith unto the churches.[319]

Here followeth a relation of a vision wherein the apostle saw our Lord in his glory with his faithful followers following him, all upon white horses, as also his glorious conquest.

19:11–12. This sheweth that he is King of Kings and Lord of Lords and had a name written that no man knew but he himself. This is his mysterious name that no man knoweth but he himself, although it is a written name.

19:13. This is that written name that no man knew but he himself, and no man yet knows it in the mystery of it but he or they that have received the white stone, and in the stone a new name written which no man knoweth saving he that receiveth it. Some people are taking the scriptures for the Word of God, but the scriptures testify of the Word of God: In the beginning was the Word, and the Word was with God, and the Word was God. The same was in the beginning with God. All things were made by him, and without him was not anything made that was made. In him was life, and the life was the light of men. And the light shineth in darkness, and the darkness comprehended it not.[320] Here the beloved apostle gives a clear description of the Word of God as it is in the bosom of the Father and also as it goeth forth from God continually as life and light, even into the minds, spirits, and souls of the children of men. And yet the unregenerate comprehendeth it not and also the visible creatures are upheld by the universal though invisible Spirit and powerful word by which they were and are created.

Oh! Immense ocean of divine goodness, life, light and wisdom, glory and power, who condescended so for the love of fallen, lost mankind as to send the Divine Word to take nature upon him and to appear in the form of a man, who in the power of his Father was able to call a man out of his grave that had been therein four days, with many other miraculous [works], all which showed his Father's glory and mighty power and himself to be the Son of God. And thus he came to his own, (i.e., the Jews, and his own received him not (i.e., not the majority), but as many as received him, to them he gave power to become the sons of God, even to them that believed on his name,

319. Revelation 3:21–22.

320. John 1:1–5.

which were born not of blood, nor of the will of the flesh, nor of the will of man, but of God.[321]

Here is a plain testimony concerning the new birth and the way to receive power to become the children of God. And as he then came to the Jews in his personal appearance, so now he is come to his own, i.e. Christians that bear his name, viz., in his spiritual appearance. And his own, or those that are called by his name, all of them do not receive him. But unto as many as do (or shall) receive him, unto them he is giving power to become the children of God, even by the same way above described. And so there are those that are following the Lamb, making war in righteousness against every appearance of evil, especially in themselves. And this king of saints was represented to John as in a vesture, dipped in blood; this represents the great battles that he hath been engaged in, even for the sake of lost mankind. This is the warrior that was foreseen by Isaiah the prophet. Who is this that cometh from Edom, with dyed garments from Bozra? This that is glorious in his apparel, traveling in the greatness of his strength? I that speak in righteousness, mighty to save, etc. The prophet seems mightily concerned to know wherefore the Lord appeared red in his apparel. He received an answer from the Holy One, who said, I have trodden the winepress alone, and of the people there was none with me. No, there was none with him. When they shed his blood, his very disciples fled from him, but now he promiseth, saying, for I will tread them in anger, and trample them in my fury, and their blood shall be sprinkled upon my garments, and I will stain all my raiment. For the day of vengeance is in my heart, and the year of my redeemed is come.[322]

19:14. These are they that follow the Lamb of God in the way of regeneration and make war in righteousness against every appearance of evil in themselves. And as they are called to it they testify against all evil in others. And the white horses they sit on signify the purity of that power that bears them up and carrieth them through in their holy warfare. And their fine white linen garments is the same that was granted to the bride, which is the righteousness of saints—see verse 8—and their being seen in heaven is their heavenly, spiritual station, for they were in their warfare, and their captain was before them.

321. John 1:11–13.

322. Isaiah 63:1–4.

19:15. This sharp sword is the word of God that hath been felt to operate, quick and powerful and sharper than any two-edged sword, piercing even to the dividing asunder of soul and spirit and of the joints and marrow, and is a discerner of the thoughts and intents of the heart. Neither is there any creature that is not manifest in his sight, but all things are naked and opened unto the eyes of him with whom we have to do.[323] Therefore I advise to a due consideration of these things, and give up all that the controversy of the Lord is against, and join to the Lord Jesus. And thou shalt be one spirit with him, and then he will rule in thee with his meek love and not with his rod of iron.

19:16. This name is given to his glorified nature, wherein he is the first begotten from the dead and the prince of the kings of the earth. And he hath raised the poor from the dust and the beggar from the dung hill and made them to sit with the princes of his people and to inherit the throne of glory.[324] And this is the Lord's doing, and it is marvelous in our eyes, for which all the faithful do render to him glory and dominion, as he is one with his Father, world without end. Amen. This is the King the Psalmist spake of. Thou art fairer than the children of men. Grace is poured into thy lips; therefore, God hath blessed thee forever. Gird thy sword upon thy thigh, O most mighty, with thy glory and thy majesty. And in thy majesty, ride prosperously because of truth and meekness and righteousness; and thy right hand shall teach thee terrible things. Thine arrows are sharp in the heart of the king's enemies, whereby the people fall under thee. Thy throne, O God, is forever and ever; the sceptre of thy kingdom is a right scepter. Thou lovest righteousness and hatest wickedness; therefore, God, thy God, hath anointed thee with the oil of gladness above thy fellows, etc.[325] Thus the Psalmist proceeds very sweetly and excellently in setting forth the majesty and grace of Christ's kingdom, the duty of his bride, etc., the perusal of which is very sweet to a soul that loveth Jesus Christ above all things in this world, which I earnestly advise all to do.

19:17–18. By the angel standing in the sun doth shew that he was an angel of light and stood in open view. And his calling with a loud voice, etc., was to

323. Hebrews 4:12–13.

324. See 1 Samuel 2:8.

325. Psalm 45:2–7.

declare the determination of the Almighty concerning the destruction of all those that make war against the Lamb and his followers.

19:19. This I take to be another similitude, as there are several ways of making war against, or resisting, the spirit of the Son of God that he hath sent into the hearts of the children of men in order that he might dwell among them. But they resist it, and when they have resisted its reproofs and strivings in themselves till they are hardened, then they make war against its appearance in others.

19:20. By the beast is intended the persecuting powers of this world or those that support the false church, who received that persecuting spirit and power from the great red dragon. And the kings of the earth and their armies are all those that resist the power of God and its divine operations, either in themselves or in others. These make war against him who sits on the white horse of his pure, righteous power.[326] And the ten horns which those sawest are ten kings, etc. These ten horns were seen upon the beast and have begun their reign, and they do hate the whore, or mother of harlots, and will make her desolate, etc., for it is according to the will of God. Yet these make war with the Lamb, and the Lamb shall overcome them, for he is Lord of Lords and King of Kings, glory to God forevermore.

And the false prophet that is taken with the beast is he that rose out of the earth with two horns like a lamb, but he spoke as a dragon and represents all false prophets that come in sheep's clothing but inwardly are ravening wolves.[327] And his two horns may signify his power that he had usurped both over church and state; this is the same that the angel called that great city which reigneth over the kings of the earth.[328] And he might well speak as a dragon, for he was the dragon's mouth or trumpet to alarm his vassals to do his drudgery and butchery against the followers of the Lamb. But now he is going into perdition, and he with the beast is to be cast alive into a lake of fire burning with brimstone. This beast and false prophet have treasured up abundance of wrath (by the dragon's persecuting spirit and power) against the day of wrath and are to be cast alive into a lake of fire. This doubtless will be a battle of shaking, as the prophet Isaiah terms it. And in every place, said

326. See Revelation 17:12–14.

327. See Matthew 7:15.

328. See Revelation 17:18.

he, where the grounded staff shall pass, which the Lord shall lay upon him, it shall be with tabrets and harps; and in battles of shaking shall he fight with it. For Tophet is ordained of old; yea, for the King it is prepared. He hath made it deep and large; the pile thereof is fire and much wood. The breath of the Lord, like a stream of brimstone, doth kindle it.[329] These and such like testimonies denote great horror, anguish, and inward burning, even as an oven, as the prophet Malachi terms it.[330]

19:21. The sword of God is his powerful word, whereby he can call for—send—what plagues or judgments he please to cut off man and beast from the earth. But some may be mystically slain by the entrance of the divine word, which slays the old man with his deeds and giveth life to the soul, or spiritual man. And such may say the body is dead because of sin, but the spirit is life because of righteousness—and yet, not their own self-righteousness but the righteousness that is granted to them by Jesus Christ. So now the beast and the false prophet are gone into perdition and their armies are slain. The persecuting power is subdued, yet there will remain a sort of people that do not acquaint themselves with God, even in the time of the Saints' Sabbath. But Satan being bound, that old serpent—the worldly-minded people let the saints alone till Satan is again loosed, as may be seen in the next chapter.

CHAPTER 20

20:1–2. The devil is a spirit, an evil spirit, though represented in the vision like a dragon. And the chain is the power of God, for nothing else can limit the power of Satan. And as these things treated on in this book are mysterious things and yet needful to be known because they belong to the churches of Christ and to every member in particular, and they were delivered or revealed by the Almighty through the ministration of [angels] (who are ministering spirits) on purpose for the good of man and are not to be understood but by the help of the divine light which is Christ, within the hope of glory: therefore, I tenderly advise that all love the true light and watch in it with the eye of the mind, very single to the Almighty. And then such will have a right

329. Isaiah 30:32–33.

330. Malachi 4:1.

understanding and a comfortable sense of the glorious things yet to be spoken to, which are yet to come, and our children may live to see glorious days if they will love Christ, the true light. For the spirit of man is the candle of the Lord, but the candle of the wicked is oft put out by the power of darkness. Therefore, for me to know the prince of the power of darkness bound and cast out of my mind by the prince of life and light will be very profitable and comfortable to me, and so every particular soul may say.

20:3. Thus I observe, that the good angel had a key to shut up the bottomless pit of heresies and delusions and power, to bind him that is the author thereof. This is the great work of God, both in the great world and in man, which is an epitome of the great world. And when an eminent man falls from a heavenly station to an earthly, carnal state and lets in a proud spirit, he hath a key to open the pit of heresies and delusions into the world and is an instrument in the hand of the evil spirit. And his doctrine is compared to smoke that dims the eyesight, and a long abiding in it may cause a total blindness.[331] So, when the heart is kept with all diligence, out of it proceeds the issues of life; so, on the contrary, when the heart is not kept lifted up to God, the prince of darkness and death gets possession, and he sends forth the issues of death and darkness. For what is man but what the Spirit maketh him to be that rules within him, though there is a striving of the two spirits for a time. Yet in time, there is and will be a conquest, and the true light will shine more and more bright in the minds of the children of men, and the prince of darkness will be so bound down in chains by the power of God that he shall deceive the nations no more till the thousand years be fulfilled, and after that he must be loosed for a little season.[332]

20:4. John doth not declare who they are that he saw sitting in judgment on the thrones, but we may find who this station was promised to. After Peter had signified to our Lord, saying, behold we have forsaken all and followed thee; what shall we have therefore? And Jesus said unto them, verily I say unto you that ye which have followed me—in the regeneration, when the son of man shall sit in the throne of his glory, ye shall also sit upon twelve thrones, judging the twelve tribes of Israel.[333] This shows who they are.

331. See Revelation 9:1–5.

332. See Revelation 20:7–8, below.

333. Matthew 19:27–28.

20:4–5. By the rest of the dead I understand those that died in sin, that where Christ is they cannot come. For it will appear toward the end of this chapter that after these thousand years the general resurrection will be, but times and seasons are in the hand of God. But this is well known, that all that believe in Christ and suffer with him in bearing the daily cross, to the thorough mortification of the old man with his deeds, do and shall know a resurrection out of a state of sin and spiritual death and darkness into a state of holiness, spiritual life, and light.[334] And this is the state that our Lord testified of, saying, verily, verily, I say unto you, he that heareth my word and believeth on him that sent me hath everlasting life and shall not come into condemnation but is passed from death unto life again. He said verily, verily I say unto you, the hour is coming and now is when the dead shall hear the voice of the Son of God, and they that hear shall live.[335]

Observe: (now is) was then the present time, and now is, is the time present always, but the work of God is still going on, and so is to come until the total separation be made. For (saith Jesus) as the Father hath life in himself, so he hath given to the Son to have life in himself and hath given him authority to execute judgment also because he is the Son of man.[336] And then our Lord declares concerning the general resurrection, saying, marvel not at this, for the hour cometh in which all that are in the graves shall hear his voice and shall come forth: they that have done good, unto the resurrection of life; and they that have done evil, unto the resurrection of damnation.[337] O dismal sentence. Oh, fly from the wrath to come by dying to sin while here, and hasten to give up all for Christ's sake, and he will give thee a part in the first resurrection, and then thou wilt partake of the blessing next mentioned.

20:6. And I believe after that thousand years are expired, they shall live with God, for ever and ever, for the second death shall have no power over them.

20:7–8. By this we may understand that the natural generation of mankind will be in the world this thousand years' time of peace and quiet, wherein those that serve God meet with no molestation from Gog and Magog, which

334. See Mark 10:21; Romans 6:6.

335. John 5:24–25.

336. John 5:26–27.

337. John 5:28–29.

name seems to signify such as did not concern themselves about heavenly affairs, the name being derived from the fathers of the Gentiles.[338] The prophet [Ezekiel] speaks of Gog's army and God's judgments against him and the feast of the fowls, etc.[339] I admire the harmony that I find there is between the Old Testament and the New, etc. It is a comfort to my mind in the observing of it. It is to be observed that those people which are here called Gog and Magog did let the Saints alone in their devotions and services that God Almighty exercised them in by his Holy Spirit, until Satan was loosed out of his prison. Then he went forth after his wonted manner to deceive the nations and to stir up strife and seditions among the people, to gather them to battle against the peaceable people of God, for the devil always envies their happiness.

20:9. This is the last destruction of mankind in this life that we have any account of, and God Almighty hath so manifestly revealed his will and determination concerning this low world and the worldly men that have their portion in this life that the apostle Peter concludes that people that are ignorant of it are willingly ignorant: for this they are willingly ignorant of, that by the word of God the heavens were of old, and the earth standing out of the water and in the water, whereby the world that then was, being overflowed with water, perished. But the heavens and the earth which are now, by the same word are kept in store, reserved unto fire against the day of judgment and perdition of ungodly men.[340] If the apostle then counted people were willingly ignorant of the will and pleasure of the Almighty, well may it be counted so now, for the true interpreter, i.e. the Holy Spirit, doth interpret the parables and mystical sayings that were formerly delivered by the impulse or movings of the same Spirit. And it is the good will of God, our Father, that it should be so; that so, as many as will believe may turn to him and be saved, and those that will not believe shall be left without excuse. For now the sealed book is opened, and the visions are written upon the tables of hearts and made plain, that he may run that readeth it. Oh! Glorious dispensation of divine light and love. Oh! My soul, prize it, and value it above all the world, and walk thou humbly with thy God, who is the dispenser of it.

338. See Genesis 10:2, 5.

339. See Ezekiel 38–39.

340. 2 Peter 3:5–7.

20:10. This deluding of Gog and Magog was, or will be, the devil's last enterprise. For then the time of his torment cometh, even when a total separation is made. For he is a busy spirit and delights to deceive and do hurt to the children of men, and it is his torment to be bound in chains and shut up in the bottomless pit of horrible darkness and desperate despair, he being once an angel of light. And he fell by pride and self seeking, self-exaltation, etc., and so was cast out of the love of God and bound under his wrath, which is compared to a stream of brimstone, and our Lord called it everlasting fire prepared for the devil and his angels. And the souls of men are and will be angels in eternity.[341] For those that are joined to the Lord are one spirit, and so, on the contrary, those that serve the evil spirit are one with him and will be with him in eternity, forever and ever, in wo and misery.

20:11. This is a mysterious and great work of God Almighty. The beginning of it is witnessed in the bosoms of all that knows the Almighty, by the judgments that he executeth upon the old earthly Adam and upon the old mirth and carnal delights which have been as a state of happiness unto them. And such believe with the apostle Peter that (this great day) of the Lord will come as a thief in the night, etc., upon all that are not prepared to meet the Lord in the way of his judgments, that hath not brought their sins to judgment while here.[342]

20:12. These books are the books of conscience, and he that opens them is God's Witness that brings all things to remembrance. And if the Lamb of God hath not been received, who takes away the sin by washing the soul in his own blood, then the creature stands guilty before this great and just judge. This book of life is likewise within: it is the spirit that bears witness within the soul that its sins are washed away by the baptism of Jesus Christ. And after they have received Christ Jesus to be their leader, example, and lawgiver, they have been such as our Lord pronounced blessed in his Sermon on the Mount.[343] And so their meek, merciful [lives] have found acceptance, and their names are written in the book of life, having the light and life within them.

341. See Revelation 1:20, 22:8.

342. See 2 Peter 3:10.

343. See Matthew 5–7.

20:13. This is the general resurrection and last judgment which our Lord and Savior foretold of, to the end—that, a very plain and agreeable testimony to this in the Revelation. There he giveth them the reason why he saith, come ye blessed, and go ye cursed.[344] It is worthy of consideration.

20:14. The first death to them that die in sin is the death of the body, and eternal punishment is called the second death. And to set forth the horror of it, it is called a lake of fire.

20:15. Oh, dreadful: why should any be unwilling to part with all for eternal life? In the second and third chapters of this book there is set down the Lord's call to the churches, as also to him that hath an ear to hear what the Spirit saith to the churches. And those that answer the heavenly call and divine requirings in simplicity, love, and faithfulness and abide constant in their spiritual warfare to the end, the Lord Jesus will so help them and strengthen them that they shall know an overcoming of all their enemies at last. And to such an one he hath promised, saying, and I will write upon him the name of my God and the name of the city of my God, which is New Jerusalem, with many other gracious promises, which are all yea and amen to the faithful. Glory to God forevermore.[345]

CHAPTER 21

21:1. That the old heavens and the old earth (literally understood) will pass away or be dissolved and that a new heaven and a new earth will be constituted in the place thereof, wherein dwells righteousness, I believe will be in the Lord's due and appointed time because it stands agreeable with his holy will and divine nature to put an end to sin and to finish transgression in an universal as well as in a particular manner; and that there shall be no more sea, with its unstable and dividing waves. But my chief concern is to witness this great work of God carried on to the perfection of it within, that is, to know my heart made new, and a new spirit to dwell within it, that by the help thereof my soul may walk humbly with God and keep within the line of judgment and righteousness, that it may be fitted to dwell with God Almighty,

344. See Matthew 25:32–41.

345. See Revelation 3:12.

and his holy Lamb, and with all the holy angels and saints forevermore. The Lord hath promised by the prophets that he would make new heavens and a new earth and that the former should not come into remembrance.[346] But be you glad (said the Lord) and rejoice forever in that which I create, etc.[347] These are precious promises, which the faithful soul has an evidence of the truth of them while here.

21:2. Thus we may observe that the new creation is the inheritance of the saints, who are espoused to Christ Jesus in a perpetual covenant never to be disannulled. For he is the only begotten Son of God, the Prince of Life and heir of all things, and all souls that are espoused to him in the covenant of divine love and life are joint heirs with him. These are great mercies; the meditation of these things bows my spirit in great reverence before the Almighty and makes me say, what is man that thou art so mindful of him?[348] And oh, that we may walk worthy of such inexpressible love and favor of the Almighty.

21:3. A tabernacle is a tent to dwell in. Moses pitched a tabernacle in the wilderness, where the Lord met with Moses and instructed him in things appertaining to that dispensation, but this is the tabernacle which God hath pitched and not man, of which the other was a figure. And this tabernacle is the holy place or sanctuary that God hath cleansed and sanctified by the washing of regeneration, in and by the word of life, and made fit for himself to dwell in. And it is in the bosom of every saint, and those are saints whom the Lord hath sanctified and they have the witness in themselves. For God hath not left his [saints] without a witness: that shows how the case stands between God and the soul.

21:4. Oh! Gracious promises—and they are revealed for the encouragement of poor travelers that go weeping and seeking the way to Zion, with their faces turned thitherward. Oh! What could the Lord have done more for the children of men that he hath not done?

21:5. What confirmation more can be desired?

346. See Isaiah 65:17, 66:22.

347. Isaiah 65:18.

348. Psalm 8:4.

21:6. Oh! The free good will of our Heavenly Father—how freely it is offered to mankind. O my soul, let no black ingratitude be in thee, to cause thee to murmur at any trial thou may meet with in thy pilgrimage. Seeing thou hast a helper near that in due time, if thou put thy trust in him, will help thee to overcome all thy enemies, live thou in faith, hope, and charity.

21:7–8. Here is faithful, plain dealing, and it is made known in time that the evil may be prevented by a timely repentance and amendment of life. Read Ezekiel 18, and see therein the justice and mercies of God. Meditate on it; there is none need to despair. Have a care of being fearful or distrustful and unbelieving. Pray to God for faith, even that faith that works by divine love, that purifies the heart and giveth the soul victory over its natural corruptions or evil inclinations, which are many. As the apostle likewise maketh mention and then saith: and such were some of you, but ye are washed, but ye are sanctified, but ye are justified in the name of our Lord Jesus Christ and by the spirit of our God.[349] Thus the Lord works in the hearts of all that are given up to him until he maketh all things new. And so it is his own works that praise him forever and will forevermore: but those that will go on in evil, until the body die, they must have their part in the lake, which burneth with fire and brimstone, which is the second death.

21:9–10. First I observe that John was taken up into the spirit when he saw these great visions, and it is the same spirit only that giveth a right understanding of this and all other heavenly mysteries. For Christ Jesus, our Lord, said to Nicodemus, except a man be born again (or from above) he cannot see the kingdom of God.[350] And again it is said, for what man knoweth the things of a man, save the spirit of man that is in him? Even so, the things of God knoweth no man, but the Spirit of God. Now, we have received not the spirit of the world but the spirit which is of God, that we may know the things that are freely given to us of God.[351] Even so it is now, and these things are so freely given to us and revealed for our good, that the Lord calls to him that hath an ear to hear what the Spirit saith to the churches. Secondly I observe that John was carried into a wilderness to see the false church, and he saw her sitting on a scarlet-colored beast, full of names of blasphemy. This is

349. 1 Corinthians 6:11; see also 9–10.

350. John 3:3.

351. 1 Corinthians 2:11–12.

to shew her bewildered state and the blasphemous spirit that dwells in those that are gone from God.

And the scarlet-colored beast denotes the persecuting powers of this world that bore her up, but John saw the true church descending from God out of heaven. This is to show that she is born of God, and so descended or came from God. So this is a spiritual city, a spiritual bride; for, saith our Lord, that which is born of the flesh is flesh, and that which is born of the spirit is spirit. Marvel not that I said unto thee, ye must be born again, etc. And no man hath ascended up to heaven but he that came down from heaven, even the Son of man which is in heaven.[352] By all which it is plainly demonstrated that whosoever is born of God is descended from him, as he is [their] spiritual father and liveth in him and by him, abiding in his heavenly station Christ Jesus, and so, and not otherwise, is a member of this true church or a polished stone in the heavenly building in this city.

21:11–12. And had a wall great and high—great and high indeed is the wall of New Jerusalem, for it is the power of God and the salvation of God, it being the day of perfect deliverance from all enemies. The promise is fulfilled that was made to Israel of old, on the like occasion. In that day shall this song be sung in the land of Judah: we have a strong city; salvation will God appoint for walls and bulwarks. Open ye the gates, that the righteous nation, which keepeth the truth may enter in. Thou (O Lord) wilt keep him in perfect peace whose mind is stayed on thee because he trusteth in thee. Trust ye in the Lord forever, for in the Lord Jehovah is everlasting strength.[353]

21:13. These twelve gates represent the twelve tribes of the children of Israel, as appears by their names being written on them.

21:14. This new Jerusalem, the city of the great king and the inheritance of all sanctified souls, both Jews and Gentiles. The Gentiles, before the coming of Christ in the flesh, were accounted as a people afar off, but our Lord hath reconciled both unto God in one body by the cross, having slain the enmity thereby, and came (saith the apostle) and preached peace, to you which were afar off and to them that were nigh, for through him we have both an access

352. John 3:6–7, 13.

353. Isaiah 26:1–4.

by one Spirit unto the Father. Now therefore ye are no more strangers and foreigners but fellow citizens with the saints and of the household of God and are built upon the foundation of the apostles and prophets, Jesus Christ himself being the chief cornerstone, in whom all the building, fitly framed together, groweth to an holy temple in the Lord; in whom you also are builded together for an habitation through the Spirit.[354] Here is a description of the living stones that have been squared and polished by the wise master builder in the mountain of God's judgments and righteousness, that they are so fitly framed that no noise of a hammer is heard when they are brought together but do so unite that they grow to be an holy temple in the Lord, yea, an habitation of God, through the Spirit. And God himself is the spirit that fills them and is indeed, all in all. My heart is broken and my spirit is melted by the divine love in a sense of what I write–Oh! That the children of men would come to Jesus Christ; that the spiritual senses may be unlocked; that all may taste and see that the Lord is good, gracious, and glorious in holiness, fearful in praises, doing wonders. And then it would be their joy and delight to serve him, to worship him in his sanctuary while here, and in eternity to praise him forevermore.

21:15. This is the Spirit of God, by which these spiritual buildings are measured, and oh! My soul, keep thou within the line of judgment and righteousness while thou art at home in the body—that thou mayest be squared and polished by the great master builder, who is greater and wiser than Solomon, who had all the stones for his magnificent temple squared or made ready, before they were brought thither; so that there was neither hammer, nor ax, nor any tool of iron heard in that house, while it was in building.[355] Oh! The mystery of thy heavenly building, O Lord; my soul admireth it, for thou art polishing and fitting thy living stones by the operation of thy pure Spirit before they are brought together, for the completing of thy glorious building.

21:16. Oh! Lord, thy wisdom, thy equal and just dealings, are admired by all that loveth thee and are enlightened by thee, who see but a glimpse of thy glory and desire to be fitted to dwell with thee forevermore.

354. Ephesians 2:17–22.

355. 1 Kings 6:7.

21:17–18. Thus the building of the city of God is with that which is most precious, represented to John as precious stones and pure gold, purged from all dross.

21:19–21. This is to set forth the glory and splendor of the city of God, both without and within, where John saw those that had gotten the victory over the beast, and over his image, and over his mark, and over the number of his name—standing on the sea of glass, having the harps of God, singing the song of Moses, the servant of God, and the song of the Lamb, saying, great and marvelous are thy works, O Lord God Almighty; just and true are thy ways, thou king of saints. Who shall not fear thee, O Lord, and glorify thy name? For thou only art holy, for all nations shall come and worship before thee, etc.[356]

21:22. A temple signifieth a place of worship, and the Lord God Almighty and the Lamb are the temple in this holy city. This, indeed, is a great mystery to all that do not know God and are not acquainted with his holy Lamb, but them unto whom the Lamb hath revealed himself, as he is in the Father and the Father in him and he in them, to these the mystery is unfolded, and it is their daily and hourly practice to worship God in his temple, which is his Spirit, and in the meekness and lowly obedience of the spirit of his Son, Jesus. This is the true temple indeed, and all that are gathered into it are true worshipers, as our dear Lord said to the woman of Samaria. But the hour cometh and now is, when the true worshipers shall worship the Father in spirit and in truth; for the Father seeketh such to worship him. God is a spirit, and they that worship him must worship him in spirit and in truth.[357] So this is the temple in the city of God, and her light is of the same nature, even the spirit of God and Christ.

21:23–24. This is a glorious day that the Lord our God hath promised long ago, and the morning of it hath appeared, and the glorious light thereof shineth in the hearts of all true believers, according to the degrees of its arising or exaltation in them, and that is according as people shake themselves from the dust of the earth and loose themselves from the bonds of it. To such it will be said, arise, shine, for thy light is come, and the glory of the Lord is

356. Revelation 15:2–4.

357. John 4:23–24.

risen upon thee. For behold, the darkness shall cover the earth and gross darkness the people, but the Lord shall arise upon thee, and his glory shall be seen upon thee. And the Gentiles shall come to thy light and kings to the brightness of thy rising, etc.[358] This is spoken to the church of God and doth belong to each particular member of it, so that we may say by experience, to the praise and glory of God and joy of our souls, that God, who commanded light to shine out of darkness, hath shined in our hearts to give the light of the knowledge of the glory of God in the face of Jesus Christ. Oh! The divine, heavenly harmony that I find between the testimonies left on record and the goodness of God experienced by following the leadings of the Lamb and living in the light and love of his spirit. And these things are not high notions, nor strained, nor farfetched but are the familiar conversation of a soul that walks in the love and fear of God and hath its inward conversation with Jesus Christ, in and by his spirit. And such are, and will be, the inhabitants of the New Jerusalem, of whom glorious things are spoken and to whom glorious things are promised. For the nation and kingdom that will not serve thee shall perish; yea, those nations shall be utterly wasted.[359]

21:25. This is to show the great love of God to all that are willing to come to him, to walk in his glorious light, being made willing to forsake the evil and cleave to the good spirit, and to bring all their glory and honor, crowns and dignities, and give them up to God Almighty and to the Lamb and esteem the riches of divine love above all things.

21:26. I do not understand that the glories and treasures of this world shall be carried to heaven or go with the soul beyond the grave; but the nations that love the truth above the world shall glorify God with what he hath lent unto them, accounting themselves only stewards of his manifold mercies and esteeming of the heavenly treasure above all the treasures in this world.

21:27. It is not said, whosoever hath wrought abomination or made a lie, etc., but whosoever doth so, and so continue in sin until the dissolution of the body or until the Holy Spirit hath ceased striving with them. But forever blessed be our Heavenly Father, who hath opened a fountain for all souls to wash in, for sin and for uncleanness. This fountain is the gift of God, and it

358. Isaiah 60:1–3.

359. Isaiah 60:12.

is open in all true believers in Jesus Christ, but unbelief shuts it up. But do thou, O my soul, go down into it. Often wash thou in it, as Naaman the Syrian did in Jordan, until thy uncleanness be quite washed away.[360] And as his flesh came again as the flesh of a little child, so thy Savior will renew thee, my soul, and make thee as the spirit of a little child. And yet depart not thou from Jordan, but bathe in it often that thou mayest be kept clean, that so thou may have thy name written in the Lamb's book of life and have free entrance into the holy city. Oh! My God, help thy poor creatures, for without thee we can do nothing.

CHAPTER 22

22:1. Which is one throne, one power, as may be seen where our Lord promised, saying, to him that overcometh will I grant to sit with me in my throne, as I also overcame and am set down with my Father in his throne.[361] This pure river of water of life is the Holy Spirit proceeding from the Father and the Son and in its self is clear as crystal, i.e., before it is sullied with the waters of Euphrates, which must be dried up in each particular soul, that the pure water may spring and run through the conduit pipe in its own native clearness. The prophet Ezekiel had a vision of the holy waters: observe it well.[362]

22:2. This tree of life is the same with the true vine which our Lord spoke of.[363] And it is an admirable tree in consideration of all its virtues: the fruit is for food, the leaves for medicine. The fruit is the same with the bread of life which our Lord spoke of and explained the meaning.[364] The leaves of this tree are not to be fed upon but are for healing of the nations. The leaves I take to be sound doctrine that hath proceeded and do still proceed from the immediate virtue and impulse of this tree of life, which being received and rightly applied hath healed many a sick and wounded soul. Oh! What wonderful kindness and love is here manifested to sick and to hungry souls. The gates of

360. See 2 Kings 5.

361. Revelation 3:21.

362. See Ezekiel 47:1–13.

363. See John 15:1.

364. See John 6:32–63.

this holy, glorious city standing open continually, the king is calling by the messenger of his covenant and by his servants, saying, ho, every one that thirsteth, come ye to the waters. And he that hath no money, come ye, buy and eat. Yea come, buy wine and milk without money and without price.[365] The Lord useth great entreaties and makes great promises to encourage disobedient man to turn to him. And in a sense and consideration of the great mercies and many loving invitations that the Lord hath made use of, to invite mankind to accept of them, hath bowed my spirit very low and drawn my soul to great admiration. Oh what is man indeed, that thou art so mindful of him, O Lord, that thou hast sent thy only Son to ransom poor captive souls and to pay the debt and proclaim liberty to him that is willing to return to thee.[366] Oh my Lord, my God, thou hast melted my spirit in a living sense of thy love and unexpressible kindness. And for all thy kindness thou hast only required our childlike love and obedience to thee, as thou art our Father which art in heaven, and that we should hallow thy great name among men and desire that thy kingdom may come and that thy holy will may be done in earth as it is done in heaven, all which is but our reasonable duty.[367]

22:3–4. This is great encouragement to all to give up the whole heart to God that he may purify it, for it is the pure in heart that our Savior promised this great blessing unto, viz., that they shall see God and his name shall be in their foreheads.[368] The name of God is known by his great power, by his love, by his judgments, and by his mercies. So his servants, he hath put his name in them and upon them, for they bear the heavenly image, having put off the old man inwardly with his deeds, even before the death of the body, and put on Christ Jesus, the true light, and are born of God and are become children of this everlasting day, which our gracious Father is willing to grant unto all souls.

22:5. This is a gracious and glorious promise indeed, and the children of God have a taste of this good word of life and of the powers of the world to come even while here and see with the spiritual eye a glimpse of this glorious light which encourageth them to press forward after a more full enjoyment of

365. Isaiah 55:1.

366. Psalm 8:4.

367. See Matthew 6:9–13.

368. See Matthew 5:8.

it—it being Christ in them, the light of life and the hope of their glory. And to shew the great unity that there is and will forever be in New Jerusalem, we may consider that although there are twelve gates, yet but one street, one river of life, one tree of life, no temple to worship in but the Lord God and the Lamb. These things are strange to carnal reason yet most true, verified by God Almighty and Christ Jesus, his only Son, and by the holy angels.

22:6. The work of the salvation of God is carried on in every age; so is the destruction of the wicked when they have filled up their measure. In this consideration, the things of God are shortly to be done in every particular, in every age of the world. As (for instance), my life shall be shortly finished, and my soul shall be gathered into its proper repository; if it is sanctified and made holy, it shall be holy still. The decree will be sealed unto it, and so on the contrary, so everyone may say within himself, the end of this world will come to me. But sometimes there are more general visitations, as in the time of Noah's flood, the overthrow of Sodom and Gomorrah, and the destruction of Jerusalem of which our Lord foretold and said, this generation shall not pass till all these things are fulfilled.[369] There is good counsel and caution given by our Lord to them that can receive it, but that the day of the general resurrection of the just and unjust, and the final judgment and separation of come ye blessed and go ye cursed will come in due time, I also believe. But I desire all to consider the caution of the apostle Peter: but beloved (said he) be not ignorant of this one thing, that one day is with the Lord as a thousand years, and a thousand years as one day. The Lord is not slack concerning his promise (as some men count slackness) but is long suffering to us-ward, not willing that any should perish but that all should come to repentance.[370] Oh! Gracious God, shall not thy long-suffering be considered, and lead many to repentance?

22:7. He that is willing or desirous to keep the sayings of the prophecies of this book will patiently wait for the coming of his Lord, and in the meanwhile endeavor to be faithful and careful in his station that his Lord hath placed him in, that his Lord may not at his coming find him unprepared.

Help thy poor creatures, my dear Lord and Saviour Jesus Christ. Fill our hearts with thy grace, that at thy coming, if it should be at midnight, we may

369. Matthew 24:34; Luke 21:32.

370. 2 Peter 3:8–9.

be as the wise virgins with our vessels full of heavenly oil, our lamps burning, our light shining—that we may be in readiness to enter in with our dear Lord, our Bridegroom, into the marriage chamber before the door is shut or the sentence sealed against our souls.[371]

22:8–9. Observe, the angel will not be worshiped but declares himself to be of the prophets and of them that keep the sayings of this book, which is a manifest testimony, yea, of an angel of God, that these revelations are manifested and sent forth into the world for the instruction of them that dwell therein and, also, that those that keep the sayings of this book—their souls will be as angels in heaven. This is encouragement to all believers, to persevere in fighting the good fight of faith, hoping and believing that he that hath begun this good work in us will perfect the same, to his own glory and everlasting praise.

22:10. Thus it appears that John was commanded to publish these sayings or visions that were revealed to him. For saith the angel, the time is at hand, yea, the time is at hand in every age of the world, yea, every year, day, and hour, taking things home to particular souls. For some are going off the stage of this world daily and hourly, but the prophecy reacheth to the end of time here, even to the last general judgment, which I take as a great favor of God, that he is pleased to let the children of men know his determinations that so all from age to age may be prepared to meet the Lord before the sentence pass.

22:11–12. Thus the Lord in his love did forewarn and tell of his coming to judgment, that the unjust and unclean may be forewarned of the danger they are in while in that state, that they may repent before it be too late, and the righteous and holy may be made sensible of their reward, that thereby they may be encouraged to continue in well doing until the coming of their Lord, for to deliver them out of all temptations and tribulations and take them to himself.

22:13–15. i.e., that die without repentance and amendment of life. Oh, that the fear of the Lord may be placed in every heart, that all may hear and also consider what the Spirit saith unto the churches.

371. See Matthew 25:1–13.

22:16. Thus I observe that our dear Lord manifested himself to his beloved disciple John (who now had tarried till he came indeed) and manifested himself to him in an eminent manner, both at the beginning and at the finishing of his revelations and now again declares himself to be both the root and offspring of David and the bright and morning star in which he manifesteth his divinity and glorious manhood.[372] Both which are excellent subjects for our meditations, that we may be acquainted with his divine nature and also believe in that power that raised his human body from the dead, by which he became the first in the resurrection. For (saith the apostle), if the dead rise not then is not Christ raised, and if Christ be not raised your faith is in vain, and ye are yet in your sins; then they also which are fallen asleep in Christ are perished. If in this life only we have hope in Christ only, we are of all men most miserable, but now is Christ risen from the dead and become the first fruits of them that slept.[373] And so the apostle proceeds in giving relation how death came, even by man, and how by man came the resurrection from the dead and so declares concerning the orderly proceedings of the divine wisdom and power and saith, the last enemy that shall be destroyed is death.[374] And he says, but some will say, how are the dead raised, and with what body do they come.[375] Then he compareth spiritual things with temporal as to several sorts of seeds that men sow into the earth, and saith, God giveth it a body.[376] Then he speaks of different glories of celestial bodies and bodies terrestrial, as also how the sun, moon, and stars differ in glory and how that one star differs from another in glory. In all which he had a spiritual meaning, even concerning the seed of the kingdom of God and the seed of the evil one, who hath sowed tares in the field of this world. And concerning the resurrection of spiritual bodies, he saith, so also is the resurrection of the dead. It is sown in corruption, it is raised in incorruption; it is sown in dishonour, it is raised in glory; it is sown in weakness, it is raised in power; it is sown a natural body, it is raised a spiritual body, etc.[377] The perusal of these and suchlike spiritual things are a comfort to my soul, and I bless the Lord, my gracious

372. See Revelation 1:11–18.

373. 1 Corinthians 15:16–20.

374. 1 Corinthians 15:26.

375. 1 Corinthians 15:35.

376. 1 Corinthians 15:38.

377. 1 Corinthians 15:42–44.

God, in that he hath made known to mankind so much of his holy will and divine purposes, that all may hear and learn to fear him.

22:17. Here is large invitations indeed. The Spirit saith come: this is an inward call by that teacher that cannot be removed into a corner, sometimes called the reproofs of instruction, which is the way to life. The Spirit and the bride say come: (that is) the Spirit in and by the church do call, the Spirit making use of some members to be as the mouth, to call to others to come taste and see how good the Lord is or how good and reviving the water of life is. And let him that heareth say come: here is a commission, if not a command, to him whose spiritual ear is opened to hear the call of God (so as to obey it), to call to others to come, hear, and obey also. And whosoever will, let him take of the water of life freely: so there is nothing wanting but the will of man. Our gracious God hath offered the water of life freely. Blessed be his name forever more.

22:18–19. Thus it hath pleased God Almighty to set a guard (as it were) upon these revelations, to keep them in their own native plainness, that so none may presume to add to them or take from them by human reason, wit, or letter-learning, but the true interpreters of them is the same Spirit by which they were given forth. And so it is of all the other scriptures, for want of which spirit many wrest the other scriptures to their own destruction.[378]

22:20–21.

AFTERWORD

An inward breathing of a soul to Almighty God, and some communication with him set down in the spring and opening of divine love and in humility.

Oh! Lord, how manifold are thy mercies. I cannot recount them up in order to thee, for thou hast brought my soul through many fiery trials and hast delivered it out of many distresses and snares which the subtle enemy brought it into. And thy word hath been quick and powerful, sharper than any

378. 2 Peter 3:16.

two-edged sword against the man of sin, the transgressing nature, for which in humility I bless and praise thy holy name, O Lord. And my soul do love thy judgments and can say to thy praise, they are just and righteous altogether. By them are thy servants warned, and in keeping them there is great reward. And now, oh! Let thy judgment be the line and righteousness the plumbline that all my thoughts, words, and deeds may be squared or measured by. For thou knowest, O my sweet Lord, that my soul loveth to wait for thee in the ways of thy judgments, that so every thing may be judged down and done away that is displeasing unto thee. For it is thy sweet love and the light of thy countenance that is the sole comfort of my soul, by which thou art daily sweetening my passage through this vale of tears and art supporting my soul by that faith which thou alone hast given, which worketh in and by thy matchless love, which is indeed unexpressible. Yet, O Lord, let me commune with thee reverently, of thy mercies and of thy judgments, for thou knows my soul loveth to draw near to thee and to bow in reverence as at thy feet, in spirit, as Mary did outwardly.[379] And oh! Thy presence is near, can my soul say, for thou art the possessor of heaven and earth! When I look into this world with that inward eye which thou, my Lord God, hast opened, then I see thy providence in thy universal spirit, by which thou upholds, feeds, and manifesteth thy whole creation. And when I retire inward I find thee, O my Beloved, my Bridegroom, sitting in the center of my mind—giving forth thy royal law, which when it is obeyed then thou causest thy glorious light to shine in and upon my poor inward man to its great joy and inward comfort, but oh! I have gone out from thee too much and have left thee, my Lord and Savior, to sit alone, knocking and calling inwardly to my soul to return in and to dwell with thee, oh! The outgoing vanities of this world and the subtlety of thy enemy and my soul's enemy (that would not have thee to reign in my heart) have kept thee too long out of thy throne, O Lord, my sweet, peaceable Savior. And now I am grieved that I ever grieved thee and do promise by thy assistance to give up my heart, will, and affections wholly to thee for the time to come, that so thou may take to thyself thy great power and rule and reign in my bosom; and that my poor, simple soul may be thy loyal subject and thy kingdom may come to me indeed; and that thy holy will may be done in me and by me here on earth as it is done in heaven while I have a being here, that my soul may be made fit to stand on the sea of glass mingled with fire hereafter, with the numberless number of thy redeemed ones. And

379. See Luke 10:38–42.

now oh! My God, my breathing is unto thee, that thou would be pleased to incline the hearts of my children and of all my fellow mortals to love thy glorious light, that all thereby may see themselves to be what indeed we are and to see this world to be what it is (while it is governed by the prince of the power of the air)—even a kingdom of vanity and as chaff before thy holy wind, which bloweth where thou pleasest and when thou pleasest, O Lord.

And oh! That all may consider and remember that thou hast said, Behold I come as a thief. Blessed is he that watcheth and keepeth his garments.[380] Oh! That we may all watch and pray, to the end of our days here, that so we and our children and the succeeding generations may be so purified, by the operation of thy grace in our hearts while here, that we may (by following the meek Lamb of thee, our God, through the many tribulations) at last get perfect victory over the beast and over his image and over the number of his name, that our souls may be made to stand before thy throne and may, by thee, be enabled to sing the new song, even the song of Moses and the song of the Lamb, and say with them that have gotten the victory, Great and marvelous are thy works O Lord God Almighty. Just and true are all thy ways, thou King of saints. Who shall not fear thee?

380. Revelation 16:15.

Personal Writings

A SHORT ACCOUNT OF MY VOYAGE INTO AMERICA WITH MARY ROGERS, MY COMPANION

[This manuscript account of Webb's first transatlantic journey is held by the Manuscripts and Archives Department of the Hagley Museum and Library. It was first transcribed in 1958 by John Riggs, who, with Charles David, prepared an edition of the journal that never circulated in print; this edition has been prepared from the original manuscript and corrects several errors in the Riggs/David transcription. The journal is missing two pages, and several words have been reconstructed where damage has been done to the manuscript. This edition includes the entire narrative account of her journal but omits the log-based entries of her return voyage to England found at the end of the manuscript. It also omits a fragmentary certificate provided by Thomas Chalkley upon her return to England, attesting to Webb's work as an evangelist in North America, because Webb included that letter of support as a preface to her commentary on Revelation, and it can be found in this volume on pages 57–59.—Eds.]

In the year 1697, upon the second day of the ninth month, I left my habitation which was in the city of Gloucester and went down to Bristol, being accompanied with my husband and many other Friends, where we stayed two weeks until the ship was ready to set sail.[1] So on the sixteenth day of the

1. Throughout her diary, Webb numbers the days of the week and months of the year rather than referring to them by their conventional names—Sunday, Monday, July, January, etc.—because of the pagan origins of those names. She numbers the months according to the Roman calendar, which still prevailed in the seventeenth century and stipulated that the New Year began in March; thus, March is Webb's "first" month, October the eighth month, November the ninth, December the tenth, and so on. Her diary begins, then, on November 2, 1697.

same month we went on board, namely: Mary Rogers and I went upon truth's service only; and John Rhoads with his family; and many more families of Friends and others which went in to dwell in Pennsylvania and set sail the same day. . . .

So coming pretty far in [the] northern climate, and it being winter, we met with many very great storms, so that the ship many times was covered with waves. And there were seamen that had used the sea twelve years [but] said they had not seen the like, so that we can witness what David said: they that go down to the sea in ships, that do business in great waters, these see the works of the Lord, and his wonders in the deep. For he commandeth and raiseth the stormy wind which lifteth up the waves thereof. They mount up to the heaven, they go down again to the depths; their soul is melted because of trouble. They reel to and fro, and stagger like a drunken man, and are at their wits' end. Then they cry unto the Lord in their trouble, and he bringeth them out of their distresses. He maketh the storm a calm so that the waves thereof are still. Then are they glad because they be quiet; so he bringeth them to their desired haven.[2] [And] in this time of trial many were in great distresses because death seemed to approach near unto them, and many discouraging words were spoken, as that we [should] be in the bottom of the sea and such like expressions. Then was the Lord pleased to make known his mighty power in the souls of a little remnant that trusted in him, and [he] gave us a strong evidence of his preserving hand and arm of power which was about us, which we [dreamed] of, which caused [us to] sing praises unto him . . .

We came to anchor . . . within the capes of Virginia all in good health, blessed be the name of God . . . for all his mercies. Not . . . his life, save one little child that was born on board the ship, for there were three children born on board that ship in that voyage. We kept meetings twice in the week all the voyage on board, both in good weather and in storms, and the power of God was mightily with us to his own glory and our comfort. So when we got up into Mobjack Bay, soon after we went on shore to one Mark Wheeler's—he was brother to my companion.

And the next first day had a meeting at his house with the people of that place, for there were no Friends there. And the Lord was pleased to reach forth a hand of divine love unto them, and some of them were very tender. And the power of the Lord reached the man of the house and wrought upon

2. Psalm 107:23–30.

him, and he [was] convinced, and he sent a letter after us to desire if the Lord pleased, we might return that way.[3] And said [we] had met with him for his pleading so much against the truth, for we had much discourse with him, and said in his letter that he did verily believe that we were servants of the living God and what we spoke was from a pure conscience, etc. We had another meeting above that at one John Corner's in the dragon swamp, where the people were very sober and had much discourse with that man and found him very high in his notions [but] very little in substance.

From thence we returned to [Mark] Wheeler's, from thence to Milford Haven, where we [hired] a boat and got over the bay and landed at Thomas Brown's in Accomack. There we bought horses for our journey. We had several meetings in that country and good service for the Lord, whose living presences was with us: blessed be his holy name forever. So from that county we traveled and came to Pocomoke in Maryland, to George [Truitt's], where we had a meeting where we were made instrumental to strengthen some in the faith. So we . . . [eastern] shore of Virginia and Maryland . . . meetings all along as we went and were exercised both [in public] and private to exhort to plainness both in speech and apparel, for it was much wanting . . . amongst those professing . . .

So, when we came over Great Choptank, we met with a greater body of Friends, and they were more plain.[4] Yet notwithstanding, we met with great exercises there also, for there were some disorderly spirits amongst them which had cast stumbling blocks in the way of the weak, and they were not taken away, which the Lord gave us a sense of. And so we made inquiry into those matters and were made instrumental in helping to remove these causes, and to lay judgment where it was due, that so the true innocent seed might be set at liberty, for there is a tender seed and a tender people thereabouts.

So we went from thence to Chester River, where we had a precious meeting. And after meeting we went to the house of Henry Hosea, and the man was cast down below his measure, almost into despair, and the enemy troubled him sore, to cause him to fret and think [hardly] of the dealings of the Lord. And on the morrow there came to see us a man that had been lately

3. Friends typically used the term *convinced* rather than *converted,* signaling a mental assent to the doctrine as well as a spiritual and emotional experience of God's saving grace.

4. The Choptank River in Maryland empties into Chesapeake Bay.

convinced, and he was lifted up above the witness. And if we spake to him to bring him down, then the other was ready to be hurt by it. And so on the other hand, if anything was spoken to the comfort of him that was cast down, the other—he would take it to set himself up. So we were in a strait, but he that is the physician of [nature], that knoweth how to apply a suitable remedy to all sorts of distempers, he wrought mightily, by his own power, in deep silence, and bowed down the haughty spirit and brake him into great tenderness and deep humility and comforted and raised up the dejected soul. And all this was done by the mighty power of God that wrought in silence. So after the Lord had laid low the mountain and raised up the valley by his own mighty power in true silence, then could we speak freely one to another of the goodness of the Lord, to his praise and to his glory. Ah, it was a day not to be forgotten by me.

Thence we went to Cecil, where we had a meeting, and thence into the territories of Pennsylvania, on the first day of the second month 1698, and had a meeting at Newcastle which is upon Delaware river, where I felt that a dark power was over the town. And the seed of God was pressed in me until I went away, and could not get clear; at that time, many Friends also did I hear complain of the hardness of that place. From thence we traveled toward Philadelphia and had many meetings all along as we went among several sorts of people, viz: Irish, Welsh, and English. And the Lord was pleased to show his mighty power, which alone pierceth hearts, and cause his word of life to run through the meetings, to the setting of the truth over all tips and shadows, and over all disorderly spirits, to the glory of God and the comfort of his people.

So that on the 16th of the second month we came to Philadelphia and on the morrow had two great and good meetings at Friends' meeting house. The next third day we went to Germantown and had a meeting amongst the Germans. They are, many of them, very tender. After that we traveled on toward West Jersey and had many good meetings along as we went. And on the 24th of the same month, we were at Burlington at Friends' meeting there in those countries. We had great meetings and good service for God, whose power and living presence was with us to his own glory and our great consolation and comfort, with many more. So, when we had passed through West and East Jersey, we, leaving our horses at Shrewsbury, sailed up by water to New York and so to Flushing, on Long Island. And after we had been there about a week, our dear friends Richard Hoskins of Philadelphia and Elizabeth Gamble of Barbados came to us, who were going for New England, so after we had visited this island we went in a sloop to Rhode Island, which is about 200 miles by water, and landed at [Newport].

[Pages 5 and 6 of the original manuscript are missing. Webb and Rogers apparently stayed in Newport and spoke at the Rhode Island yearly meeting before leaving a letter with local Friends, exhorting them to labor diligently in their ministry. After the missing pages, Webb's journal continues with a copy of their letter:—Ed]

be not slack herein, but labor together in the name, power, and wisdom of God. That God over all may be glorified, and your souls with ours may be comforted together in the Lord, is the fervent prayers of your exercised Friends,

Elizabeth Webb
Mary Rogers

Newport on Rhode Island
The 13th of the 4th month 1698

So after this yearly meeting we traveled towards Boston and had a meeting at Seekonk under a tree, whereabouts forty or fifty of the inhabitants of the place came to us, but the priest was angry.[5] Yet, notwithstanding, truth made some entrance upon them, and some of them said that if we would have a meeting there when we returned, we should have one of their houses. We lodged that night at an inn. The next day we went to Boston, where we had two great meetings which were more peaceable than any that had been there a great while before. From thence we traveled to Lynn, where we had a precious meeting. And I felt the showers of God's love so to shed itself abroad over New England, that had I been a man I thought I could have went into all corners of the land to declare of it, for indeed it is the great day of New England's visitation to them that will receive the truth in the love of it, wherein it is freely offered. From Lynn we went to Salem where we had a

5. This priest is presumably Thomas Greenwood—the Congregational minister of Rehoboth, Massachusetts (where the inhabitants of Seekonk and Pawtucket worshipped).

meeting, thence to Salisbury, where we found a great number of new-convinced people. And they were very hungry, and the hand of the Lord was very open to them. Thence we went to Hampton and so to Dover and many other places thereabout.

And all eastward of Salem they were got into garrisons for fear of the Indians which were at war with them. So we went in jeopardy of our lives, to visit them, but the Lord preserved us: blessed be his name forever. At Dover and some other places they were so hardened in sin, by flocking to garrisons and letting their minds out of the fear of God into the fear of men, that I could see nothing but death and destruction hang over them unless they do repent and come to fear the living God and to trust in him, and was made to declare that unless they did repent and turn, etc., their garrisons would not save them. But at Salisbury and Amesbury the people were very tender, but there was not a Friend there to sit down with them to wait upon God. So we exhorted them to sit down together and wait for their heavenly teacher, which is near, which they promised us to do. So we left them, and when we returned to Salem it was with me to write this following letter to them at Salisbury and thereabout.

To Jacob Morel and his wife, with the rest that are convinced of the blessed truth in and about Salisbury

Dear Friends,

I have traveled in the path that you are now entering into, which is the path of the just that is as a burning and as a shining light which (as you keep in it) will shine more and more until the perfect day.[6] In which day you will see that all these things that have been set up in the night of apostasy must be done away, both the old heavens and the old earth wherein unrighteousness dwelleth, and new heavens and a new earth will be created, wherein dwelleth righteousness. And as you come to know old things to be done away by the washing of regeneration in the word of life, you will come to enter into the kingdom of God as a little child, and your cries will be unto the Lord daily and hourly, that you may feel his living, divine presence which is life to your souls. And as you are thus exercised before the Lord in prayers and supplications, you will come to see in the light that you dare not use the double lan-

6. Proverbs 4:18.

guage to please proud man, that you do not use to the Great God in your approaches to him. For the Lord is come to restore unto his people a pure language, yea, and to restore judges as at the first and counselors as at the beginning.

Therefore, I exhort and counsel you as one that have found favor with God, that you meet often together and wait for the counsel of the spirit of truth, which is come to lead the followers of Jesus into all truth. And when you meet together and when you are asunder, be sure you think upon the name of the Lord. For in times past, those that feared the Lord met often together, and the Lord hearkened and heard, and a book of remembrance was written for those that thought upon his name. And they shall be mine, saith the Lord, etc.[7] Oh, dear Friends, dwell low, dwell low in true humility, innocency, and meekness, and the teachings of the Lord you will come to know, which will be to you beyond what I can utter.

But my heart is open in the love of God towards you, and I could write abundance to you concerning the dealings of the Lord by me, but at present shall forbear. But know this, that all the covenants of God, made to me, were made upon condition—that is, as I do keep near to him. For it is not the changing of the name that will serve the turn but oh, the nature of Christianity, the nature of the leaven of the kingdom, which Christ spake of, is that which giveth acceptance with God.[8] Oh, the virtue of it! It is certainly able to leaven soul, body, and spirit into its own heavenly and divine nature, as we keep near to the Lord in it. Ah, pure praises be given unto the living God, that hath made a remnant living witness of it and hath cast our lots under the dispensation of it. And we can say our lot is taken in pleasant places; we have a goodly heritage.

And now dear friends, pray to the Lord in it; wait upon the Lord in it. Speak and act in it, for it is the true light or spirit or grace, which are one, and as it doth manifest the works and words of darkness in you and to you, be sure to take up the cross of Christ against them which is the great power of God unto salvation. And then you will feel that peace which the world cannot give, neither can the world take it away. But on the contrary, if you do not deny yourselves and do not take up your daily cross and follow Jesus Christ, then this light will be your condemnation, for it is the condemnation

7. Malachi 3:17.

8. See Matthew 13:33.

of the world.[9] Into which light you are called, and as you walk in it and bring your deeds unto it, you will be the children of it, and your fellowship will be with the Father and with the Son. And the blood of Jesus Christ will cleanse you from all sin and give you an inheritance amongst them that are sanctified—and that it may be so with you all is the fervent prayers of your true Friend in the blessed truth,

Elizabeth Webb

Salem, the 2nd day of the 5th month, 1698

So after this, we returned to Lynn, where we had another precious meeting. Thence we went to Boston and had a heavenly meeting there. It is the day of Boston's visitation, after her great cruelty to the servants of the Lord. From Boston we went to Scituate and had a meeting there on a first day, and the next third day we had a most heavenly meeting about six miles from Scituate, where several of their church members were, and some of them were much tendered by the sweet streams of life that ran through the meeting that day.

From thence we went to Rhode Island and had several good meetings, and left friends and some others very tender, and entered into a sloop to go to Long Island—and by the way put into Block Island and had a meeting there on a first day, and many people were very tender. The master of the sloop promised to come on shore after us to the meeting by that time the people were gathered, but for lucre's sake he did not come. For there were Indians that did catch fish on the first day and did sell them cheap to him, which he did salt up in barrels and carry to York to get gain. He gave the Indians rum for them and made them drunk; as we came from the meeting we saw them and told him of it. So we arrived at Long Island the 27th day of the 5th month, and the master went down to New York, and soon after he came there, as he was hoisting up, a bag of wool fell down from a door three story high and dashed his brains out against the stones of the street. Our dear Friends Richard Hoskins and John Roadman saw him a little before and also presently after. So he died in his full strength, about middle age; his name was Roger Counter, not a Friend.

We had many precious meetings on Long Island, but one day we had a meeting at Matinecock near Oyster Bay. Here the Ranters came and made a

9. See John 3:19.

disturbance—some singing and ranting, others howling with hideous noises, all in confusion and disorder. The transformation of the devil is such in these Ranters that it cannot be imagined, nor scarcely credited, but by those that have seen it. I was speaking after they had given over ranting once, and they fell at it again. And I stood still a while, and the power of God was over their power, and I was made to testify, that God is a God of order and not of confusion. And truth came over their heads, and we had a good meeting afterward through the goodness of God, blessed be his powerful name forever.

So after we were clear of Long Island, we went to New York, and there got a boat to go down to Shrewsbury, which is in East Jersey, being accompanied with several good Friends, viz. Richard Hoskins, who had traveled through New England with us, and John Roadman and Robert Field, both of Long Island. So after we had a meeting at Shrewsbury we went to Crosswicks. Here our dear Friend and fellow traveler Richard Hoskins left us and went home to Philadelphia. And after we had stayed their first day meeting we went to Burlington, and had a meeting there, and then crossed Delaware River and so into Pennsylvania again and had many good meetings before we came to Philadelphia, where we arrived the 21st day of the 6th month 1698. Here we met with our dear Friend William Ellis. Here we tarried about a week and had many good meetings with Friends and others.

And when we came to Newcastle (where used to be such a cloud of darkness, even darkness which many felt)—so when we came thither again my spirit was more easy, and the Lord opened in me that he would remove the gin and take away the snare, for the day of their visitation was come. And on the morrow, it being the first day of the week, we had a great meeting in the town hall, and the Lord performed his promise. For the love of God and the life of Jesus ran freely through the whole meeting, and the brightness of the glory of God broke through the thick darkness. And I was made to declare to them that it was the day of God's love, and his visitation to them, and exhorted them to prize it. And so left them very tender and went away over the River Delaware to Salem and to Cohansey, and had very good meetings there, and then returned back to New Castle and so traveled upward toward Philadelphia, and had one meeting at Bartholomew Coppock's and another at Hartford amongst the Welsh people, and there went to Philadelphia again, which was our center, or our American home. So after we had tarried their youth's meeting (which was a very glorious meeting) we went up into the country, and Dr. William Ellis with us, and visited some meetings and returned to Philadelphia again. And by this time, Dr. Aaron Atkinson was come, who had been sick in Maryland.

So after the fifth day's meeting was over, we all prepared to go to the yearly meeting, which was then held at Burlington in West Jersey, which began the 18th day of the 7th month 98, and a glorious and precious meeting it was. It was attended with Friends from Virginia, Maryland, Pennsylvania, Long Island, and East and West Jersey. Here it came weightily upon my companion, Mary Rogers, to go to Barbados. So she laid it before a meeting of ministering Friends, and we were sensible that it was of the Lord. And so we are made willing to give up to his holy will and requirings. So after this great and weighty meeting was over, Friends parted in much love and unity. And our dear Friends, William Ellis and Aaron Atkinson, went toward New England, and my companion and I, with many more, came down to Philadelphia. And the next first day we had a great meeting at Concord, and the tendering power of God ran through the meeting and bowed down the souls of many, and raised up the seeds of life unto dominion, to bless and praise the name of the Lord. So we parted in a good sense of the heart, tendering love and power of the living God, and so on the morrow we went to George's Creek to Edward Gibb's, his house, and had a meeting there on the third day.

And on the fourth day, my companion, with many more Friends, went toward the yearly meeting in Maryland, but I was both sick and lame, for I had traveled hard, beyond the ability of my body. And with heats and colds and wet and dry I had taken a surfeit, and it was fallen into my leg, and it was in my body also. And so I was constrained to tarry behind to recruit. So, when I had tarried here about ten days, my Friends, viz. Thomas Ducet, Margaret Beardsley, Mary Rogers, Elizabeth Lloyd, with several others—they returned from the yearly meeting and came to George's Creek to Edward Gibb's, his house, the place where I had tarried, and abode with [me] one day, and had a good meeting in the evening together with the neighbors. And on the morrow, it being the eighth day of the eighth month, we parted.

And Mary Rogers, with the rest of the Friends, went toward Philadelphia, and I, with Elizabeth Lloyd, who was now to be my companion—we went to George Warner's in Maryland in order to be at Cecil meeting on the first day, which we were.[10] And a precious meeting it was; after meeting

10. Born in England in 1677, Elizabeth Lloyd arrived in colonial North America with her family in 1683. She was the daughter of Thomas Lloyd, a Quaker who served as the president of Pennsylvania's provincial council and the colony's chief executive from 1684 to 1688 and from 1690 to 1693.

we went down to Henry Hosea's, near Chester River, where we had a meeting on the third day of the week and eleventh of the eighth month. And a very precious meeting it was, glory and honor be given to the name of the living God, who never leaves nor forsakes those that put their trust in him. That evening came Thomas Turner, and we had a meeting at Henry Hosea's on the fifth day, where we tarried together until the seventh day.

And then I and my companion Elizabeth Lloyd went down to James Ridley's, and Thomas Turner tarried at Henry Hosea's, his house, waiting to take shipping for England. And after we came to James Ridley's, we tarried there a week because I was not recovered of my lameness and had two great and good meetings at Tuckahoe. And upon the twenty-first of this eighth month our dear Friends Richard Hoskins and Samuel Carpenter came to us. And on the morrow we with many Friends passed over Great Choptank and went about twenty miles to a marriage—and second day returned and lodged at John Pitt's, where we tarried on the third day, where I wrought several letters to Friends in and about Philadelphia. And on the fourth and fifth days we were at a quarterly meeting at Choptank's great meeting house, where the great power of God did overshadow us to his own glory, and the mutual glory and comfort of Friends.

The next first day we had a meeting at the bayside, where abundance of people came, and many of them were very tender, for the Lord reached forth his arm of divine love unto them. On the morrow, being the thirtieth of the month, we went over the great bay and landed at Richard Galloway's. And on the morrow we went to a quarterly meeting at Herring Creek, which held two days, and on the sixth day we had to give a meeting at South River—lodged at Doctor Moore's where we had a great meeting at West River, where the power of the Lord was mightily manifested to his glory and our comfort. After meeting we went back to Dr. Moore's; his wife was not a Friend, yet she desired us to have a meeting in the family, which we had, and the love of God was mightily manifested amongst us.

Second day, [the seventh of the] ninth month, we traveled to Patapsco—had meeting there on third day. Fourth day we traveled about fifty miles through the wilderness; about ten miles of the way there was no path. Came at night to Herring Creek, and on the fifth day we traveled to the clefts of Maryland to a monthly meeting, at Richard John's, his house, which held two days. And the Lord was good to his people and dealt very plainly with them. First day following we had a meeting at Patuxent, where we had abundance of people come, and the Lord was very good to them, in opening the way of life and salvation very plainly to them. Blessed be his holy name forever.

[On the fifteenth day of the month, third day of the week,] we crossed over Patuxent and traveled through the woods and lodged at night a house by the way. [On the sixteenth of the month, fourth day,] we traveled to Potomac and tarried there that night. [On the seventeenth of the month, fifth day,] we crossed Potomac, landed at John Harvey's, and had two meetings at Joshua Hudson's, one on the sixth day and the other on a first day. Here we parted with our dear friends Samuel Carpenter, Richard Johns, and some others and traveled to Rappahannock—tarried all night at Hugh French, his house. On the morrow, it being the twenty-first of the ninth month, we traveled to Mattaponi to George Wilson's, where we had a meeting. Thence we traveled to New Kent, where we had three meetings. Thence we went to visit a sick woman about eight miles from New Kent and had a meeting there and returned to Charles Fleming's, at New Kent.

The second of the ninth month we traveled to Curles [Neck] and lodged at Jane Pleasant's and on the morrow had a meeting at their meeting house. From thence we went to James Howard's where we had a meeting on the first day of the tenth month. Here a great sense of the great work of God came weightily upon me, and I covenanted with the Lord that if he would be pleased to make way for me and give me a suitable companion, I would give up my days in his service. Lord enable me to keep covenant with thee.[11]

From hence we traveled to John Butler's—had a meeting at his house. From thence we went to Merchant's Hope in James River, where we had a meeting and good service for God, whose power and presence do attend his people, which alone fits for every good word and work. From thence we traveled to Walter Bartlett's. On the morrow had a meeting at Robert Lacy's; thence we went to Chuckatuck, where we had two meetings. From thence we went to the Widow Buskin's, where we had a meeting.

After meeting we went to Nathan Newby's, and on the morrow, being the tenth day of the tenth month we traveled into Carolina fifty miles through the wilderness. Came at night to Ann Wilson's, and on the morrow crossed

11. As Webb notes later in the journal, Lloyd was not given to public speaking, and Webb apparently found this reticence on her part trying. Her offer to covenant with God and to serve him more devotedly in exchange for his blessing is fairly typical for persons of faith during this period, whether Quaker or not.

Pequimon's and had a meeting at Francis Tom's, his house.[12] There are a very tender people, and the love of God flowed forth abundantly toward them. From thence we went down to Little River, through the swamps and deep waters, and had a meeting at Henry White's. Thence we went to Pasquotank, where we had a meeting, and on the morrow had another meeting at Henry White's. And from thence we returned to Francis Tom's: had another meeting there, where the power of the Lord was so over the meeting that it was beyond words. Oh, that I, with the rest of his servants, may never forget his great goodness, which is handed forth to them that truly fear his great name. On the morrow we had a meeting at Ann Wilson's—six meetings in Carolina.

On the eighteenth of the tenth month we returned back to Virginia, lodged at Nathan Newby's, and from thence we went to Dorothy Buskin's and thence to Eliza Hollowell's, where we had a meeting. And . . . on the morrow had a meeting at the Widow Buskin's, and on the morrow after went on board the ship, called the *Elizabeth and Mary,* Frederick Johnson being master, to see her and to see what conveniency I might have if I went home in her. On the morrow we had a great meeting at Elizabeth River, it being their Christmas Day, and on that day abundance of people came, and the Lord was pleased to blow his trumpet among them, and the everlasting gospel was livingly sounded in their ears, to the glory of God and the comfort of his people.

Next third day we had a meeting at Isaac Reek's, and on the morrow had a meeting at Chuckatuck. And on the sixth day we had a meeting at Robert Lacy's at Lyons Creek. Next first day, being the first day of the eleventh month 1698, we had a meeting at Pagan Creek; in both this one and the former, God was wonderful in his goodness. And second day passed over James River to Jamestown, where we left our dear Friends R. K. and Samuel Newton, and Elizabeth Lloyd and I hired a man and two horses and went to Edward Thomas, his house, that night, and on the morrow our fellow traveler came to us. Next fifth day we had a meeting at Edward Thomas's, in York River in Virginia. And next first day had a meeting about ten miles from hence, and after meeting went home with Ann Akehurst—had a meeting at her house. Next third day and next sixth day we had a meeting about seven miles from Ann Akehurst. After meeting, went down to Kecoughtan and

12. Although the Pequimon River is no longer identified by that name, it was likely located in or near Chowan County in North Carolina.

lodged at a public home where I took a great cold, which put me into a fever and sore throat and violent headache, which held for a week.

On the [morrow], went to George Walker's, whose son had married George Keith's daughter, where we had a meeting with the world's people, for there are very few there that owns truth.[13] Second day, being the sixteenth of the eleventh month, 98, we tarried here and I wrote many letters to Friends and kin or . . . to send by our friend and fellow traveler Richard Hoskins, who was ready to go home. On the morrow we returned back to Ann Akehurst, and our dear Friend Richard Hoskins brought us eleven or twelve miles on our way and returned to George Walker's, there to wait for a wind to carry him over the bay.

On the morrow, I had a good meeting at Ann Akehurst, having no helper in meetings now but the Lord alone, my innocent companion Elizabeth Lloyd having no public testimony. We tarried about Warwick River and York River until the sixth day of the twelfth month and had many meetings and good service for God. For several about Warwick River were pricked to the heart, and were thoroughly convinced of the blessed truth, and came to sit with those few Friends that there were in their silent meetings, amongst whom was Thomas Cary and Elizabeth Cary, wife of Miles Cary. And Miles was also convinced, but he had many great places among men, which he did speak of leaving, but it is hard to flesh and blood, and so I was doubtful of him.

[On the] seventh of the twelfth month we came from Warwick River and came over James River, and so at night came into the mouth of Nansemond River. It rained all day, and when night came it was very dark, so that the Friends that came with us could not find the creek to go on shore. But at length we espied a light which we counted was in the ships we intended to go in, so they steered towards it and found it so. We went on board, very wet and cold, and stayed there until the moon and tide was up, and then the master, Fredrick Johnson, sent one of his men to pilot up to the shore. We landed about midnight at Elizabeth Holloway's.

On the fifth day we went to the monthly meeting at Chuckatuck. Returned after meeting, it being very cold, wet, and sleety weather. First day we had a meeting in the branch at Thomas Page's—after meeting went to

13. George Keith was a prominent Quaker who held several public offices in the colonies. In the 1690s, he left the Society of Friends and published a tract admonishing Quakers not to buy or sell slaves.

Thomas Jordan's, and on the morrow went to see John Jordan. At night fell a great snow, and on the morrow we returned to Thomas Jordan's, and it did freeze so sharply that the drops of water did freeze as fast as they dropped on us. Fourth day we had a meeting at Daniel Sanburn's. And the wind coming about to the south, by the fifth or sixth day, it was so hot that we did sweat as we rode along the way. And such alterations there are very often, which renders the country very unhealthy toward the south of Virginia and Carolina.

Sixth day we had a meeting at Richard Ratliff's. Next first day we had a meeting at Pagan Creek and third day had a meeting at Lyons Creek, the good presence of God accompanying us to his glory and our comfort. Blessed be his holy name forever. Fourth day we returned to Thomas Jordan's. Fifth day crossed Nansemond to Elizabeth Holloway's. Sixth day had a meeting at Dorothy Buskin's in the southern branch of Nansemond River. First day had a meeting at Elizabeth Holloway's, where we tarried until fourth day, making preparations for our voyage, fourth day being the first day of the first month.

We went to Chuckatuck, where we met with our Friends Roger Gill and Thomas Story, which were newly arrived out of Old England. Sixth day had a meeting at Dorothy Buskins with the aforenamed Friends, where the mighty power of God was made manifest to the honor and exaltation of his great and glorious name, as at other times. . . . We had a meeting at Elizabeth River with [the] world's people, where the love of God was shed abroad in a wonderful manner, to the tendering of many hearts. Oh my soul is overcome in the sense of the shedding abroad of the love of God in America.

Second day we [crossed] over Nansemond and went to John Copeland's, where we met our dear Friends Thomas Chalkley of Old England and Richard Gore of Pennsylvania, which we were glad to see. Had two meetings with them about Nansemond, and on the fifth day we all went up by water to Chuckatuck, to the monthly meeting, which was very large and precious. After meeting we parted with Richard Gore, and Thomas Chalkley returned with us, in order to go for England with us, being now pretty clear of America for the present.

Seventh day, being the eleventh of the first [month], we, taking our leave of Friends, came from John Copeland's down to the ship, which was fallen down near Kecoughtan. Daniel Sanburn and his wife, Richard Ratliff, and his son Richard came down with us and tarried on board with us all night. And on the morrow morning, it being the first day of the week, twelfth of the first month, we sat down together and felt the divine spring of life and love to open and run with love to God and one another, in which our souls and spirits were sweetly refreshed and united to God and one unto another. In which we parted, with fervent prayers to almighty God for the preservation of his people.

We waited near Kecoughtan until the nineteenth day of the first month for a wind, and on the eighteenth day we went on shore to George Walker's and tarried there all night. And on the morrow we intended to have had a meeting there, it being first day. But the wind came up fair, and the master sent for us on board about the tenth hour in the morning. So we sat down together on board the ship, and the Lord was very good to us. We cast anchor that night near the capes of Virginia, and on the morrow, it being the twentieth of the first month, 1699, we left the capes of Virginia and went out to sea, having a gentle gale of wind for that day and the next—sailed about twenty-nine miles. But on the fourth day of the week and twenty-second of the month, the wind began to be a little boisterous, and my two friends John Copeland and Elizabeth Lloyd fell very sick. This day we saw a great whale and sailed about 103 [miles].

SHORT MEMORIAL

A Short Memorial of the Dealings of God with me in the days of my Youth, which I leave behind me for Young people to Consider of and do Advise all to take the Counsel of Solomon: Remember thy Creator in the days of thy Youth, while the evil days come not, nor the years draw Nigh when thou Shalt Say, I have no pleasure in them [forever].[1] No pleasure indeed in Vanity; when a dying hour Draws Nigh, then all below the Sun will appear to be but Vanity.

[The original undated manuscript of Webb's "Short Memorial" is held by Haverford College. Excerpts from this text appeared in *The Friend,* a nineteenth-century Quaker periodical, but it has never before been published in full.—Eds.]

But I believe your tender Father will grant to you a visitation of his divine love, as he did to my soul; for he is no respecter of persons. And the sin of ignorance he winks at, but he calls people betimes unto repentance and draws souls to come to Jesus Christ by His cords of divine love. There is none can come to me (said Jesus) except the Father, which hath sent me, draw him: and I will raise him up at the last day. It is written in the prophets (said he), and they shall be all taught of God. Every man, therefore, that hath heard and learned of the Father cometh to me.[2]

In my childhood I had my education under the Episcopal ministry, which then was called the Church of England, and went to school to a minister of the Church and went to hear him preach on the first days of the week. And I well remember that when I was about ten years of age, some divine notion

1. Ecclesiastes 12:1.

2. John 6:44–45.

began to be in my mind, according to my childish capacity, which the evil spirit warred against. For when I would say my forms of prayer which I was taught, then I should grow drowsy, but if I would give up my mind to think of childish vanities, then I could keep awake well enough, which doubtless was because my mind began to be devoted to God. And I began to think upon my latter end and used to think, if I had been in the days when Christ was on the earth, I would have been one of his followers. And I began to love to read the scriptures and to go to church with my Bible, and when the minister did pray, I well remember my heart would be given up and devoted to the Lord, especially when he did say the Lord's Prayer (so called).

So I continued in the faith which I had received by education until I came to be about fourteen or fifteen years of age, about which time a brighter light shined in my childish understanding. And I took notice that Christ Jesus said to his ministers, freely ye have received, freely give; as also that the Lord promised to teach his people himself; and many such testimonies that are left on record, by which I was convinced that the ministry of the church that I did belong to was not the true ministry.[3] My forms of prayer also did not suit with my condition, unless it were the Lord's Prayer, which I always had a great esteem for. So I went to church still, until a dread fell on me when I was in the worship house, and I thought it was just upon me if it did fall upon my head.

So I, after that, walked alone for some time, and a sweet spirit was in my bosom, and a divine light shined in my understanding, which gave me to see my vanities. Then I remembered the baptismal vows that were made for me in my infancy: how that I should renounce the Devil and all his works, the pomps and vanities of this wicked world, and all the sinful lusts of the flesh and should keep God's holy will and commandments. I thought this, indeed, is the way to be a member of Christ and a child of God and an inheritor of the kingdom of heaven, but oh! I want power to enable me to forsake all these things and to keep God's holy will and commandments. So it was made known to me by the true light that I must walk humbly with, or as before, my maker and take up the daily cross that would crucify the vain delights of the world to me and me to them, for the cross of Christ is the power of God to salvation to all them that believe. Now, although this was hard to my natural temper, which was very airy and vain, yet I was made willing and did bear the daily cross and walk alone for some considerable time.

3. Matthew 10:8.

And the spirit of Christ, the true light which God, the Father of my spirit, had sent into my heart, was then in me a spirit of grace and supplication which made intercession in me and for me with earnest longings and groanings which many times could not be uttered. But one expression that used to run through my mind very often was thus: O Lord, preserve me in thy fear and in thy truth. And I much desired to know the people that were true to God, for I thought Jesus Christ was become the beloved of my soul. And I often cried, O Lord, where dost thou feed thy flocks? Where dost thou cause them to rest at noon? For why should I be as one that turns aside from the flocks of the companions? Oh! The drawing cords of divine love! How did it draw my soul with longings for the fuller enjoyment of the divine knowledge of the true and right way, not seeing my own inabilities to walk therein, having felt no condemnation for the sins of my ignorance. So I thought myself very strong, even able to give up my life for Jesus, my love to him was so strong (at least I thought so). And while my soul abode in this retired frame—bearing the daily cross and walking humbly with my God—I had great peace and divine comfort, insomuch that the enjoyment of the divine love was more to me than my natural food or any outward enjoyment whatsoever.

And in those times of the singleness of my heart and inward retirement with the good spirit, I had manifestations of things that were to come, which I have since seen come to pass. Oh! It is a great privilege to have the eye of the mind single, looking unto Jesus, who is the true light and true interpreter of the testimonies left on record in the scriptures of truth and also the revealer of the mystery of godliness and the mystery of iniquity. And so it was that while I walked alone, praying to God Almighty day and night for the knowledge of his will and that he would be pleased to make known to me the right way, that leadeth to eternal life and salvation—for that was it alone which my soul wanted—I was convinced that the principles which the Quakers hold was the truth and their ministry was the true ministry.

But my habitation at that time was not near to any of their meetings, but it had so happened that when I was about 12 years of age I had gone with my mother (who went only when she was Invited) to two or three of their meetings. And the doctrine of one of their ministers proved (as the wise man terms it) as bread cast upon the waters, which was found by me many days after.[4] For the sound of the voice seemed to be in my mind when I was alone,

4. Ecclesiastes 11:1.

and some of the words came fresh into my remembrance, and both the voice and the words suited with the sweet spirit which then had the exercise of my mind. I also met with a little book of theirs, which I read, and I thought the doctrine therein contained suited with the doctrine of the apostles. So I was convinced but had no acquaintance with any of said people so could not have the privilege of any instrumental assistance, for I did not find freedom to open my condition to any of my acquaintance but got alone as much as I could with my Bible. For I thought I had a better sense or understanding of what I read in a way of quiet perusal than I had when I did read aloud in the family, and I can never forget the sweet visits of the holy spirit to my soul many time when I was alone. Oh! It loves a single soul, and this divine love is exceeding sweet, clean, and pure. My soul tasted of it in these, my young and tender years, even to a rapture several times.

But oh! My poor, simple soul dwelt in a weak vessel and had a subtle adversary near it and many of his instruments not far off, who used to scoff at my silent behavior. And some of my relations counted I should grow melancholy or go into a consumption, so they did their endeavor to divert me and they, with my own reasoning, prevailed—to my unexpressible sorrow afterward. For reasonings came into my mind after this manner: that I was young in years and that I might take a little more delight in the world; it was time enough to live such a strict and sober life; I might serve God when I was older; and such like reasonings with flesh and blood that do not love to bear the daily cross. So I let go my inward exercise of watching and left off retirement and let my love go outward, to worldly things, and vanity sprung up again in my mind. And the divine, meek, sweet, loving spirit withdrew, and I could not find it again when I pleased, although I did seek for it sometimes, for I could have been pleased with the sweet comforts of its love, though I did not like to bear the daily cross.

And because I was convinced that it was the Quakers' principles, and I did believe that they enjoyed the sweetness of divine love at their meetings, therefore I sometimes went a great way to a meeting, to seek for divine refreshment there. But to no purpose, for my soul was become dry and quite barren as to any heart meltings which I had felt before, when I used to walk humbly with my Lord, Jesus Christ, whose meek spirit and divine love had been as precious ointment poured into my heart while I dwelt within, with him. Oh! But now he had withdrawn himself and was gone, and my soul remembered his sweet savor, wanted to enjoy it again, but could not find it neither at home nor abroad. Oh! The remembrance of those times of darkness, dryness, doubtings, and confusions causeth me to admire at the goodness of the Lord in preserving from Despair. For so it was, that if I had mirth one day, I had sorrow on the morrow, and in such a bewildered, dry, barren state of mind I remained about three years. Oh! Unexpressible sordid, which was then and afterward, as I may relate something of.

So, when I was about nineteen years of age, it pleased the all-wise God to send his quickening spirit again into my heart. And his light shined into my mind, and all my transgressions were set in order before me, and I was made deeply sensible of my undone estate without the great mercy of my offended Father and my grieved, lamb-like Redeemer. Oh! Then I mourned over him whom I had pierced. Then I cried, Wo is me! I have slain the babe of grace; I have crucified the Lord of life unto myself afresh. Although I had not put him to open shame—for I had been preserved in moral honesty in all respects, so that my acquaintance counted me a very honest, blameless girl, and I could be trusted with anything, even with untold gold (as they used to say)—but the searcher of hearts found me so guilty that I doubted there was no mercy for me. And the testimony of our Lord Jesus I found to be very true, viz. except your righteousness exceed the righteousness of the scribes and Pharisees, ye shall in no wise enter into the kingdom of heaven.

But after many days and nights of great sorrow and anguish of soul (such as cannot be expressed by me), having no creature to make my moan unto, it came into my mind to lie down at the gate of mercy and give up my soul into the hand of God. And I said, Oh! Lord, if I perish, it shall be at the gate of thy mercy, for if thou cast me into hell I cannot help myself. I will give up to thee; do thy pleasure by me. Thy judgements are just and righteous altogether, for I have slighted thy sweet love [forever]. Thus I made confession of my transgressions unto my God and sank down into the judgements. And in the midst of judgements, the Lord remembered mercy! For he caused his divine love to spring up again in my bosom, by which my heart was broken which before was very hard. And this spring of divine life and sweet compassion: the heavenly water refreshed my dry and barren soul, and my hope was revived, for which I did then and do still magnify the name of my merciful Father and holy Redeemer, whose compassions fail not—they are here every morning. Great is his faithfulness, and he is wise and just in his dealings with the children of men; I am a witness of [it] by many experiences. Glory be given to the name of the Lord my God and to the Lamb forevermore.

But I soon entered into the wilderness again, for thus it was: I went to live with the people called Quakers and frequented meetings and felt divine refreshments in my soul, which was given of God in order to strengthen it in bearing the daily cross. But the natural part took hold of the joy, and (as it is usual with the old man if he is not kept under the cross) so he turned the grace of God into vanity and elevation of mind. And I thought, surely, now all is well: I am taken into the favor of God and am now walking among his people. So, I thought all the hard exercises were over and was much elevated in my mind but kept it all to myself, and it was well I did, for I saw afterward that this was the way by which the Ranters went out.[5] So after this joy abated I went to retire, to seek some solid comfort, but my soul's Comforter had withdrawn himself and was gone, and I was left in a vast, howling wilderness where I was miserably buffeted by Satan, who brought darkness into my mind and deprived me of all my faith and brought in such reasonings into my mind to cause me to believe nothing but what I could see with the eyes of reason. So I questioned the truth of all things that are left on record in holy writ because I could not see by the eye of reason how Jesus Christ should be the Son of God. At least he prevailed so far that I was like to sit down in the Jews' opinion of Christ. Oh! The prince of the power of darkness is an horrible companion for a human soul. Oh! The horror of darkness that my soul felt, especially in the nights, when many times I thought the evil spirits were about me, and I sometimes questioned whether I should live to see the light of the morning. Yet, I found no freedom to speak of those great troubles to any but the Lord alone, to whom I cried day and night for faith and for deliverance, but not one tear that could fall from mine eyes—my heart was like a fiery oven.

Oh! The days of sorrow and nights of anguish that my soul went through none can be sensible of it but those that have gone through the like, and it was the Lord's great mercy that I had not been lost forever. But there was a little hope in the bottom or center of my mind that caused me to hope that I should be brought through these hard exercises sometime or other, and this little glimmering of light and hope was as an anchor to my soul. So after I had undergone these sort of inward exercises about three months, it pleased my gracious God one day, when I was alone, to cause his divine light to shine in my understanding in a more than common degree of it. And his divine love sprang up in my heart, and the holy spirit of life and light even

5. The Ranters, another nonconforming sect with roots in the English Civil War, were widely criticized for a general lack of moral values. See Christopher Hill, *The World Turned Upside Down: Radical Ideas During the English Revolution* (1972; repr., New York: Penguin, 1991), 184–258.

overshadowed my soul, and all doubtings and reasonings and all the powers of darkness fled before it. And I did believe in the power of God and was made to say, oh! Almighty God, thou that madest the world by thy word art able by the same word of power to take upon thee what form thou pleases, and oh! That the Lord should lay hold on our nature in order to unite us to himself! Again the sense of this laid me very low, and this great visitation and the sense of his great condescension to me and to mankind brought me under great obligation to fear and love God Almighty and Jesus Christ, his only Son, above all things in this world.

And so I came to know that the true and saving faith which giveth victory over Satan, it is the gift of God, and it sprung in his divine love which he was pleased to fill my heart with at that time. And ever since I have found by experience that the more I have gave up my heart in love to God Almighty and Jesus Christ, his only Son, my Redeemer (who said without me ye can do nothing), the stronger my faith hath been in him. For since those early or youthful days I have met with great trials and exercises and have found by experience that God Almighty requires the whole heart, will, and affections, that the spirit of his Son, Jesus Christ, may have the rule therein until he hath put all his enemies under his feet and his and our Heavenly Father become all in all, which is a great work and is carried on by degrees as the creature is able to bear it. And as the old man dies daily, so the new man is raised up that lives in resignation to the will of God, for as the apostles testified, the natural man receiveth not the things of the Spirit of God for they are foolishness to him, neither can he know them because they are spiritually discerned.[6] So without the spirit of the Lord Jesus we can do nothing that is well pleasing to God; therefore, the work of mortification and regeneration is of absolute necessity to salvation. For, said our Lord to Nicodemus, verily, verily I say unto thee, except a man be born again he cannot see the kingdom of God.[7] So I endeavored more and more to give up into the divine hand that, so, I might be weaned from all vain delights and worldly pleasures, so that sometime I could say, O Lord, my soul is as a weaned child, as a child that is weaned of his mother.

In this single, simple state, my mouth was opened first to pray to God Almighty my Heavenly Father in public and to praise his name for his great mercies and sometimes to exhort others to trust in the Lord and to be

6. 1 Corinthians 2:14.

7. John 3:3.

obedient unto him [forever]. So after I had been publicly concerned for some years at home, it came upon my mind to go into the north of England, and I gave up in obedience to go. And in that (as well as in other journeys) I found my spiritual guide to go with me and to direct my course. And the Lord my gracious God did bear up my spirits and carry me through by his own power and wisdom only and alone. Oh! The remembrance of the goodness of the Lord to my soul in those early days are not to be forgotten by me. And in those times I had many visions of spiritual things when the outward man was asleep, and sometimes it seemed as though I was in great combats with evil spirits, and the good spirit used to give my soul the victory many times when the body was asleep, which used to be comfortable to me when I did awake. And many remarkable occurrences I met with in that journey of diverse kinds, in the remembrance of which I bless the name of my God at this time and have cause so to do forevermore.

And when I came to the far end of my journey, then I dreamed that I saw Jesus Christ and a Friend that I knew, walking together before me in a very pleasant green walk. And I quickened my pace and came up between them, and I thought that it pleased the Lord to take notice of me and to show great kindness to me, which was a great comfort to my soul, although it was in a dream. And he appeared as a plain man of middle stature, of a sweet, amiable, innocent countenance and kind behavior, such as my soul could both love and reverence. So on the morrow I met with that Friend and saw the fulfilling of that vision with the eye of my mind, for the Lord was very gracious to my soul, forever blessed be his holy name. And I found by many experiences that in those days I had certain manifestations of things in dreams, by which many times I was forewarned of things that I saw come to pass.

I traveled alone that time in great care to please God and in great humility and simplicity. And it was a good time to me, and I set it down as a memorial of the goodness of God to a poor young creature of the weaker sex. Oh! I can say, it is good to trust in the Lord and to give up in simplicity to his requirings. And this I can say by experience, that the more simple or childlike my soul have been and free from care of pleasing or fear of displeasing man, even wholly resigned up into the hand and will of God, the more it hath been fitted and furnished by the Lord alone and laid hold on as his instrument. But on the contrary, when I have been in care to please or in fear of displeasing man, the gift of God—which in its simplicity or singleness ariseth from the spring of eternal life—it hath been muddied with a mixture of carnal reason, and then poor work is made. So I exhort you, my surviving Friends, to live in pure obedience and perfect resignation to the divine will in all its requirings, for herein is our peace.

And in the year 1697, in the sixth month, as I was sitting in a meeting in Gloucester (the place of my habitation), my mind was gathered into perfect stillness for some little time, and my spirit was as if it had been carried away into America. And my heart was (as it were) melted with the love of God, and it flowed and seemed to reach over the great ocean. And I was constrained to kneel down and pray to the Lord for the prosperity of his seed in America, and that concern never went out of my mind day nor night until I went in the Love of God to travel there. So universal is the divine love that it reacheth over sea & land (and my soul can say thy commandments, O Lord, are exceeding broad). But when I did look at this thing with an eye of reason it seemed very strange to me, for I knew not the country, neither any creature that dwelt there, and I reasoned much concerning my own inabilities, and what people would say if I should leave my husband and family, and many such things. But when I did let such reasonings take place I had nothing but darkness and trouble and could not feel the divine spring, no, not in a meeting, until I gave up.

And as soon as I did resign my will to the divine will and requirings in this thing, then the light and life of truth would spring up in my bosom, by which I knew that it was the requirings of the only true God. But I was so timorous and fearful and stood in the reasoning part so long until these words did run through my mind with authority, viz. the fearful and unbelieving shall have their portion with the hypocrites in the lake that burns with fire and brimstone, which is the second death. This brought a dread on my mind; then I told my husband of my concern and how close it was laid upon me. So after some time of consideration he gave consent that I should go.

But a little while after, I was taken with a violent fever which brought me so weak that most that saw me thought I should not recover. But I thought my day's work was not done, and my chief concern in the time of the sickness was about going to America. But some were troubled because I had made it so public, because they thought I should die and then people would speak reproachfully of me and my profession. And they said if I did recover, the ship would sail before I should be fit to go on board, but I thought if they would but carry me and lay me down in the ship, I should do well enough. And the Lord was very gracious to my soul in the time of my sickness, for he promised that his presence should go with me.

So, at last, all the difficulties passed over, and I went from Bristol in the ninth month 1697 with my companion, Mary Rogers. The dangers we were in at sea, and the faith and courage which the Lord gave to my soul, would be too large here to relate, but this I may say by way of encouragement to faithfulness: that I had an evidence of the preserving arm of the Lord to be present, that faith was given me in the midst of great dangers. Oh! It is good to trust in the Lord and to be obedient to him, for obedience is indeed better than sacrifice.[8]

It was about the middle of the 12th month that we, through the good providence of God, arrived at Virginia. The many remarkable occurrences that happened in that journey would be too large to enumerate, but one I may mention in order to manifest the universal love of God to mankind and his great condescension in satisfying my inquiring mind, which was thus: as I traveled along in Virginia from one meeting to another, I saw great numbers of black people that were in slavery, and it was then strange to me, and I wanted to know if the visitation of the grace of God were afforded to them or not. And I several times went in unto their little outhouses (called Negro quarters) to see if I could discern any good in them by their deportment, but I could not see by that way. So when I had traveled along about four weeks, as I was in bed one morning, in a Friend's house, even after the sun was up and did shine into the room, I fell into a slumber. And I dreamed that I was a servant in a Great House and was drawing water at a well to wash the upper rooms of the house, and I heard a voice which bid me go and call others to help me to draw water. And I thought that I went presently but as I was going along in the way, in a very pleasant meadow, a great light shined round about me which exceeded the light of the sun. And I walked in the midst of it, and as I went forward I saw a chariot drawn by horses coming to meet me. And I was in care lest the light that shone about me should frighten the horses and cause them to throw down the people, but when I came near to them, I knew they were the servants that I was sent to call. And they were both white and black people, and I said to them, why have ye stayed so long? And I thought they said, the buckets were frozen; we could come no sooner.

So, by this vision, I was satisfied that the call of God was to the black people as well as to the white. And I saw the fulfilling of the vision in part before I returned to Old England, for we had an evening meeting at a Friend's house in New England and the Negros came in, and I felt a stream of divine

8. See 1 Samuel 15:22.

love run to them. And one young man, a black, was so reached to by the love of God through Jesus Christ that his heart was so broken that the tears did run down like rain. And he was convinced of the truth and lived honestly in it and walked among Friends to his dying day and left a good savor behind him, and his wife and children kept to meetings when he was gone. These things have lived on my mind, to set them down as a memorial of the great and universal love of God, who would not that any should perish, but that all should come to the knowledge of the truth and be saved.

But the question—that put forth by Isaiah the prophet—hath often come into my mind with the answer thereto annexed, which is worthy of consideration: Whom shall he teach knowledge, and whom shall he make to understand doctrine? Answer: them that are weaned from the milk and drawn from the breasts, or hath been. For precept must be upon precept, line upon line, here a little and there a little. For with stammering lips and another tongue will he speak to this people, to whom he said, this is the rest wherewith ye may cause the weary to rest, and this is the refreshing. Yet they would not, (but mark, them that would not, what it was to them); the word of the Lord was to them line upon line, precept upon precept, that they might go and fall backward and be broken and snared and taken.[9] These things are left on record for instruction, and God Almighty and his living word is the same yesterday, today, and forever.[10] Praise ye the Lord, all ye that are obedient to his divine word, for though Almighty, God is our God forever. He will be the guide of all his obedient ones, even unto death, and will redeem their souls from the power of the grave and will receive them into his mercy where they shall praise him forevermore, world without end. Amen.

Bless the Lord, O my soul, and forget not all his benefits who forgiveth all thine iniquities, who healeth all thy diseases. And, O Lord, my gracious God, grant that the succeeding generations may not be ungrateful unto thee, that none may be like the nine lepers that were cleansed by Jesus Christ, our Lord, and did not return to give glory to thy name.[11] But Oh! That all may in great humility and reverence return unto thee thanks and praise for every benefit and mercy they do daily and hourly receive. For surely thou art the giver of every good and perfect gift and art worthy of praise forever and forevermore. Amen.

9. Isaiah 28:9–13.

10. Hebrews 13:8.

11. See Luke 17:12–19.

And my dear children and young people, I exhort you to give up your hearts to the Lord, for that is what he requires. And as you do so and answer the requirings of God, the father of your spirits, then you will know the work of regeneration to be carried on gradually by Jesus Christ, who is spiritually present with the soul at all times—even in the deepest of its exercises, leading it gently on in the way of the daily cross and causing it to rest in the will of God, whose will is the sanctification of his people. And in due time, as the soul is obedient to his holy will and requirings, he will make the mind and understanding that was like a barren wilderness to become as a fruitful field, according to his promise by the prophet Isaiah. And I, with many more, have found by experience that all the promises of God are faithful and true, for the days are come there spoken of, viz. the spirit is poured upon us from on high, and judgment shall dwell in the wilderness and righteousness remain in the fruitful field. And the work of righteousness shall be peace, and the effect of righteousness quietness and assurance forever. And my people (said the Lord) shall dwell in a peaceable habitation and in sure dwellings and in quiet resting places: when it shall hail, coming down on the forest. And the city shall be in a low place. Blessed are ye that sow beside all waters, that send forth thither the feet of the ox and the ass.[12]

All these sayings are to be spiritually understood. The Jews formerly were accounted as a fruitful field until they departed from the Lord; then the primitive Christians, until they apostatized and became a Babel. Then the Mystery Babylon was seen in the wilderness upon a scarlet colored beast, and now judgement is gone forth against that wilderness and shall dwell therein, for those that worship that beast or his image have no rest day nor night [forever].[13] These things are and will be without, in the great world, but let me come nearer and desire to know the judgments of God to dwell in my heart, that hath been as a wilderness, that it may for the future be a fruitful field unto God, my maker, and unto Jesus Christ, my Redeemer. And that his righteousness may remain therein, let every one be thus exercised, and such will feel the effects of this righteousness to be quietness and assurance forever, and their situation or habitation inwardly will be in a low place, and that is near the spiritual waters. These things are neither whimsies nor fictions but are verity and truth, as the resigned souls do witness from day to day. Glory

12. See Isaiah 32:15–20.

13. See Revelation 14.

to God forevermore, who have given to us his spirit, which is the true interpreter of the scriptures of truth.

And, my dear children and friends, I having a concern in my mind in the tender love and goodwill to your souls, I leave these lines by way of counsel for you to peruse and consider of when I am gone. And I advise that you pass time of your sojourning here in fear, knowing and often thinking that you are but as pilgrims and sojourners here on earth and that you have (each of you) an immortal part that must remain forever, the salvation of which cometh from the Lord alone, who hath called (and is calling) to all, saying look unto me, all ye ends of the earth, and be ye saved; and also testifies, saying as I live, saith the Lord, I would not the death of him that dies but that all should return, repent, and live. Turn ye, why will ye die?[14] Oh how gracious and merciful is the Lord who is the father of our spirits. Acquaint yourselves with him, my dear children. Love him and fear to offend him, and you will feel the spring of his love and mercies in yourselves as I have felt it many times, to the melting of my spirit and humbling of my soul, for which I have cause to speak well of his name and praise him forever and ever more and to say with the psalmist: bless the Lord, O my soul, and all that is within me, bless his holy name. Bless the Lord, O my soul, and forget not all his benefits: who forgiveth all thine iniquities, who healeth all thy diseases, who redeemeth thy life from destruction, who crowneth thee with loving kindness and tender mercies [forever].[15] The Lord is merciful and gracious, slow to anger and plenteous in mercy. He will not always chide, neither will he keep his anger forever. He hath not dealt with us after our sins nor rewarded us accord to our iniquities, for as the heaven is high above the earth, so great is his mercy toward them that fear him [forever]. Like as a father pitieth his children, so the Lord pitieth them that fear him, for he knoweth our frame, he remembereth that we are dust. As for man, his days are as grass; as a flower of the field, so he flourisheth. For the wind passeth over it, and it is gone, and the place thereof shall know it no more. But the mercy of the Lord is from everlasting to everlasting upon them that fear him, and his righteousness unto children's children, to such as keep his covenant and to those that remember his commandments, to do them.[16]

14. Isaiah 45:22; Ezekiel 33:11.

15. Psalm 103:1–4.

16. Psalm 103:8–18.

Therefore, my dear children, I exhort you to fear to offend God always, for you will meet with temptations of diverse kinds to seek to draw your love from the Lord Jesus Christ into this vain world and to fill your minds with vain and foolish thoughts or earthly mindedness or wrath [forever]. All which springs from the evil spirit and are contrary to the nature and springing or operations of the Holy Ghost and are very troublesome to all those that desire to love God Almighty and Jesus Christ, his only Son, our Redeemer above all things in this world. And those impositions of Satan, viz. vain and evil thoughts, makes the heavenly lover to cry mightily unto the Lord, saying: O that thou wouldest please to wash my heart from wickedness and worldly mindedness, that so vain thoughts may not lodge within me. And thus the soul groans to be delivered from vanity and is desirous to find acceptance with God, as the prophet Micah was of old, whose concern was to know wherewith he should come before the Lord and bow himself before the high God. Shall I (said he) come before him with burnt offerings, with calves of a year old? Will the Lord be pleased with thousands of rams or with ten thousands of rivers of oil? Shall I give my firstborn for my transgression, the fruit of my body for the sin of my soul? Here was a close examination of his own duty, to which he received answer: He hath showed thee, O man, what is good. And what doth the Lord require of thee but to do justly and to love mercy and to walk humbly with thy God?[17] How it is needful for all mankind to consider this answer well, in all its branches.

For as there is justice due from one man to another, so in especial manner there is a justice due to Almighty God which is too much forgot among mankind, notwithstanding our dear Lord likewise commanded to render to Caesar the things that are Caesar's and unto God the things that are God's.[18] (Oh! The forgetfulness of mankind!) Now we owe our all unto our God, and he hath required our hearts, will, and affections. Then, it is my reasonable duty that I owe to God to render to him all that which he hath reserved for himself and not to give it to the god of this world, who is my soul's enemy, and so rob my best friend and benefactor of his right.[19] (Oh! The folly of mankind!) And to love mercy is a Christian duty which is attended with a great blessing. Thirdly, and walk humbly with thy God: this is an inward walking or spiritual conversing with God, who is a spirit. And he hath sent

17. Micah 6:6–8.

18. Matthew 22:21.

19. 2 Corinthians 4:4.

the spirit of his Son into the hearts of the children of men, and as many as loves this Holy Spirit and keeps low in their minds, it will lead them in the midst of the paths of judgment and cause their souls to inherit substance and will fill their treasures with the riches of heavenly love which is the sure foundation of that faith that worketh by it and the ground of that hope that is an anchor most sure and steadfast.

Oh! My soul can say to the honor of God and for your encouragement who desire to walk with God that here is nothing wanting in those holy (though despised), humble, lowly walks. My soul hath many times been greatly refreshed in this low valley where the soul drinks plentifully of the water of that river, the streams of which make glad the whole heritage of God. Here is also found the tree of life, whose fruit is good for food (for the inward man) and its leaf for medicine. Here is also the sweet lily that toils not, and why? Because it waits patiently for the celestial rain. I have thought many times, surely these were the Enochian walks, when Enoch walked with God in this low world.[20]

Oh! My soul hath found so much sweetness in walking humbly with the Lord my God that I can do no less than leave this call to my succeeding generations and say, come taste and see how good the Lord is to all humble, obedient souls. Oh! Resign your will to the divine will in all things. Follow meek, holy Jesus, and learn of him, and you will find rest for your never dying souls. And let me exhort you, my children, in the words of that kingly prophet David, who said, trust in the Lord and do good; so shalt thou dwell in the land. And verily, thou shalt be fed. Delight thyself also in the Lord, and he shall give thee the desires of thine heart. Commit thy way unto the Lord; trust also in him, and he will bring it to pass. And he shall bring forth thy Righteousness as the light and thy judgment as the noonday. And again, rest in the Lord and wait patiently for him. Fret not thyself because of evil doers who prospereth in his way because of the wicked man who bringeth wicked devices to pass. Cease from anger and forsake wrath; fret not thyself in any wise to do evil, for evil doers shall be cut off, but those that wait upon the Lord shall inherit the earth. For a little while and the wicked shall not be, etc. But the meek shall inherit the earth and shall delight themselves in the abundance of peace.[21] These testimonies, with abundance more that are left on

20. Genesis 5:22. Webb's description of this valley is redolent with the imagery of Revelation and the New Jerusalem; see Revelation 22:1–2.

21. Psalm 37:3–11.

record (for admonition), they are very comfortable and very true, for all the promises of God are yea and amen unto the state and condition of mind unto which they do belong.

Therefore I advise each particular to read the scriptures and search thy heart and make application and meditate on what thou readest, and the true light will manifest thy state and condition to thee if thou wilt deal plainly with thyself and art not willing to hope with the hope of the hypocrite, which shall perish, but consider the testimony of our Lord Jesus Christ to Nicodemus, who came to Jesus by night and made a notable confession to him. But our Lord Jesus dealt very plainly with him, saying, verily, verily I say unto thee, except a man be born again he cannot see the kingdom of God. Nicodemus wondered at that saying and said, how can a man be born when he is old? Can he enter the second time into his mother's womb and [be] born? Jesus answered, verily, verily, I say unto thee except a man be born of water and of the spirit, he cannot enter into the kingdom of God. That which is born of the flesh is flesh, and that which is born of the spirit is spirit. Marvel not that I said unto thee, ye must be born again (or from above, as in the margin). The wind bloweth where it listeth, and thou hearest the sound thereof but canst not tell whence it cometh and whither it goeth: so is everyone that is born of the Spirit.[22] These testimonies are verity and truth, and every soul ought to be concerned to look inward to know whether this babe of grace be formed in it or not.

But may any say, how shall I know whether I am born of the Spirit or not? For answer I say, every newborn babe (that is born alive), as soon as it is born, it breatheth and cries and seeketh for nourishment according to its kind and capacity. I say its kind because that which is born of the flesh or from beneath seeks and hath its nourishment from beneath, even from its mother, this low world. So, that soul that is born from above, it likewise breathes, pants, and cries, hunger and thirsteth after the sincere milk of the word of God. And as that which is born of the spirit is spirit, so it is fed with spiritual food and hath its inward dependence on its spiritual father for a daily supply of spiritual food. And as a natural child grows gradually, both in stature and in understanding, so doth the babe of grace, or new creature. And one all wise never fails of giving the new creature its daily bread and also takes care to nurture it by his law. And if, at any time, it meets with any wound by the enemy (which it meets with for want of watchfulness), then he searcheth it

22. John 3:3–8.

and cleanseth it by his heart-searching word and purifying judgments. And when the creature submits and resigns into his hand and pure will and makes a covenant to walk more carefully and humbly with him. He then pours in of his wine and oil. Oh! How many experiments have my soul had of his fatherly dealings, both in mercy and judgment. Oh! He have laid me under great obligations to serve him and to glorify his holy name forevermore.

And now, my dear children, my [travel/travail] in spirit is that Christ may be [found] in you. Great is the value of your souls, and great is the love of God manifested through Jesus Christ not only without us but also Christ in us, the hope of glory. Great indeed is the mystery of godliness, which is hid from the wise and prudent of this world and is revealed unto babes and to such as fear to offend their Heavenly Father, even to such as do pray with sincere and upright hearts as our Lord taught his disciples. Our Father which art in heaven, hallowed be thy name. Thy kingdom come, thy will be done in earth as it is done in Heaven, which kingdom comes not with observations to say, lo here or lo there, but the kingdom of heaven is within mankind, although a usurper rules in too many hearts.[23] But oh, the cries of that soul that is born from above are very ardent unto the Lord the Almighty God, that he would be pleased to disthrone the usurper and cast him out and spoil his goods and take to himself his great power. And rule thou in my heart, saith the poor soul, for I am weary of this usurper, for he hath kept to this world and to my own corrupt nature too long, and now I am one of those that labor, am weary and heavy laden, and I want rest for my soul. Such souls the Lord hath called and will call, saying come unto me, and I will give you rest. Take my yoke upon you, and learn of me; for I am meek and lowly in heart, and ye shall find rest unto your souls. (O gracious promise!) And farther, for encouragement, says, for my yoke is easy and my burden is light.[24] I have experienced the truth of this testimony, for which I bless the name of the Lord my God, but the yoke of the god of this world I have found to be very heavy.

Now it is good to know and consider what the yoke of Christ was while he was visible among the children of men, seeing he is the Christian's pattern and leader. Well then, we find that he came not to do his own will but to do the will of him that sent him and to fulfill the work he was sent to do.[25] He

23. Matthew 6:9–10; Luke 17:20–21.

24. Matthew 11:28–30.

25. John 5:30.

taught and he practiced, thy will be done in earth as it is done in heaven.[26] Now this I have found by experience, viz. that the will of God is a pure, holy will, and his will is the sanctification of his creature. And it is the reasonable duty of all mankind wholly and fully to resign up their will to the will of God and so to be as obedient children to their father or loyal subjects to their prince. And as many as do so, it quite alters the disposition and frame of their minds. For the will of man in the fallen nature is a perverse will, and the different dispositions that are among mankind makes the contentious Babel. Yea, I have observed some that could not please themselves, so confused a thing is poor man in his unregenerate state. But when the will of the creature is wholly resigned to the will of its maker and the soul, being enlightened by him who is the true light, comes to see its own folly and in some degree hath a glimpse of the glory, the power, and wisdom of God—then it is often saying, let thy will be done in me and by me in all things, O Lord. For thou knowest what is best for me, and I do believe that all things shall work together for good to them that love and fear thee.[27] So the soul resteth in the will of its maker and is at peace. As the psalmist said, acquaint thyself with God and be at peace.[28] And so, as this little child (whose sins are forgiven for the mediator's sake) abides in obedience, the Lord enlargeth his heart by his own love and enableth the soul to run in the way of his commandments with great delight. And so the work of Christ is made easy, and the meek spirit of the Lamb of God takes place in the mind and enables the soul to follow its captain in fully believing that the Lamb and his followers shall have the victory in the latter end. And so the poor soul perseveres every day, praying for daily bread and that its Heavenly Father would forgive its trespasses as the creature forgives those that trespass against him [forever].

And I advise you, my children, to take good notice of the positive testimony of Jesus Christ our Lord in this last case, who says, for if ye forgive men their trespasses, your Heavenly Father will also forgive you. But if ye forgive not men their trespasses, neither will your Father forgive you your trespasses.[29] Oh! When I consider these sayings, with many other sayings of our Lord in that most excellent sermon which he (the best minister that ever stood on the stage of this world) preached on the mountain, my heart is sorrowful to see

26. Matthew 6:10.

27. Romans 8:28.

28. Webb misattributes this quote, which is found in Job 22:21.

29. Matthew 6:14–15.

how little notice is taken of them so as to put them in practice, notwithstanding the conclusion which is on this manner. Therefore, saith our Lord, whosoever heareth these sayings of mine and doth them, I will liken him unto a wise man which built his house upon a rock. And the rain descended, and the floods came, and the winds blew and beat upon that house, and it fell not, for it was founded upon a rock. And everyone that heareth these sayings of mine and doth them not shall be likened unto a foolish man which built his house upon the sand. And the rain descended, and the floods came, and the winds blew and beat upon that house, and it fell, and great was the fall of it—a great fall indeed, to fall into the bottomless pit.[30] Well, what shall poor creatures do? For ourselves we can do nothing, no, the old man can do nothing. He must die daily, for every degree of life and strength which the new man receives is obtained through the degrees of the death of the old man and by resignation to the divine will.

We are only safe in the divine hand, for then the Holy Spirit, even the spirit of the Son of God, worketh in us, for us, and by us, to will and to do according to his good will and heavenly pleasure. And so the work is the Lord's, who said, lo I come. In the volume of the book it is written of me, I delight to do thy will, O God.[31] And so, in some degree, when his spirit rules in a child of God, a little brother of Jesus Christ, it becomes pleasant and delightful to do the will of God, who is a fountain of divine love, light, and life. And as you continue in his love and fear, your hearts will be enlarged, your capacities widened, your understandings enlightened more and more, and the inward man so enlivened that the soul will have cause to say, thy ways, O Lord, are ways of pleasantness, and all thy paths are peace.[32]

And as you read the holy scriptures their spiritual meaning will be opened in you, to you by the same spirit by which they were given forth. For unto this Holy Spirit the scriptures are of no private interpretation, for it is the true key by which souls are opened and by which all mysteries that appertain to life and godliness are revealed. And I can truly say to the praise and glory of God, who hath given such a great gift to mankind, that this spirit of truth is a sweet spirit and is the true Comforter which leads the lovers and followers of it into all truth and is the searcher of hearts and trier of reins and the revealer of the thoughts of the heart and intentions of the mind. And it is a

30. Matthew 7:24–27.

31. Psalm 40:7–8.

32. Proverbs 3:17.

righteous judge and a swift and true witness against every appearance of evil. It is the light or eye of God, which runs to and fro in the earth, beholding every thing as it is. Solomon, he called it the wisdom and said, the fear of the Lord is the beginning of knowledge, but fools despise wisdom and instruction; and advised his son, saying hear the instruction of thy father and forsake not the law of thy mother, for they shall be an ornament of grace unto thy head and chains about thy neck. My son, if sinners entice thee, consent not [forever].[33] See the second and third chapters of the proverbs of Solomon, and lay hold of his counsel, for it is good and very sweet. For wisdom is indeed a tree of life to them that lay hold upon her, and happy is every one that retaineth her.

My soul (though dwelling in a weak vessel) hath loved and admired the wisdom of God even from my childhood, and I have cause to say, wisdom is indeed a loving spirit and will not acquit a blasphemer or vain talker of his words. For God is witness of his reins and a true beholder of his heart and hearer of his tongue, for the spirit of the Lord filleth the world. And that which upholdeth all things hath knowledge of the voice [forever] (true testimony of the lovingkindness and injustice of God). And my dear children and friends who I leave behind for a little season, I advise you to love the divine wisdom that cometh from above. And desire to be guided by it in all things, and then will [it] draw your affections and set it on things that are above. And your treasure being in heaven, your hearts will be there also, and then you will long to be brought home into the full enjoyment of your beloved, which is or ought to be our Lord and Savior, Jesus Christ, where God Almighty is known to be all in all. Even so wisheth, and so prayeth your tender mother and true Friend,

Elizabeth Webb

POSTSCRIPT

A peaceable quiet life being so valuable to me, it rested upon my mind in love to set down some footsteps that thereunto hoping that some may take notice of it for their own good.

33. Proverbs 1:7–10.

Thou shalt keep him in perfect peace whose mind is stayed on thee because he trusteth in thee.[34] The way that I have found which leads to this perfect peace is (in short) perfect resignation to the divine will in all things, but great conflicts I have known between the flesh and the spirit before I could attain to a state of pure resignation. The good spirit within me often exhorted or commanded my soul, saying, let patience have her perfect work; be entire, wanting nothing but what is agreeable to the mind and will of God.[35] And it was often brought into my mind that if the captain of our salvation was made perfect through sufferings, how much more need had I to go through sufferings for the mortification of the old man with his deeds.[36] So I desired to give up all into the divine hand—body, soul, and spirit, with all things that I might call mine in this world—and desired to take all things well that might come or be permitted to come, as crosses, disappointments, wants, [forever], believing that all things do and shall work together for good to such as love and fear God.[37]

So I found by experience that when a soul is wholly given up into the hand of God, then no torment can touch it if it keeps on its guard, keeps out its grand enemy and all his instruments. And when he suggests a vain thought, then the soul rejecteth it and retireth into the name of the Lord, as into its strong tower, praying and saying, O Lord, save me from this enemy that would draw me into vanity and so bewilder my soul again, and so bring it under thy rod, and cause it to [loathe] the light of thy countenance. And so, by retiring in the fear of the Lord, it is safe and remains in its meekness and sweetness. And if it meets with any anger, either from friend or foe, it dare not go out to meet such with their own weapons or in an angry spirit but retires and sinks down into the word of patience and so hides its self from the anger. And if it meets with losses or crosses any way, it looks inwardly to the divine being and says, O Lord, thou knows what is best for me better than I know what is best for myself; thy will be done and not mine. So this quiets the mind and is well pleasing to Almighty God, who beholds the sincerity of his creature and gives it to feel that his salvation is near. Then saith the soul, as one did of old, it is good that a man should both hope and quietly wait for

34. Isaiah 26:3.

35. James 1:4.

36. Hebrews 2:10.

37. Romans 8:28.

the salvation of God. Yea, it is good for a man that he bear the yoke in his youth [forever], which testimonies are true and very comfortable to the traveling soul.[38]

So I exhort you, my sons and all my friends, to take all things well at the all-wise and all-powerful hand, and never murmur at his dealings. And as you search the Scriptures with a good intent and an humble mind, you will observe the manner of the dealings of the Almighty God with his people from age to age and also how plain and positive his promises are, which [are] always made upon condition, and unto the several states of the mind. As for proof, read the fifth chapter of Matthew and many other places in the scriptures of truth, which are left on record for the instruction of the present and future generations. But the life and power to enable the poor soul to obey the will of God and to walk humbly with him consisteth in receiving Jesus Christ in his spirit and in loving of him above all worldly enjoyments, who said to the Jews, search the scripture, and in them ye think to have eternal life. They are they which testify of me, and ye will not come to me that ye might have life.[39] So the life, power, and peace of the soul is received by uniting with Jesus Christ in a covenant of holy, heavenly love. And if the soul be faithful to this holy love which is not its Bridegroom, then he affords his own divine presence in which is divine life and comfort such as cannot be set down in words.

But we have a subtle enemy and our own corrupt nature to watch against, and a soul must come to love the judgments as well as the mercies of God before the mind can come to be stayed on God. This I have known by experience, with many more, for which I bless the name of the Lord my gracious God. So, my dear children, walk in love one toward another and to all mankind, as Christ also hath loved us and laid down his life for us, even when we were enemies to God, and hath not only commanded his followers to love and pray for enemies but hath also left us an example which, if you follow, the god of peace and love will dwell with you, yea, in your bosoms and will be your strength and stay, your guide and conductor, even in the way that leads to everlasting rest. Glory be given to God Almighty forevermore. Amen.

38. Lamentations 3:26–27.

39. John 5:39–40.

LETTER TO HER CHILDREN, AUGUST 24, 1724

[This letter was first published in *The Friend*, a Quaker periodical of the nineteenth century. Because the original has not been located, the capitalization and punctuation of the published letter have been preserved.—Eds.]

My tender, motherly love is to you all, and my prayers are to your heavenly Father that he may be pleased to take you under his care and keeping, and grant you a day of visitation by his grace and good Spirit. This, I verily believe, he will do; and it will enlighten your understanding; show you the vanity of your minds, and draw you with the cords of divine love to seek after salvation, which comes by Jesus Christ and by him alone. The Lord hath sent his Spirit into some of your hearts, whereby he hath begotten desires in you after the knowledge of him, who is the way to the kingdom of heaven, the Truth and the life. My dear children, as you are believers in his first coming, or outward appearance, according to the record of the Scriptures of Truth, which I exhort you to read often, so have a near and dear regard to his Holy Spirit in your hearts. This will incline you to love and fear God, and to learn to know him, who is the Father of your spirits, and the great Benefactor of soul and body. It is He who hath fed us all our life long, and it is in him we live, move and have our being. Few consider this as they ought; but the great love of God in the redemption and salvation of the souls of the children of men, is so stupendous, that it is beyond my capacity to set forth. Yet he hath condescended so low, as to reach forth his hand of love to little children, and will yet do it to all that love him, and lead them gently on. As a tender Father, he will feed their souls with the milk and honey of his Divine Word. This my soul witnessed in my young and tender years, even in such raptures of Divine love, that it was many times more to me than my outward food, or anything this world could afford. Oh, my dear children, partakers of my frail nature, let me tell you, that flesh and blood is very apt to grow uneasy under the yoke of Jesus Christ. His yoke is easy to the obedient soul, and his burden is light, when the old man is mortified, and the creature has learned of him, who is meek and lowly in heart. They then find sweet peace, and rest to their souls, even in resignation to the will of God. This our Lord and Savior taught, both by precept and practice. He came not to do his own will, but the will of Him that sent him, and he leads all his followers in the same way.

Now, my dear children, although I have nothing of my own to boast of, except it be weakness and infirmities, under which my soul mourns many times, yet as a tender mother, I show you the way by which my Savior hath led my soul to rest and peace with him. This was by the high way of the holy cross of our Lord Jesus Christ. The preaching of this was formerly to the Jews a stumbling block, and to the wise Greeks foolishness,—but to as many as believed, both Jews and Greeks, the power of God and the wisdom of God. I believe it was so to those who walked in the way of self-denial, and loved the Spirit that led in the midst of the paths of judgment, which gives to those who love it, to inherit substance. My dear children, the lesson I have learned, is to give up my heart to God, to resign up my will to his will, to love him above all things, and in all states to be content, believing that all things shall work together for good to those that fear and love him. As the heart, mind, will and affections are given up to Almighty God, which is our reasonable duty, the Holy Spirit doth work in the creature to will, and to do according to his own will and heavenly pleasure. His will and work is the mortification of the old man with his deeds, and the sanctification of the inner man, the hidden man of the heart. [As this is perfected,] he gives to the soul the oil of joy for mourning, the garment of praise for the spirit of heaviness, and the esteem of such who are willing and obedient. This is the Lord's doing, and it is marvelous in our eyes. For this the souls of all that love him, are filled with praises to him that liveth forever and ever.

My dear children, though you are young in years, yet often remember your latter end. Pray earnestly to Almighty God, that he may sanctify your souls, and redeem your minds and affections from the things of this lower world, set them on things above, and that he may be your portion, and the lot of your inheritance. Then you will have cause to say, "the lines are fallen for us in very pleasant places; we have a goodly heritage."[1] Then, if we should never see each other again in this world, we shall meet again, after a short, though troublesome life, in that paradisiacal life, that shall never have an end. There the souls of those that have passed through many tribulations, and have known their garments washed and made white in the blood of the Lamb, which taketh away all sins, behold the ineffable glory of God. They sing a new song, even the song of the Lamb, that none can learn, but those who are redeemed from the earth.[2]

Oh! my dear children! this redemption, this salvation that comes by Jesus Christ, is the only pearl of great price. For this, a wise man would give up his all to purchase. When he hath bought it by giving his heart to God, O, then, the care and watchfulness needed in keeping it, that no worldly Delilah steal away the heart from the Lord. We have many enemies whilst here, the flesh, the world and the evil spirit. Our best friend, Jesus Christ, exhorted all to "watch and pray," "lest," saith he, "ye enter into temptation."[3]

My dear children, although I love you dearly, yet I know the love of God, your heavenly Father, far exceeds mine. To his holy hand I commit, and commend you, with my own soul. Love him, and fear to offend him, for he is just in all his ways and equal in all his doings. Although at the sins of ignorance he winketh, yet if any sin after he or she have received the knowledge of his mind and will, that soul must be redeemed through judgment, and the baptism of the Holy Ghost and fire. This is the spiritual baptism of our Lord and Savior Jesus Christ. His fan is in his hand, and he will thoroughly purge his floor, and will gather his wheat in his garner, but the chaff he will burn with unquenchable fire. Take notice of the word unquenchable. Our God is a consuming fire to all the works, and workers of iniquity. It is unavoidably so, for nothing that is impure, shall enter the heavenly kingdom. The Lord is no respecter of persons. When Moses, that meek man, was provoked to speak unadvisedly, he suffered for it; when David looked out, and [was led astray,] he suffered great judgment and troubles for his offense. It is the comfort of all who love the just and righteous judgments of God, that in the midst of judgment, he remembereth mercies. In the type, even under the law, his mercy-seat was set above his judgment-seat. This causeth many to

1. Psalm 16:6.

2. Revelation 14:1–3.

3. Mark 14:38.

sing songs of praise and thanksgiving to him, both here and hereafter, even to all eternity. That this may be our lot and portion together, with all our friends and acquaintances, is the earnest breathings of my soul. This I send as a token of my good will to you, and good desires for you, and remain your tender mother,

Elizabeth Webb

P.S.—Remember my dear love to all our friends and neighbors, as you have opportunity. Be kindly affectioned one to another, and to all people. Remember that God is love, and he that dwelleth in love, dwelleth in God, and God in him. Our Lord and Savior is the Son of God's love, and he that hath the Son of God, hath eternal life. He that hath not the Son, hath not this life, but the wrath of God abideth in him. So, my dear children, watch and be sober, and hope to the end. Gather yourselves together and read this in the same love in which I have written it. The Lord Jesus be with you all to the end of your days here, and redeem you to himself.

SUGGESTIONS FOR FURTHER READING

Ames, Marjon. *Margaret Fell, Letters, and the Making of Quakerism.* New York: Routledge, 2017.

Angell, Stephen W., and Pink Dandelion, eds. *The Oxford Handbook of Quaker Studies.* New York: Oxford University Press, 2013.

Brekus, Catherine A. "Writing Religious Experience: Women's Authorship in Early America." *Journal of Religion* 92, no. 4 (2012): 482–97.

Bruyneel, Sally. *Margaret Fell and the End of Time: The Theology of the Mother of Quakerism.* Waco: Baylor University Press, 2010.

Frost, J. William. "Quaker Books in Colonial Pennsylvania." *Quaker History* 80, no. 1 (1991): 1–23.

Garman, Mary, Judith Applegate, Margaret Benefiel, and Dortha Meredith, eds. *Hidden in Plain Sight: Quaker Women's Writings, 1650–1700.* Wallingford, Pa.: Pendle Hill Publications, 1996.

Gerona, Carla. *Night Journeys: The Power of Dreams in Transatlantic Quaker Culture.* Charlottesville: University of Virginia Press, 2004.

Gill, Catie. *Women in the Seventeenth-Century Quaker Community: A Literary Study of Political Identities, 1650–1700.* Burlington, Vt.: Ashgate, 2005.

Glines, Elsa F., ed. *Undaunted Zeal: The Letters of Margaret Fell.* Richmond, Ind.: Friends United Press, 2003.

Graves, Michael P. *Preaching the Inward Light: Early Quaker Rhetoric.* Waco: Baylor University Press, 2009.

Herbert, Amanda E. "Companions in Preaching and Suffering: Itinerant Female Quakers in the Seventeenth- and Eighteenth-Century British Atlantic World." *Early American Studies* 9, no. 1 (2011): 73–113.

Huggins, Shannon. "The Power of Preaching: Female Identity, Legitimacy, and Leadership in American Quakerism, 1700–1776." Ph.D. diss., Auburn University, 2010.

Landes, Jordan. *London Quakers in the Trans-Atlantic World: The Creation of an Early Modern Community.* New York: Palgrave Macmillan, 2015.

Larson, Rebecca. *Daughters of Light: Quaker Women Preaching and*

Prophesying in the Colonies and Abroad, 1700–1775. Chapel Hill: University of North Carolina Press, 1999.

Mack, Phyllis. "Religion, Feminism, and the Problem of Agency: Reflections on Eighteenth-Century Quakerism." *Signs* 29, no. 1 (2003): 149–77.

Pestana, Carla Gardina. *Quakers and Baptists in Colonial Massachusetts*. New York: Cambridge University Press, 1991.

Peters, Kate. *Print Culture and the Early Quakers*. New York: Cambridge University Press, 2005.

Rose, Judith. "Prophesying Daughters: Testimony, Censorship, and Literacy Among Early Quaker Women." *Critical Survey* 14, no. 1 (2002): 93–110.

Trevett, Christine. *Women and Quakerism in the 17th Century*. York, U.K.: Ebor Press, 1991.

Wigginton, Caroline. *In the Neighborhood: Women's Publication in Early America*. Amherst: University of Massachusetts Press, 2016.

Wilcox, Catherine M. *Theology and Women's Ministry in Seventeenth-Century English Quakerism*. Lewiston, N.Y.: Edwin Mellon Press, 1995.

Wright, Luella M. *The Literary Life of the Early Friends, 1650–1725*. New York: AMS, 1966.

Wright, Sheila. "'Truly Dear Hearts': Family and Spirituality in Quaker Women's Writings, 1680–1750." In *Women, Gender, and Radical Religion in Early Modern Europe*, edited by Sylvia Brown, 97–114. Boston: Brill, 2007.

INDEX